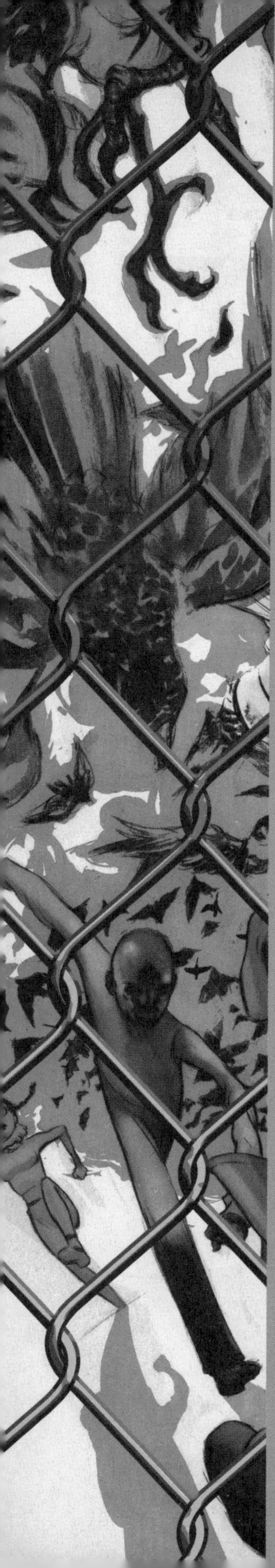

JACK OF FABLES

THE (NEARLY) GREAT ESCAPE

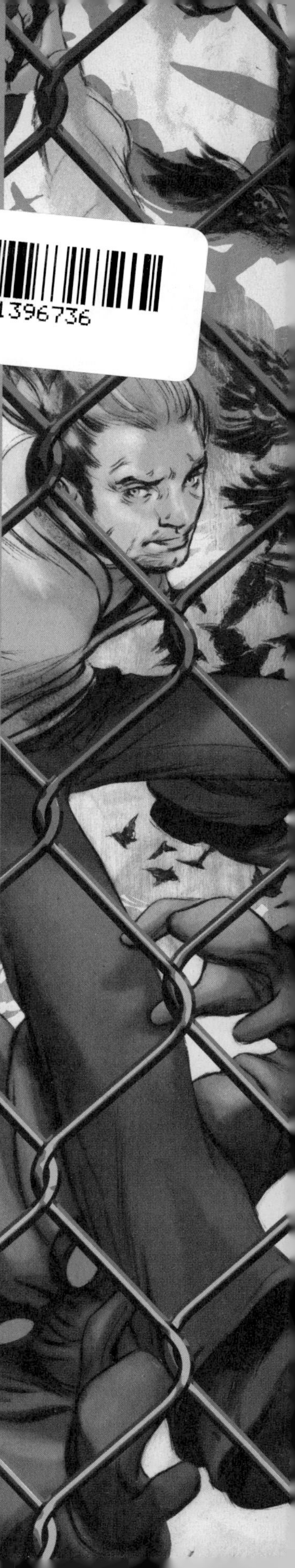

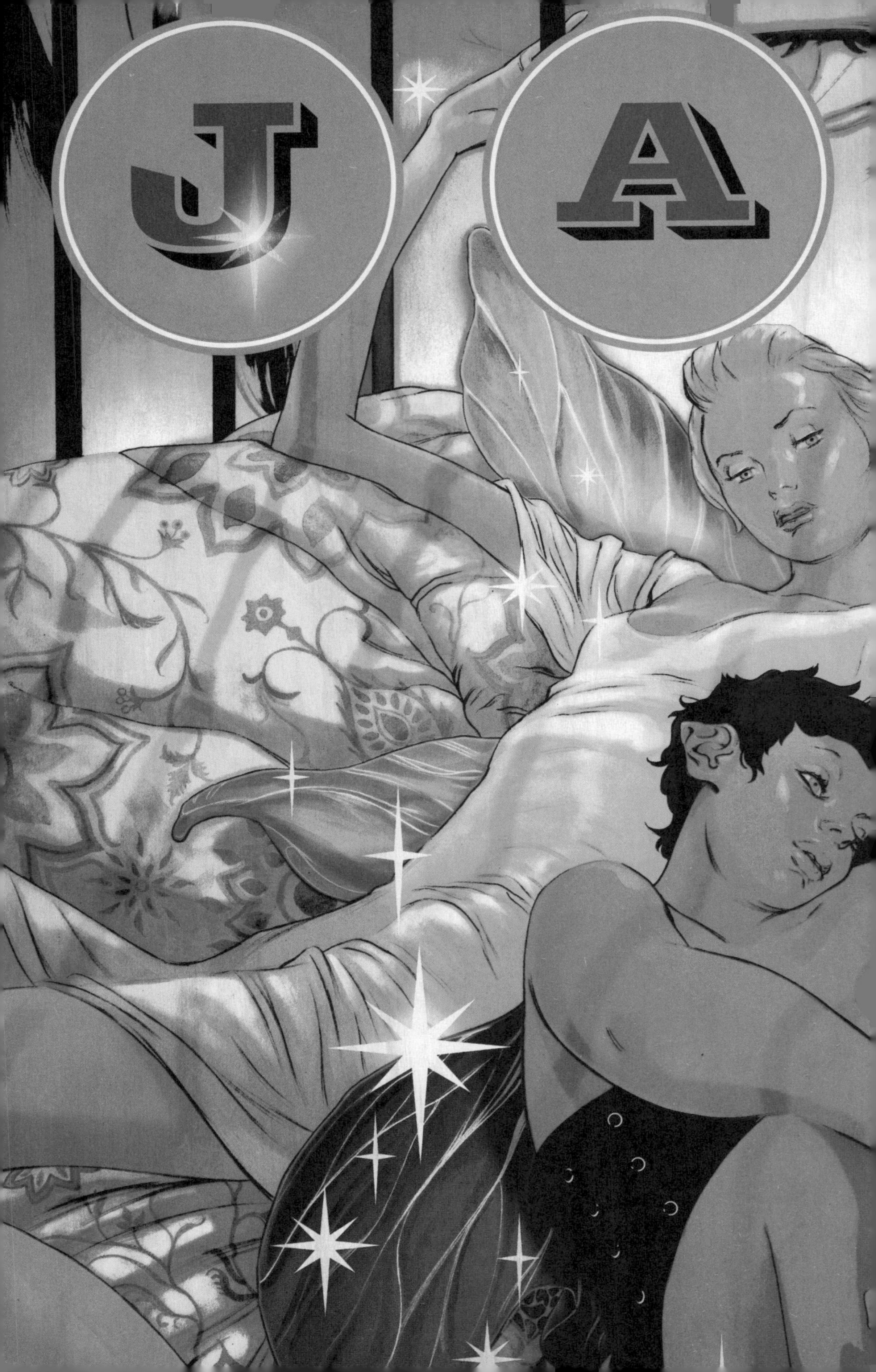
J
A

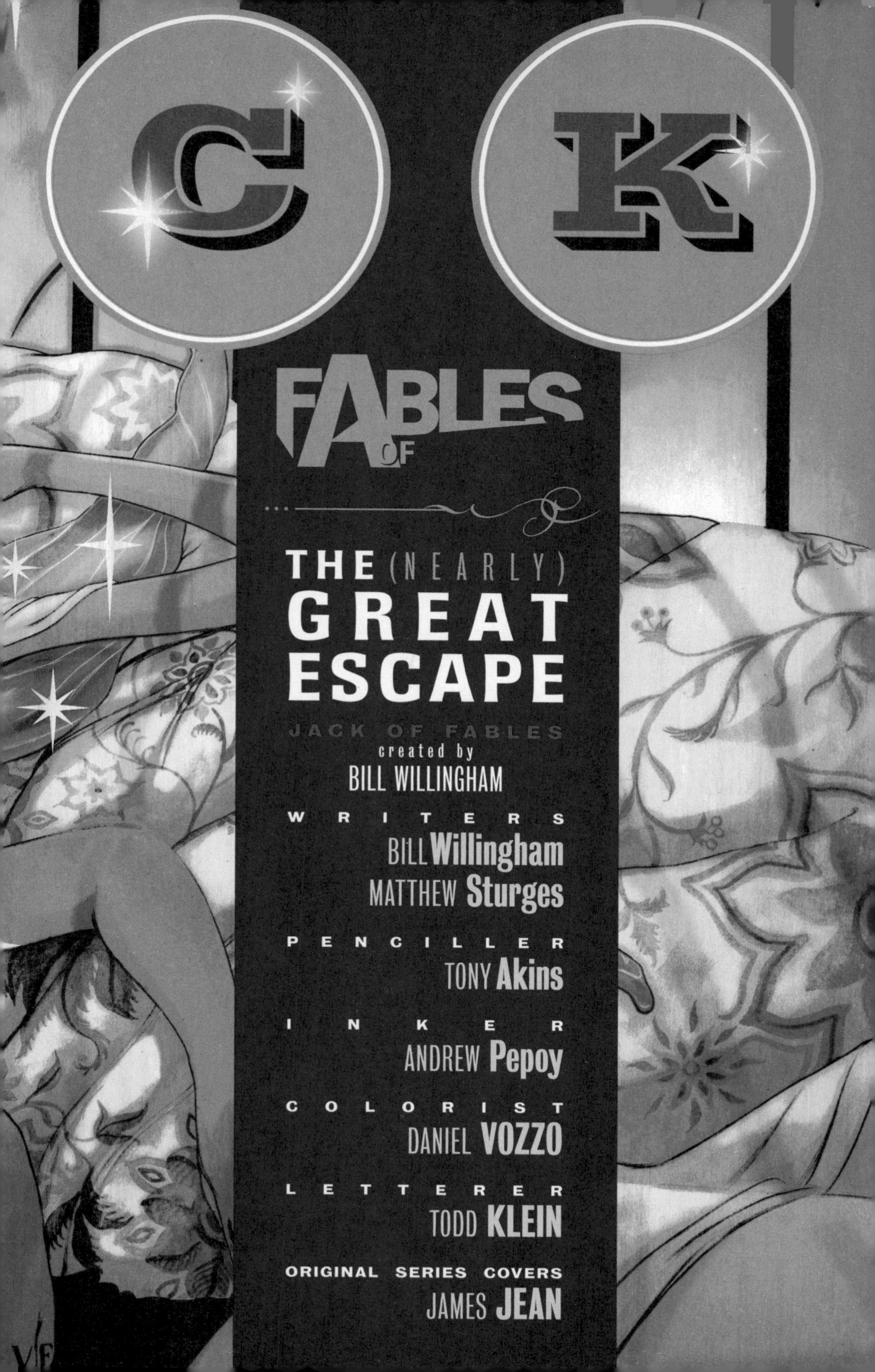

THE (NEARLY) GREAT ESCAPE

JACK OF FABLES
created by
BILL WILLINGHAM

WRITERS
BILL Willingham
MATTHEW Sturges

PENCILLER
TONY Akins

INKER
ANDREW Pepoy

COLORIST
DANIEL VOZZO

LETTERER
TODD KLEIN

ORIGINAL SERIES COVERS
JAMES JEAN

Cover illustration and logo by James Jean.
Publication design by Brainchild Studios/NYC.

JACK OF FABLES: THE (NEARLY) GREAT ESCAPE

Published by DC Comics. Cover, compilation and character sketches copyright © 2007 DC Comics. All Rights Reserved.

DC Comics, 1700 Broadway, New York, NY 10019
A Warner Bros. Entertainment Company.
Printed in Canada. First Printing.
ISBN: 1-4012-1222-0
ISBN 13: 978-1-4012-1222-3

TABLE OF CONTENTS

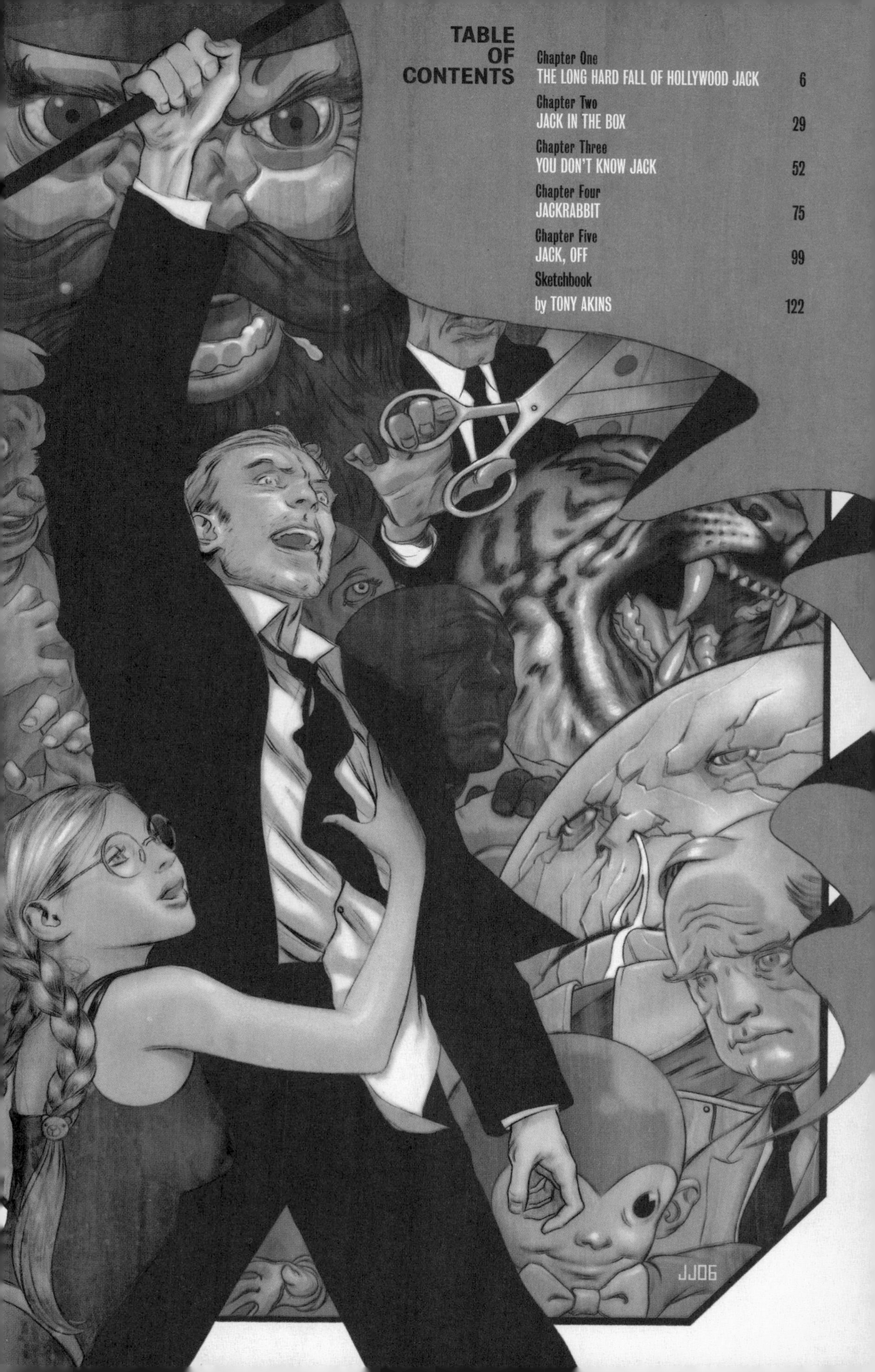

JJ06

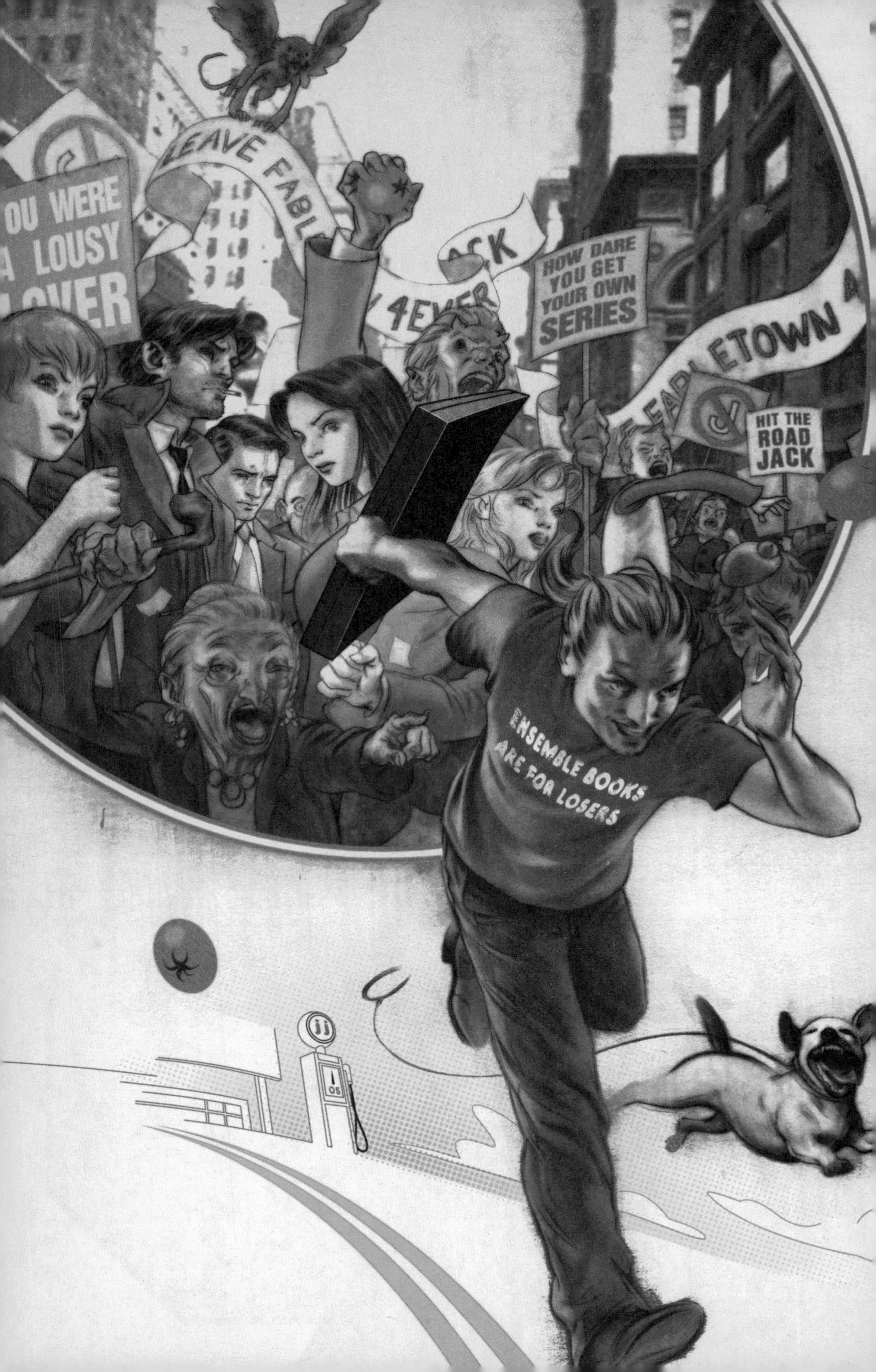
OU WERE
A LOUSY
LOVER
LEAVE FABL
ACK
4EVER
HOW DARE
YOU GET
YOUR OWN
SERIES
ETOWN
HIT THE
ROAD
JACK
ENSEMBLE BOOKS
ARE FOR LOSERS

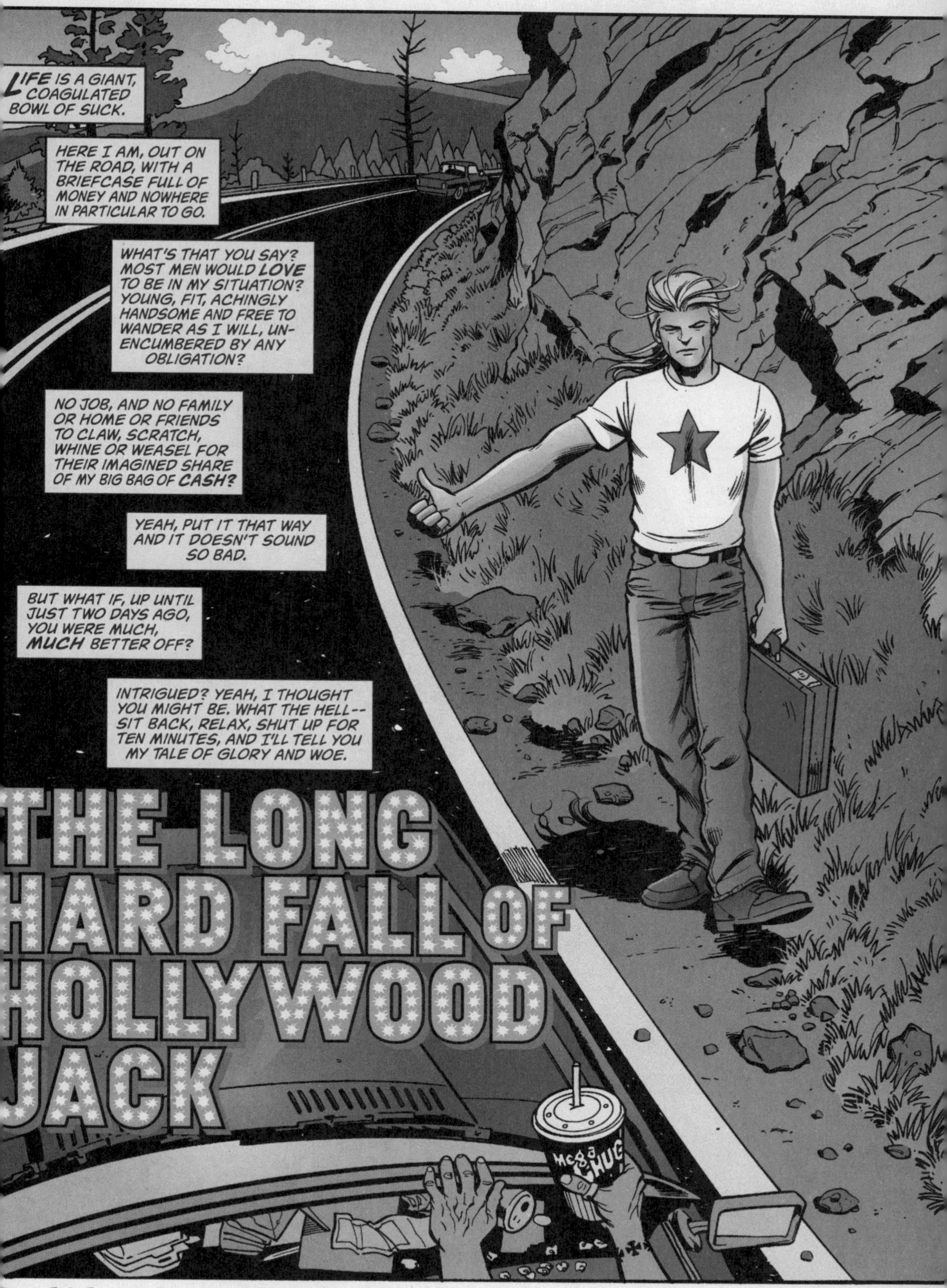
LIFE IS A GIANT, COAGULATED BOWL OF SUCK.
HERE I AM, OUT ON THE ROAD, WITH A BRIEFCASE FULL OF MONEY AND NOWHERE IN PARTICULAR TO GO.
WHAT'S THAT YOU SAY? MOST MEN WOULD LOVE TO BE IN MY SITUATION? YOUNG, FIT, ACHINGLY HANDSOME AND FREE TO WANDER AS I WILL, UN-ENCUMBERED BY ANY OBLIGATION?
NO JOB, AND NO FAMILY OR HOME OR FRIENDS TO CLAW, SCRATCH, WHINE OR WEASEL FOR THEIR IMAGINED SHARE OF MY BIG BAG OF CASH?
YEAH, PUT IT THAT WAY AND IT DOESN'T SOUND SO BAD.
BUT WHAT IF, UP UNTIL JUST TWO DAYS AGO, YOU WERE MUCH, MUCH BETTER OFF?
INTRIGUED? YEAH, I THOUGHT YOU MIGHT BE. WHAT THE HELL--SIT BACK, RELAX, SHUT UP FOR TEN MINUTES, AND I'LL TELL YOU MY TALE OF GLORY AND WOE.
THE LONG HARD FALL OF HOLLYWOOD JACK
MEGA HUG

In which our hero is offered a ride, turns it down, takes it anyway, and ends up finding many new Fables, including one we've already met before.

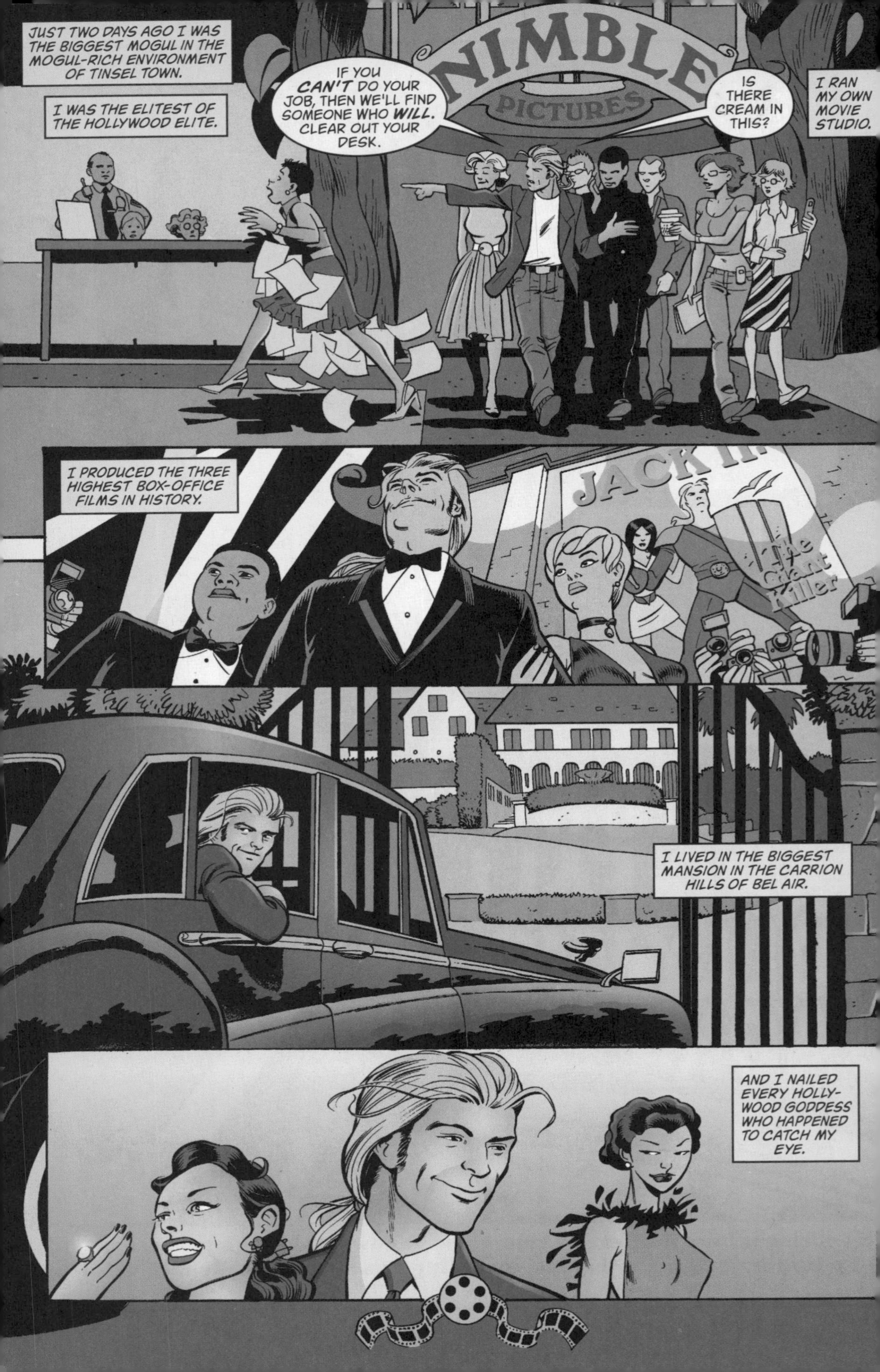
JUST TWO DAYS AGO I WAS THE BIGGEST MOGUL IN THE MOGUL-RICH ENVIRONMENT OF TINSEL TOWN.
I WAS THE ELITEST OF THE HOLLYWOOD ELITE.
NIMBLE PICTURES
IF YOU CAN'T DO YOUR JOB, THEN WE'LL FIND SOMEONE WHO WILL. CLEAR OUT YOUR DESK.
IS THERE CREAM IN THIS?
I RAN MY OWN MOVIE STUDIO.
I PRODUCED THE THREE HIGHEST BOX-OFFICE FILMS IN HISTORY.
JACK III
The Giant Killer
I LIVED IN THE BIGGEST MANSION IN THE CARRION HILLS OF BEL AIR.
AND I NAILED EVERY HOLLY-WOOD GODDESS WHO HAPPENED TO CATCH MY EYE.

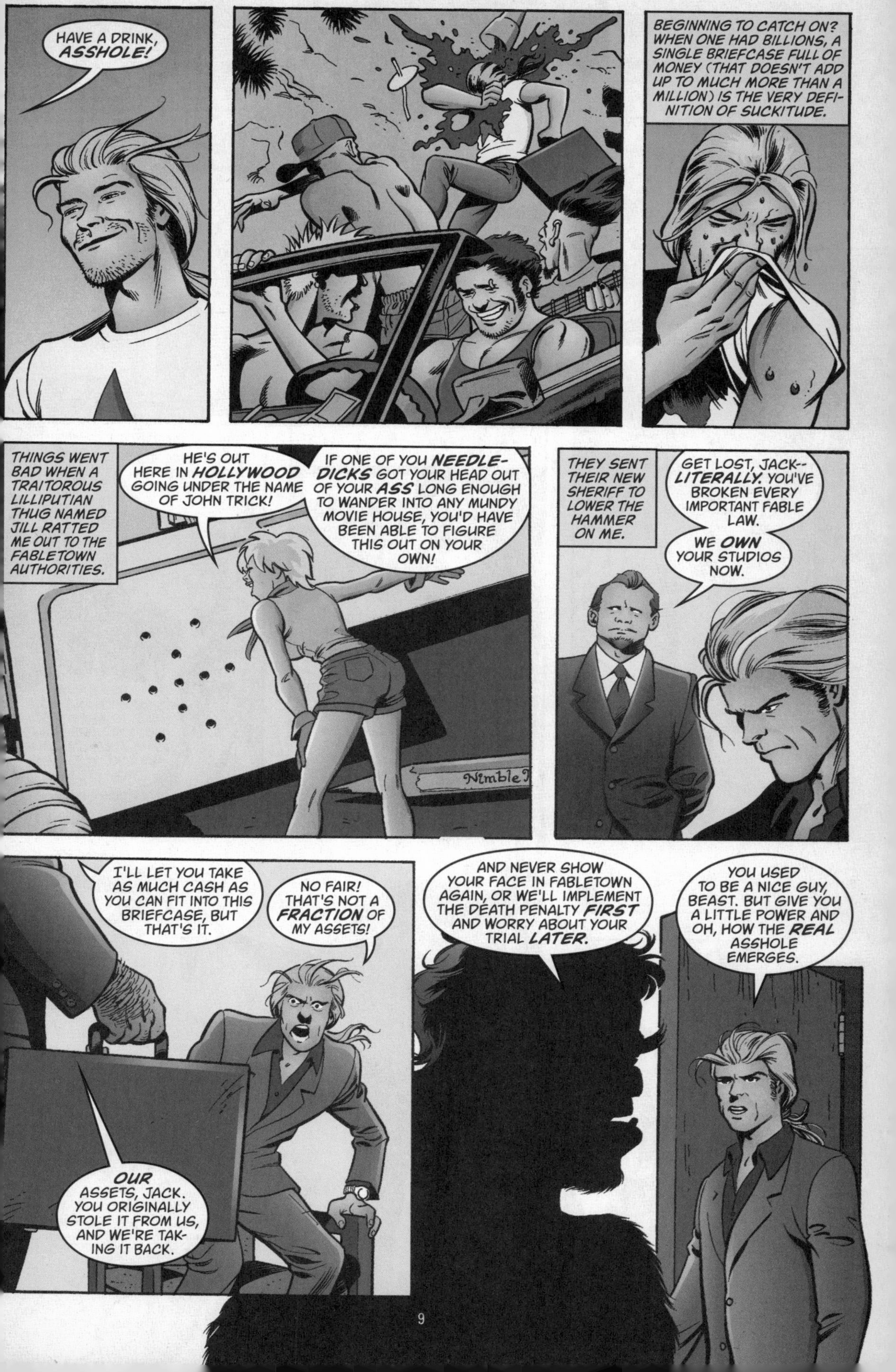
HAVE A DRINK, ASSHOLE!
BEGINNING TO CATCH ON? WHEN ONE HAD BILLIONS, A SINGLE BRIEFCASE FULL OF MONEY (THAT DOESN'T ADD UP TO MUCH MORE THAN A MILLION) IS THE VERY DEFINITION OF SUCKITUDE.
THINGS WENT BAD WHEN A TRAITOROUS LILLIPUTIAN THUG NAMED JILL RATTED ME OUT TO THE FABLETOWN AUTHORITIES.
HE'S OUT HERE IN HOLLYWOOD GOING UNDER THE NAME OF JOHN TRICK!
IF ONE OF YOU NEEDLE-DICKS GOT YOUR HEAD OUT OF YOUR ASS LONG ENOUGH TO WANDER INTO ANY MUNDY MOVIE HOUSE, YOU'D HAVE BEEN ABLE TO FIGURE THIS OUT ON YOUR OWN!
Nimble
THEY SENT THEIR NEW SHERIFF TO LOWER THE HAMMER ON ME.
GET LOST, JACK-- LITERALLY. YOU'VE BROKEN EVERY IMPORTANT FABLE LAW.
WE OWN YOUR STUDIOS NOW.
I'LL LET YOU TAKE AS MUCH CASH AS YOU CAN FIT INTO THIS BRIEFCASE, BUT THAT'S IT.
NO FAIR! THAT'S NOT A FRACTION OF MY ASSETS!
OUR ASSETS, JACK. YOU ORIGINALLY STOLE IT FROM US, AND WE'RE TAKING IT BACK.
AND NEVER SHOW YOUR FACE IN FABLETOWN AGAIN, OR WE'LL IMPLEMENT THE DEATH PENALTY FIRST AND WORRY ABOUT YOUR TRIAL LATER.
YOU USED TO BE A NICE GUY, BEAST. BUT GIVE YOU A LITTLE POWER AND OH, HOW THE REAL ASSHOLE EMERGES.

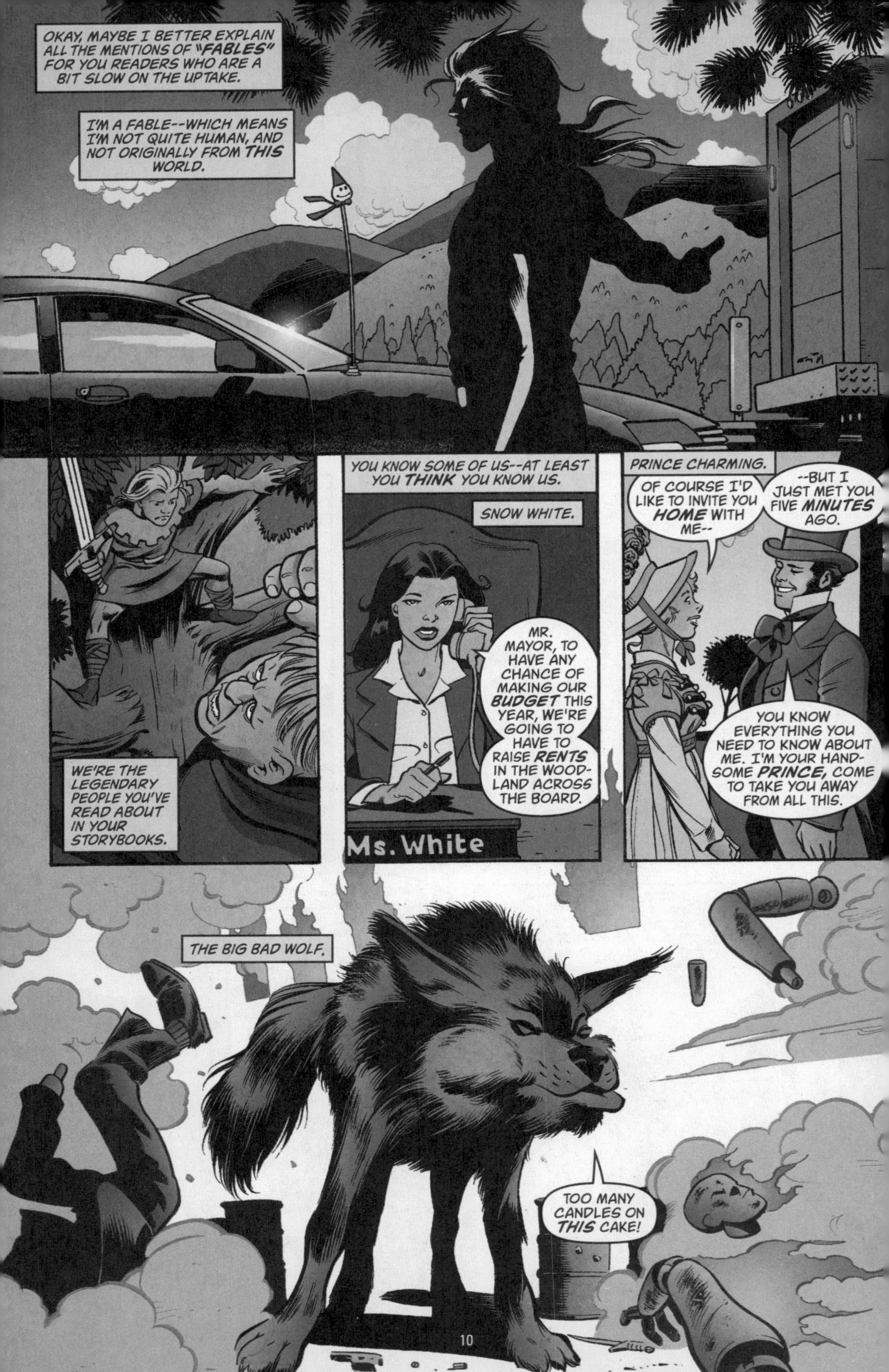
OKAY, MAYBE I BETTER EXPLAIN ALL THE MENTIONS OF "FABLES" FOR YOU READERS WHO ARE A BIT SLOW ON THE UPTAKE.
I'M A FABLE--WHICH MEANS I'M NOT QUITE HUMAN, AND NOT ORIGINALLY FROM THIS WORLD.
WE'RE THE LEGENDARY PEOPLE YOU'VE READ ABOUT IN YOUR STORYBOOKS.
YOU KNOW SOME OF US--AT LEAST YOU THINK YOU KNOW US.
SNOW WHITE.
MR. MAYOR, TO HAVE ANY CHANCE OF MAKING OUR BUDGET THIS YEAR, WE'RE GOING TO HAVE TO RAISE RENTS IN THE WOODLAND ACROSS THE BOARD.
Ms. White
PRINCE CHARMING.
OF COURSE I'D LIKE TO INVITE YOU HOME WITH ME--
--BUT I JUST MET YOU FIVE MINUTES AGO.
YOU KNOW EVERYTHING YOU NEED TO KNOW ABOUT ME. I'M YOUR HANDSOME PRINCE, COME TO TAKE YOU AWAY FROM ALL THIS.
THE BIG BAD WOLF.
TOO MANY CANDLES ON THIS CAKE!

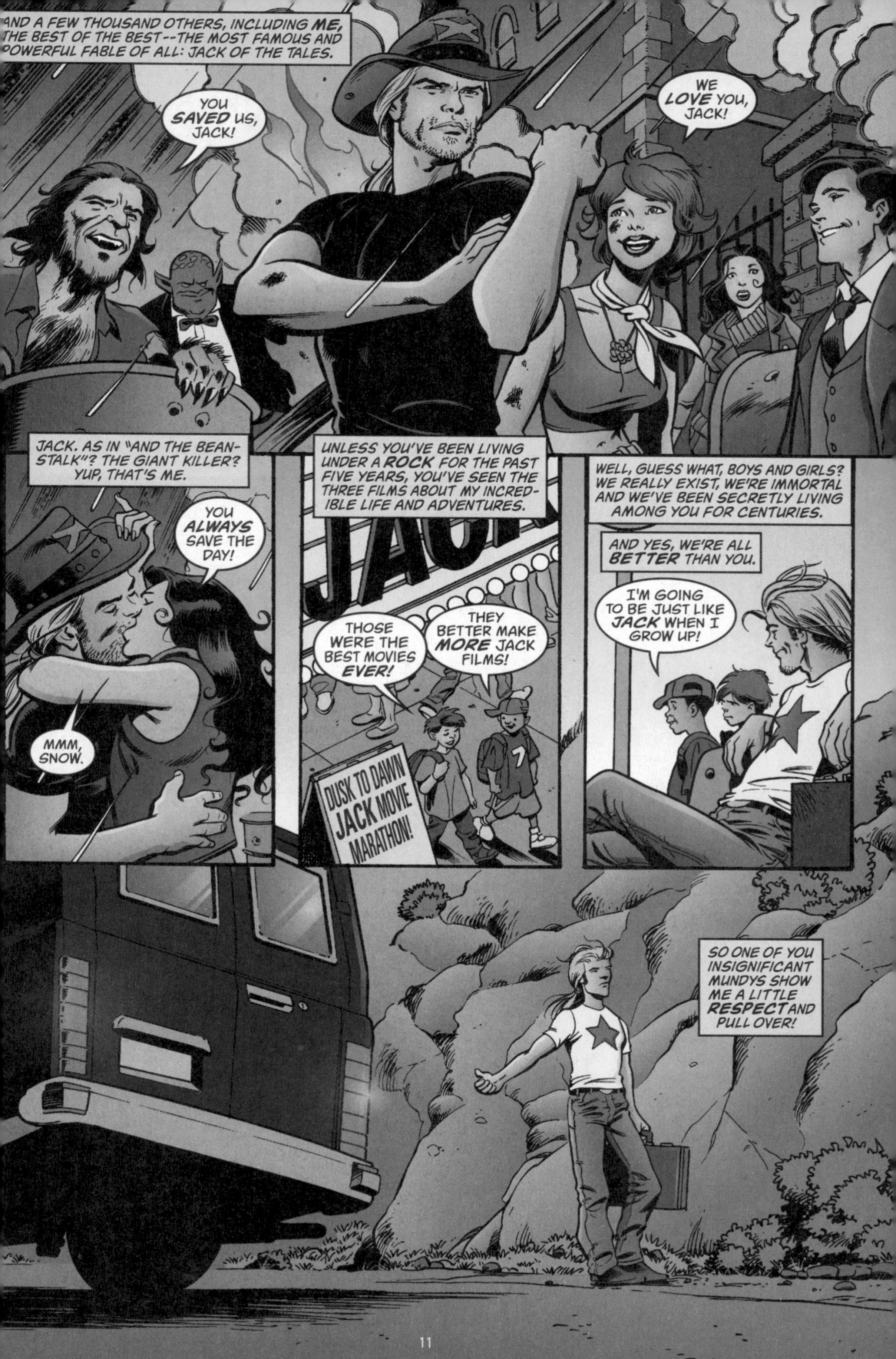

AND A FEW THOUSAND OTHERS, INCLUDING ME, THE BEST OF THE BEST--THE MOST FAMOUS AND POWERFUL FABLE OF ALL: JACK OF THE TALES.
YOU SAVED US, JACK!
WE LOVE YOU, JACK!
JACK. AS IN "AND THE BEAN-STALK"? THE GIANT KILLER? YUP, THAT'S ME.
YOU ALWAYS SAVE THE DAY!
MMM, SNOW.
UNLESS YOU'VE BEEN LIVING UNDER A ROCK FOR THE PAST FIVE YEARS, YOU'VE SEEN THE THREE FILMS ABOUT MY INCRED-IBLE LIFE AND ADVENTURES.
THOSE WERE THE BEST MOVIES EVER!
THEY BETTER MAKE MORE JACK FILMS!
DUSK TO DAWN JACK MOVIE MARATHON!
WELL, GUESS WHAT, BOYS AND GIRLS? WE REALLY EXIST, WE'RE IMMORTAL AND WE'VE BEEN SECRETLY LIVING AMONG YOU FOR CENTURIES.
AND YES, WE'RE ALL BETTER THAN YOU.
I'M GOING TO BE JUST LIKE JACK WHEN I GROW UP!
SO ONE OF YOU INSIGNIFICANT MUNDYS SHOW ME A LITTLE RESPECT AND PULL OVER!

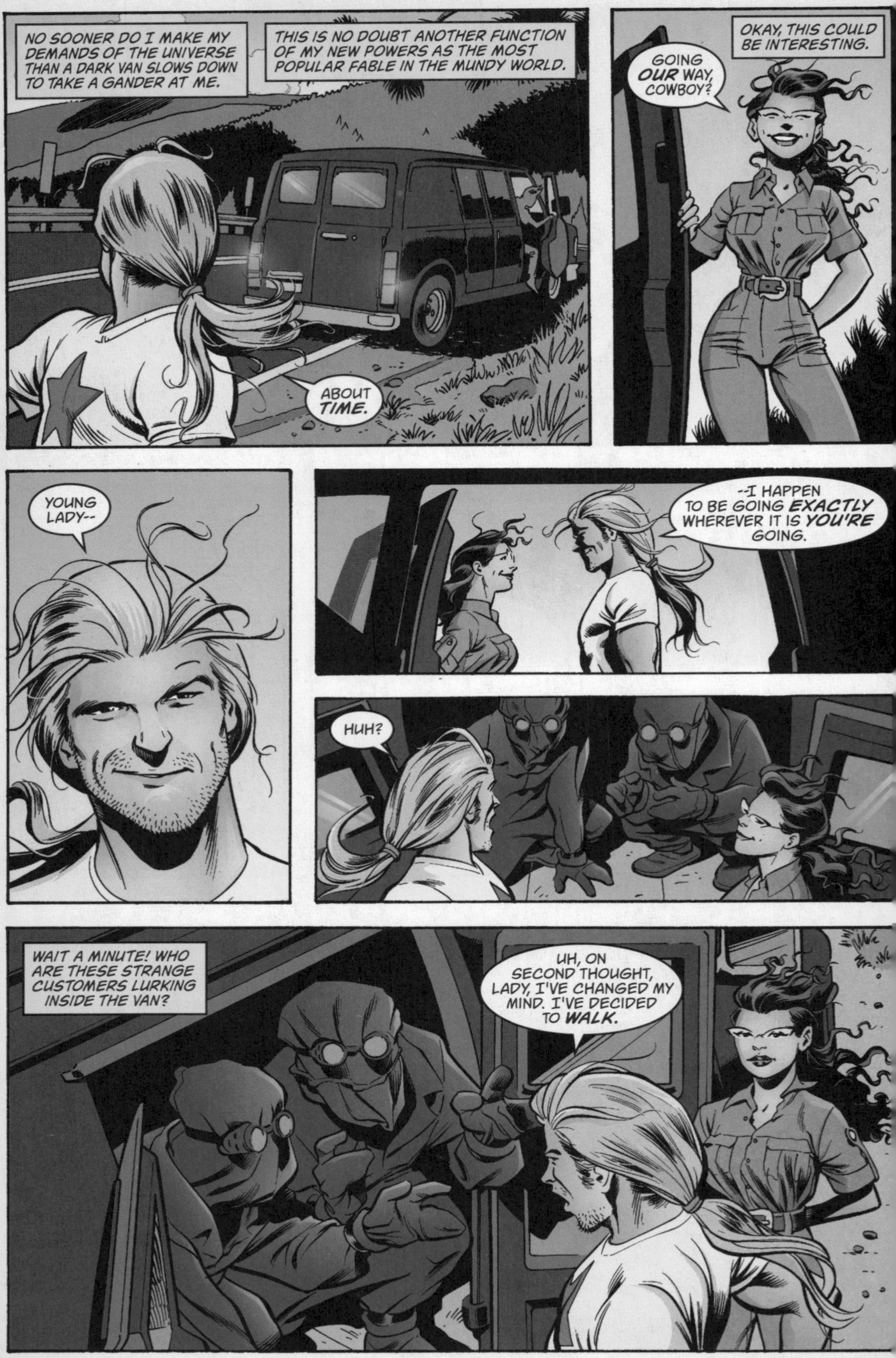
NO SOONER DO I MAKE MY DEMANDS OF THE UNIVERSE THAN A DARK VAN SLOWS DOWN TO TAKE A GANDER AT ME.
THIS IS NO DOUBT ANOTHER FUNCTION OF MY NEW POWERS AS THE MOST POPULAR FABLE IN THE MUNDY WORLD.
ABOUT TIME.
OKAY, THIS COULD BE INTERESTING.
GOING OUR WAY, COWBOY?
YOUNG LADY--
--I HAPPEN TO BE GOING EXACTLY WHEREVER IT IS YOU'RE GOING.
HUH?
WAIT A MINUTE! WHO ARE THESE STRANGE CUSTOMERS LURKING INSIDE THE VAN?
UH, ON SECOND THOUGHT, LADY, I'VE CHANGED MY MIND. I'VE DECIDED TO WALK.

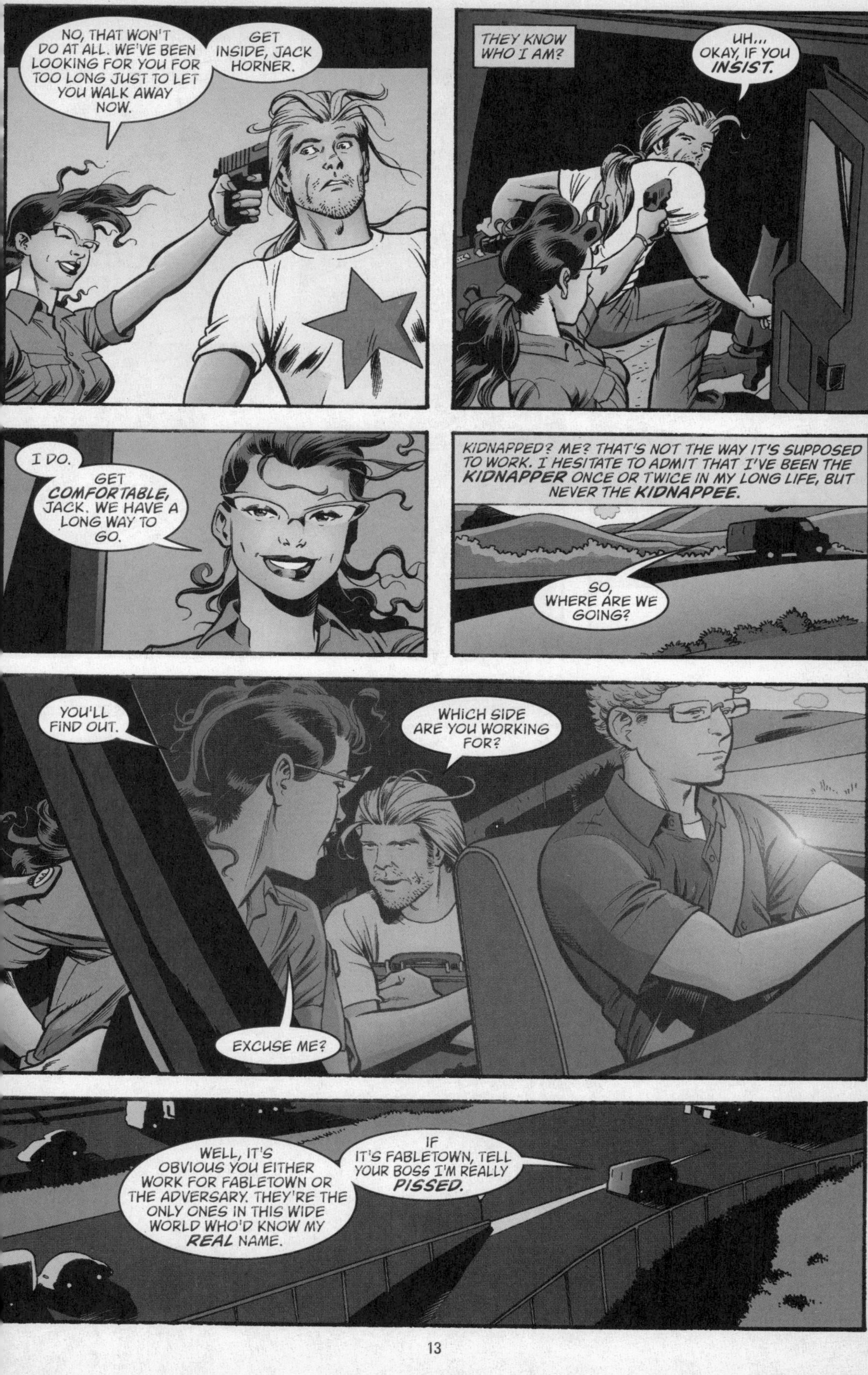
NO, THAT WON'T DO AT ALL. WE'VE BEEN LOOKING FOR YOU FOR TOO LONG JUST TO LET YOU WALK AWAY NOW.
GET INSIDE, JACK HORNER.
THEY KNOW WHO I AM?
UH... OKAY, IF YOU INSIST.
I DO.
GET COMFORTABLE, JACK. WE HAVE A LONG WAY TO GO.
KIDNAPPED? ME? THAT'S NOT THE WAY IT'S SUPPOSED TO WORK. I HESITATE TO ADMIT THAT I'VE BEEN THE KIDNAPPER ONCE OR TWICE IN MY LONG LIFE, BUT NEVER THE KIDNAPPEE.
SO, WHERE ARE WE GOING?
YOU'LL FIND OUT.
WHICH SIDE ARE YOU WORKING FOR?
EXCUSE ME?
WELL, IT'S OBVIOUS YOU EITHER WORK FOR FABLETOWN OR THE ADVERSARY. THEY'RE THE ONLY ONES IN THIS WIDE WORLD WHO'D KNOW MY REAL NAME.
IF IT'S FABLETOWN, TELL YOUR BOSS I'M REALLY PISSED.

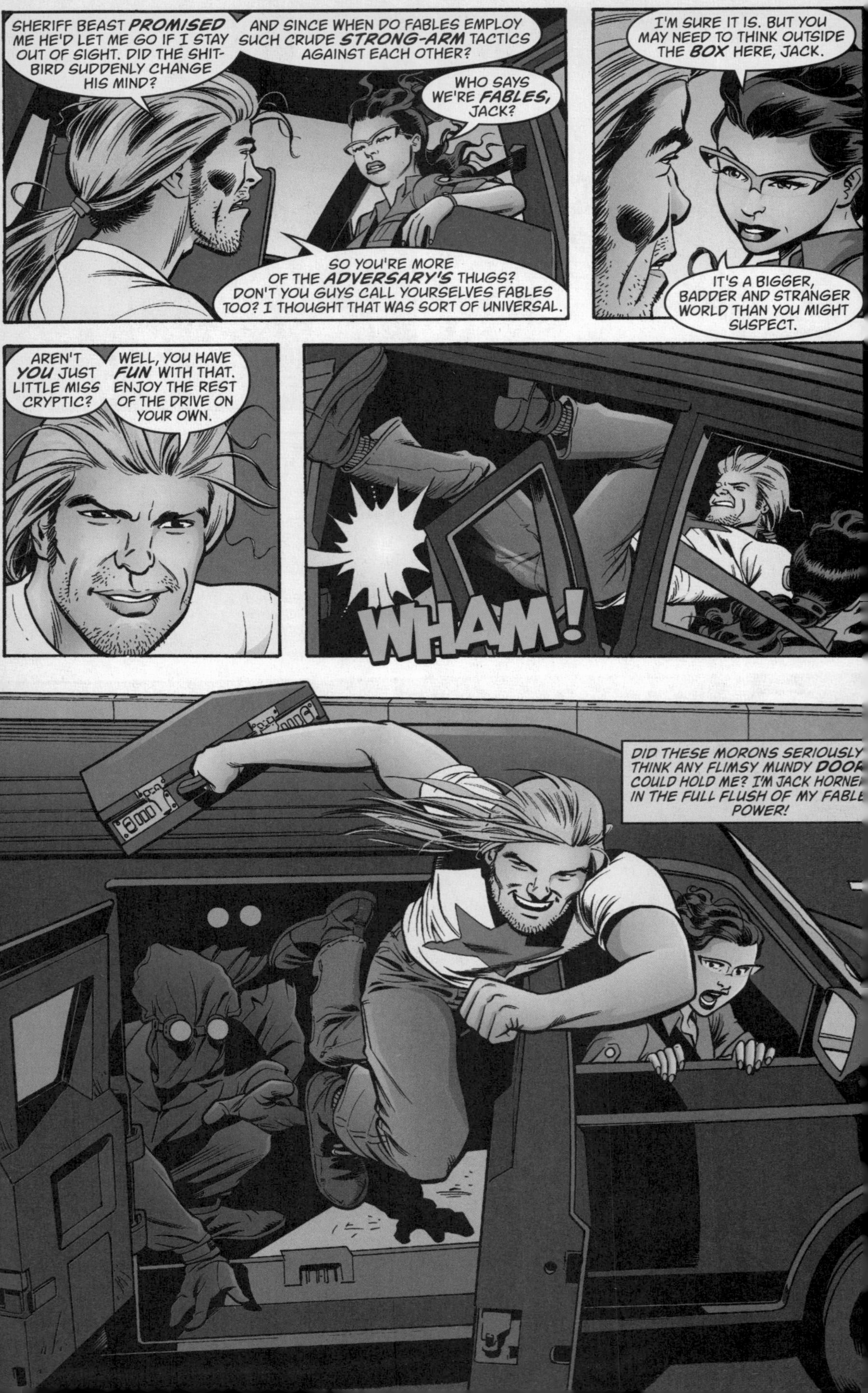

SHERIFF BEAST PROMISED ME HE'D LET ME GO IF I STAY OUT OF SIGHT. DID THE SHIT-BIRD SUDDENLY CHANGE HIS MIND?
AND SINCE WHEN DO FABLES EMPLOY SUCH CRUDE STRONG-ARM TACTICS AGAINST EACH OTHER?
WHO SAYS WE'RE FABLES, JACK?
SO YOU'RE MORE OF THE ADVERSARY'S THUGS? DON'T YOU GUYS CALL YOURSELVES FABLES TOO? I THOUGHT THAT WAS SORT OF UNIVERSAL.
I'M SURE IT IS. BUT YOU MAY NEED TO THINK OUTSIDE THE BOX HERE, JACK.
IT'S A BIGGER, BADDER AND STRANGER WORLD THAN YOU MIGHT SUSPECT.
AREN'T YOU JUST LITTLE MISS CRYPTIC?
WELL, YOU HAVE FUN WITH THAT. ENJOY THE REST OF THE DRIVE ON YOUR OWN.
WHAM!
DID THESE MORONS SERIOUSLY THINK ANY FLIMSY MUNDY DOOR COULD HOLD ME? I'M JACK HORNER IN THE FULL FLUSH OF MY FABLE POWER!

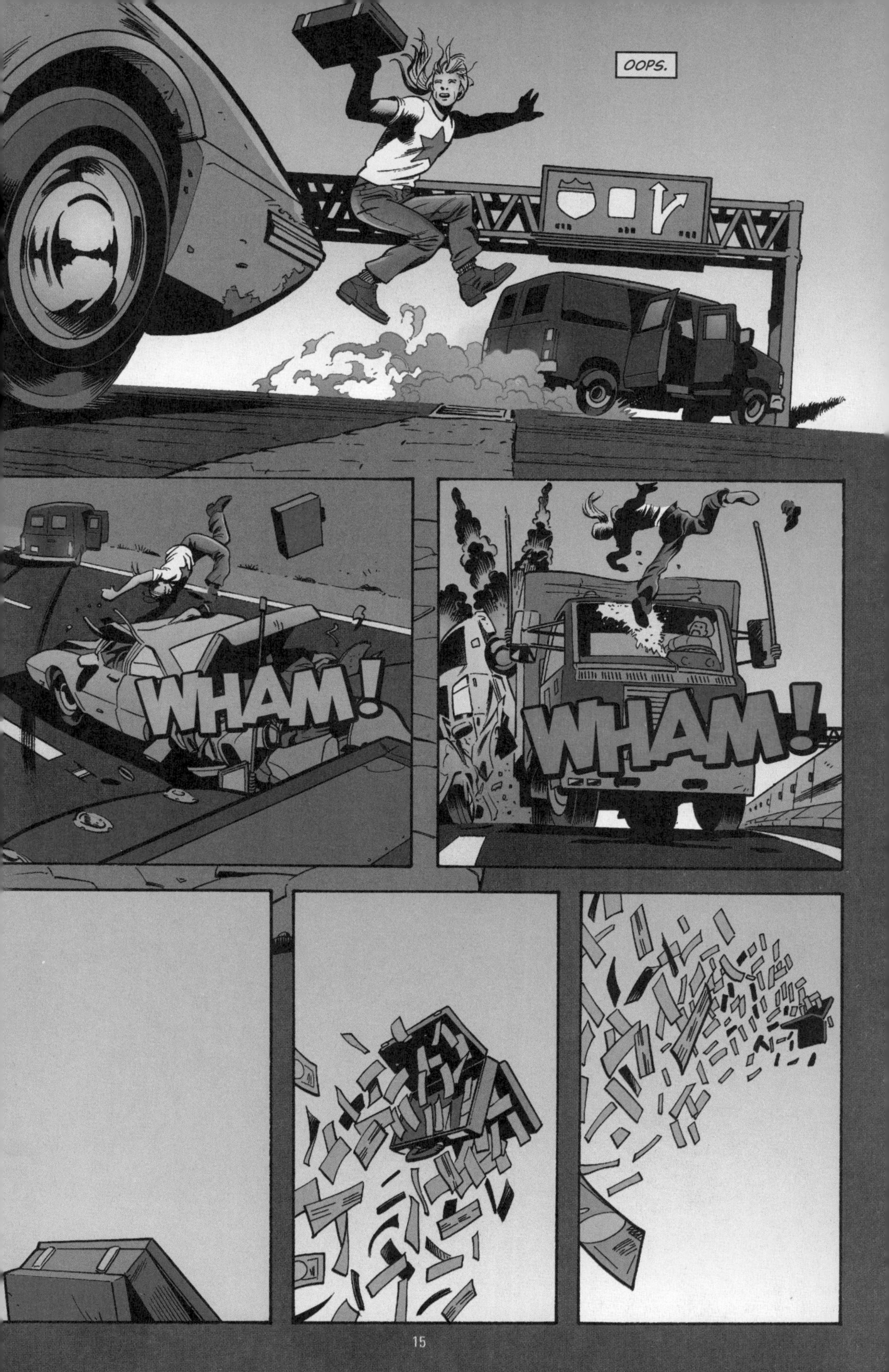
OOPS.
WHAM!
WHAM!

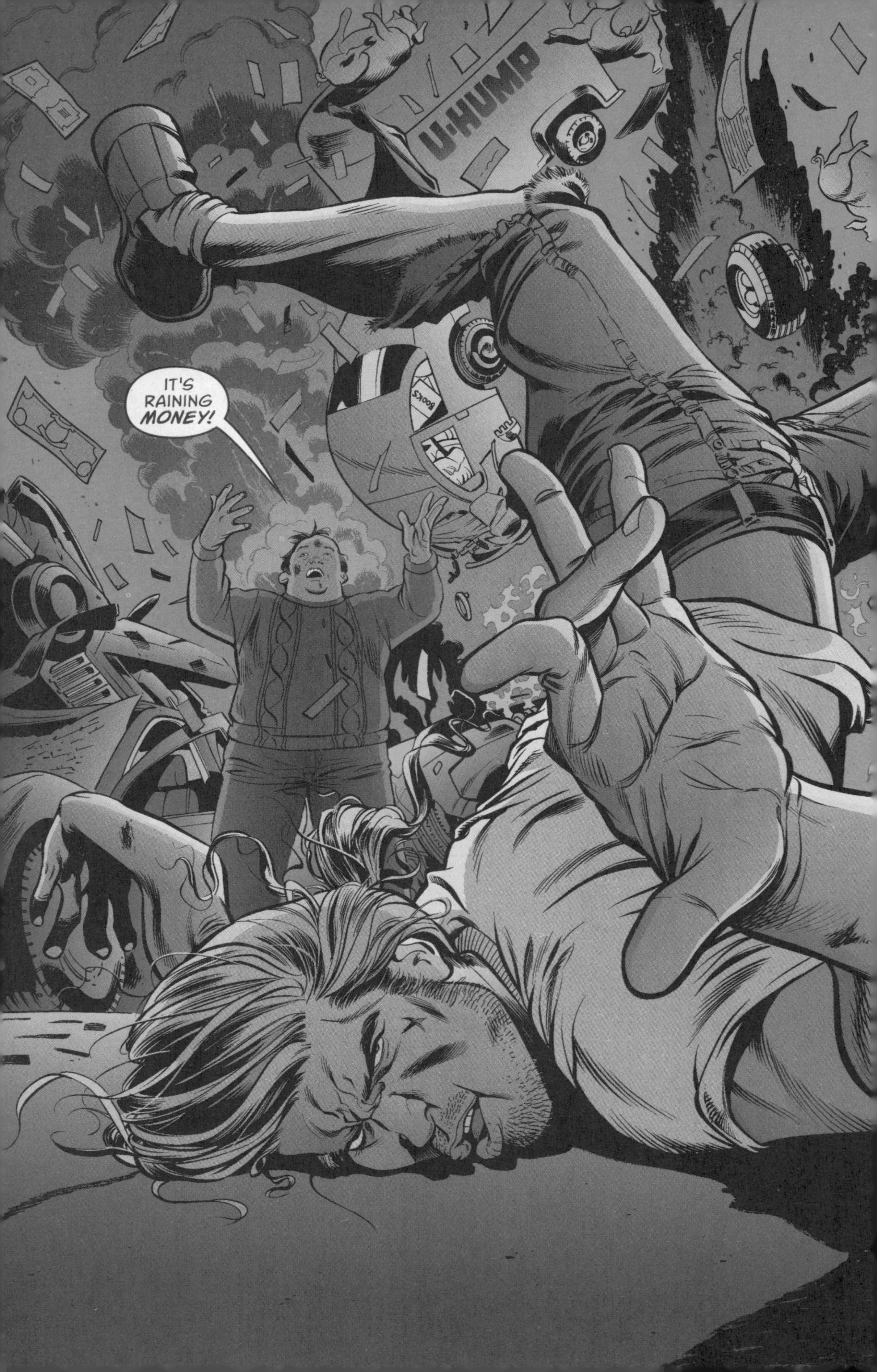
U-HUMP
IT'S RAINING *MONEY!*

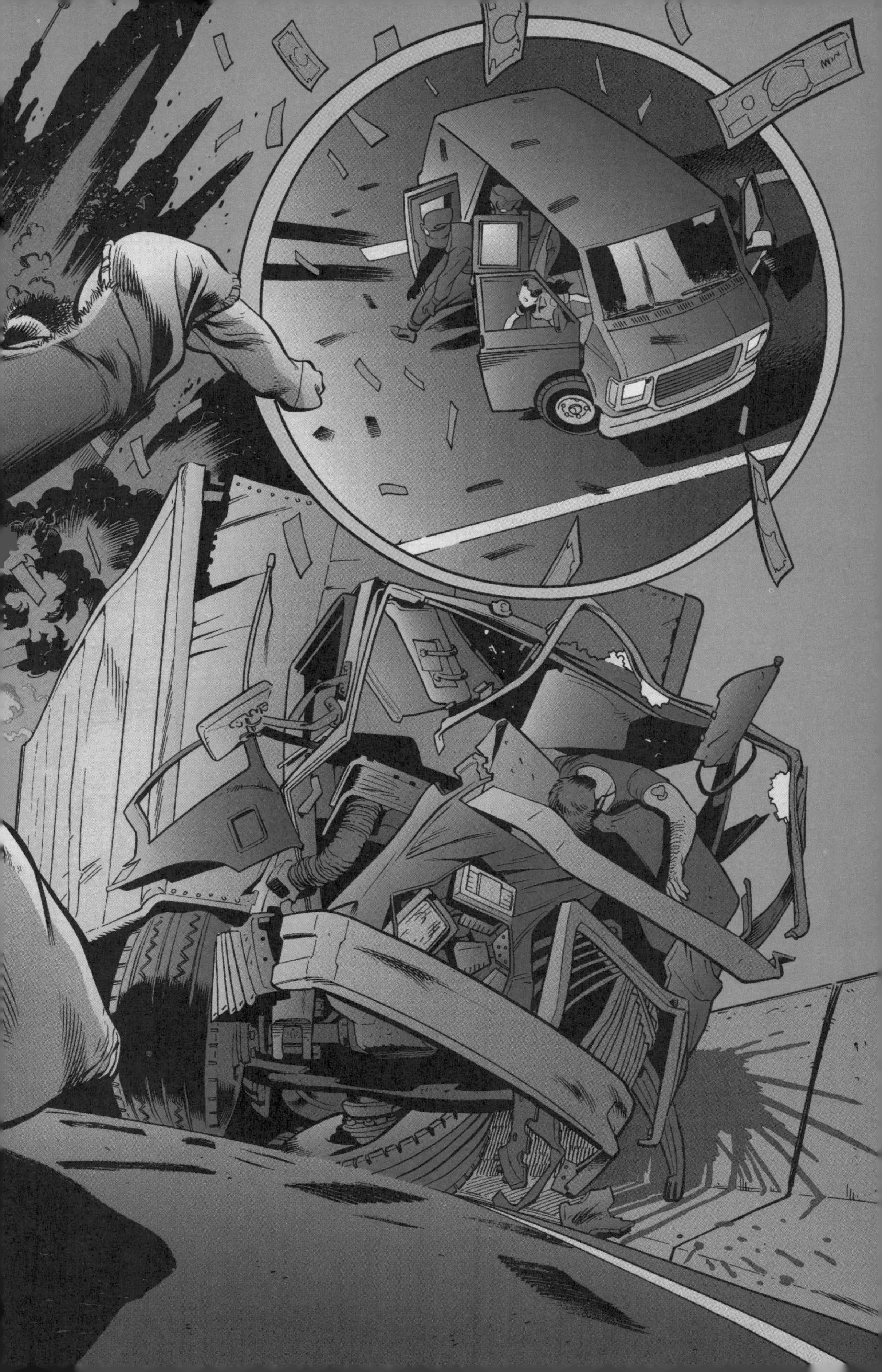

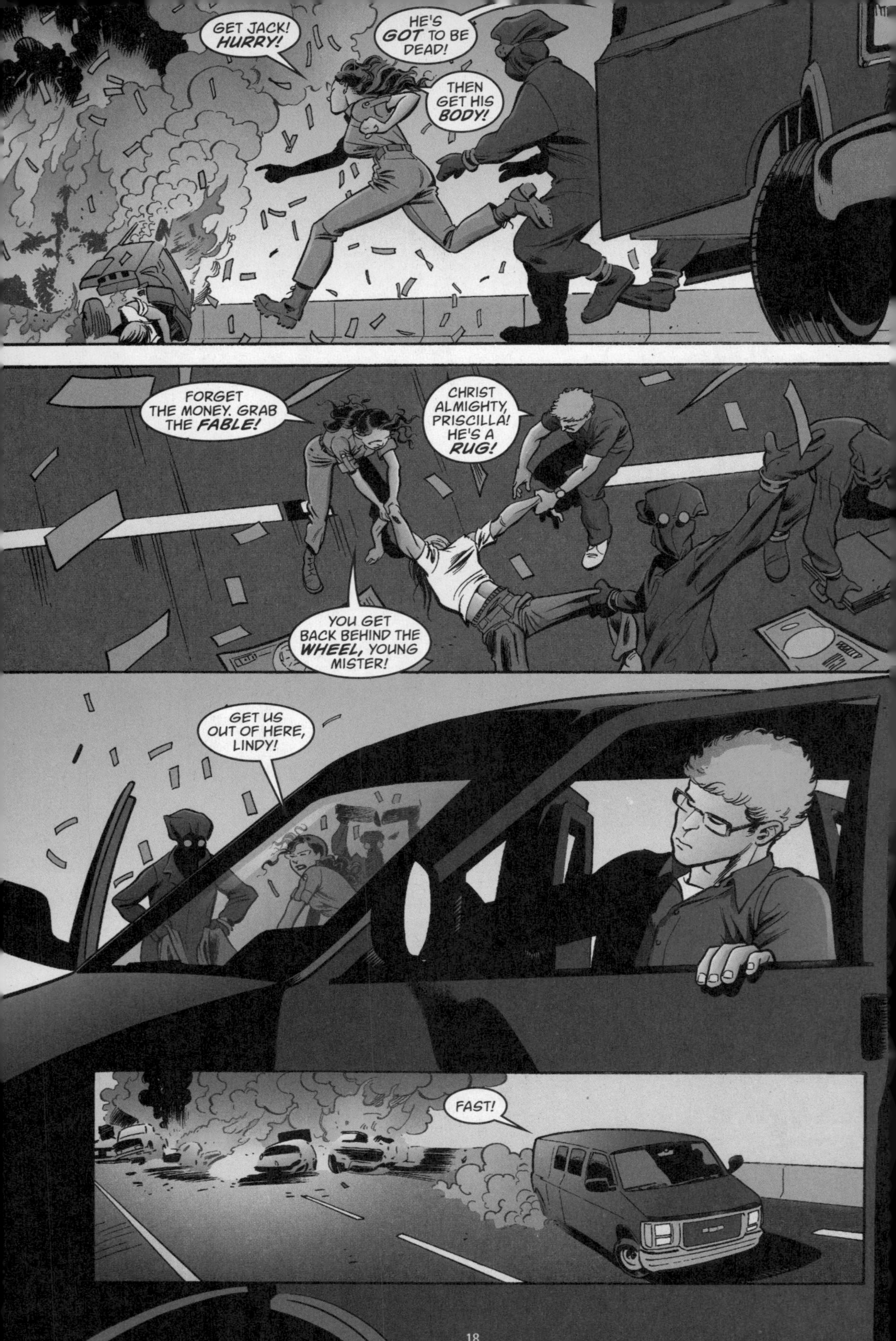
GET JACK! HURRY!
HE'S GOT TO BE DEAD!
THEN GET HIS BODY!
FORGET THE MONEY. GRAB THE FABLE!
CHRIST ALMIGHTY, PRISCILLA! HE'S A RUG!
YOU GET BACK BEHIND THE WHEEL, YOUNG MISTER!
GET US OUT OF HERE, LINDY!
FAST!

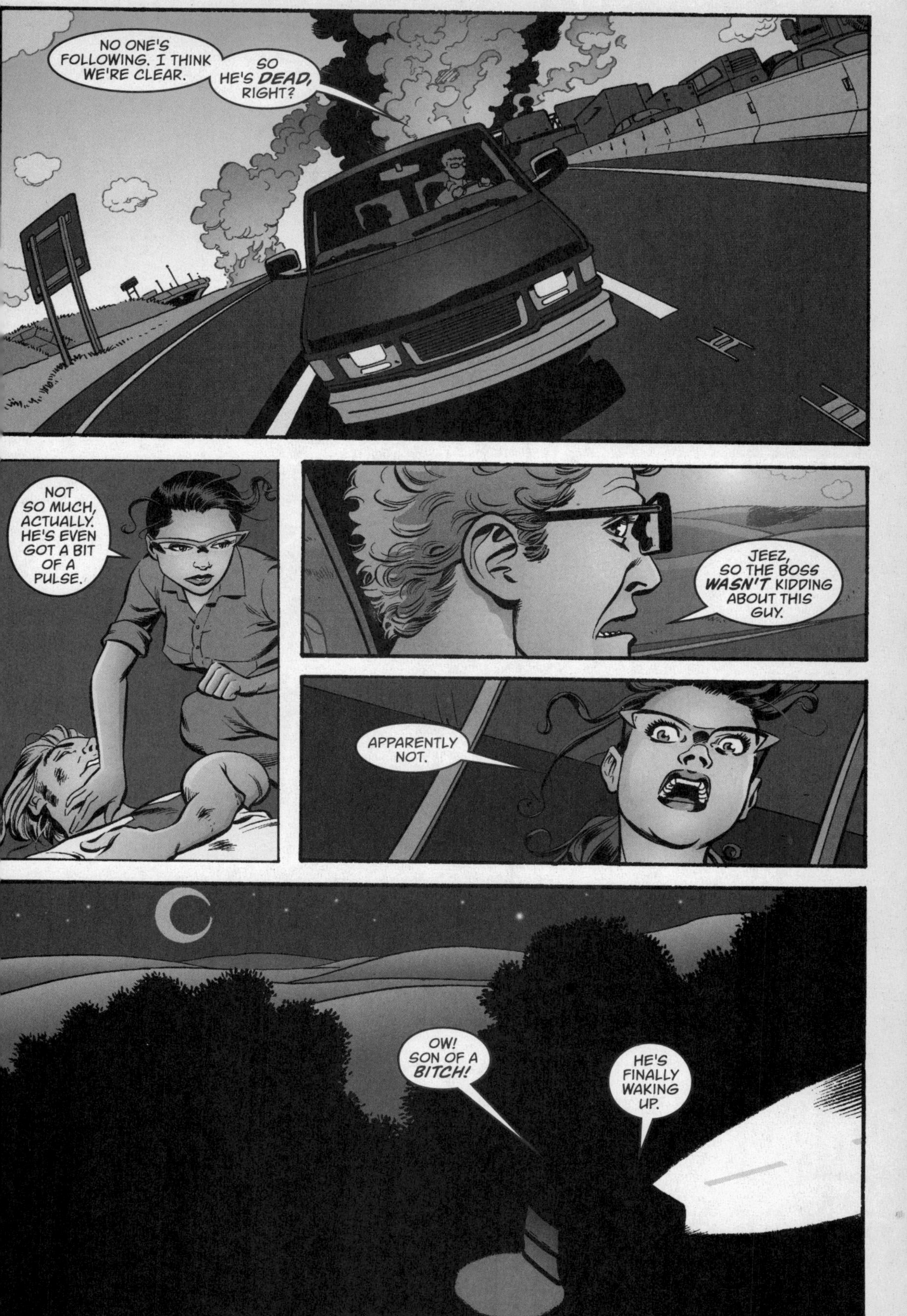
NO ONE'S FOLLOWING. I THINK WE'RE CLEAR.
SO HE'S DEAD, RIGHT?
NOT SO MUCH, ACTUALLY. HE'S EVEN GOT A BIT OF A PULSE.
JEEZ, SO THE BOSS WASN'T KIDDING ABOUT THIS GUY.
APPARENTLY NOT.
OW! SON OF A BITCH!
HE'S FINALLY WAKING UP.

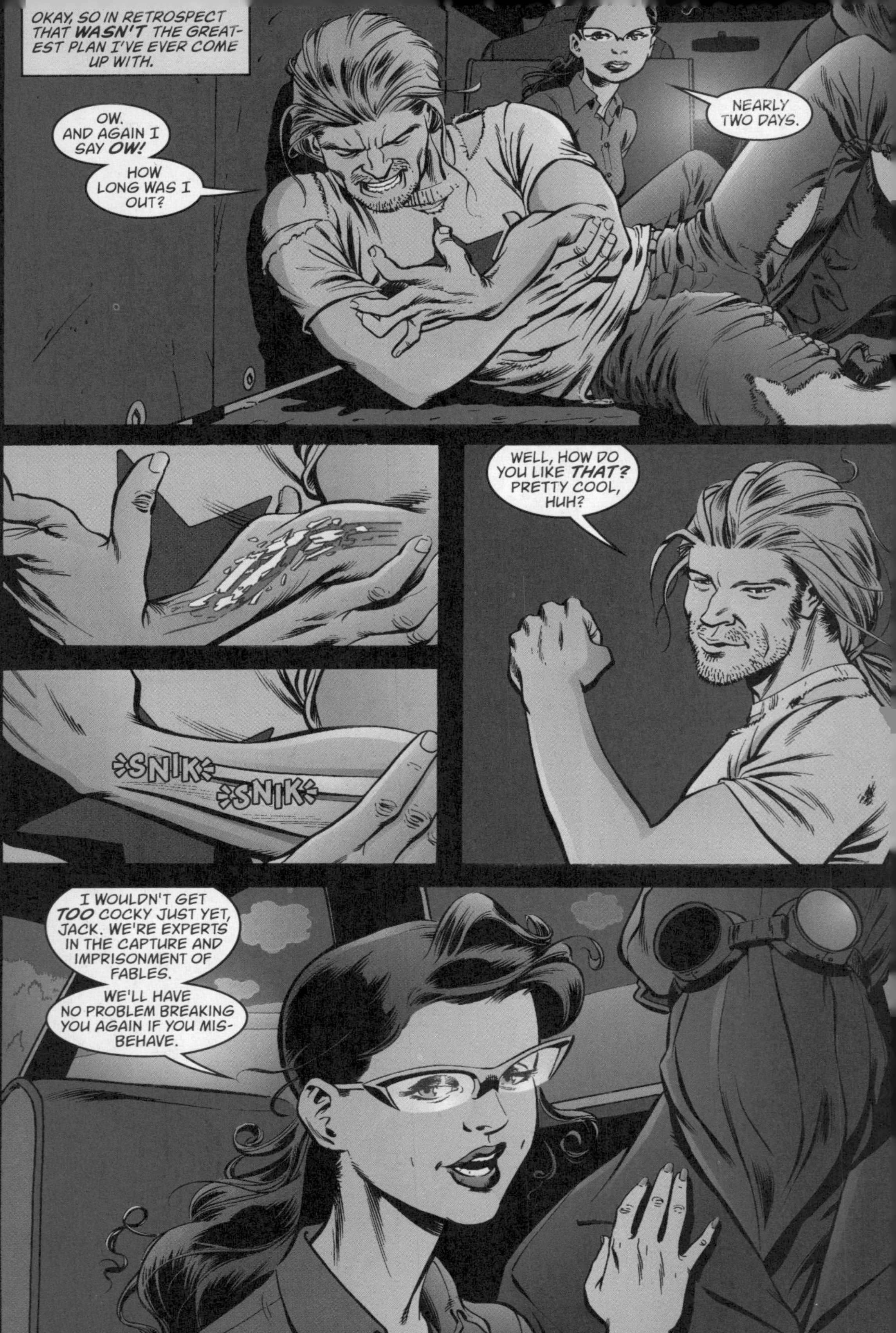
OKAY, SO IN RETROSPECT THAT WASN'T THE GREATEST PLAN I'VE EVER COME UP WITH.
OW. AND AGAIN I SAY OW!
HOW LONG WAS I OUT?
NEARLY TWO DAYS.
SNIK
SNIK
WELL, HOW DO YOU LIKE THAT? PRETTY COOL, HUH?
I WOULDN'T GET TOO COCKY JUST YET, JACK. WE'RE EXPERTS IN THE CAPTURE AND IMPRISONMENT OF FABLES.
WE'LL HAVE NO PROBLEM BREAKING YOU AGAIN IF YOU MISBEHAVE.

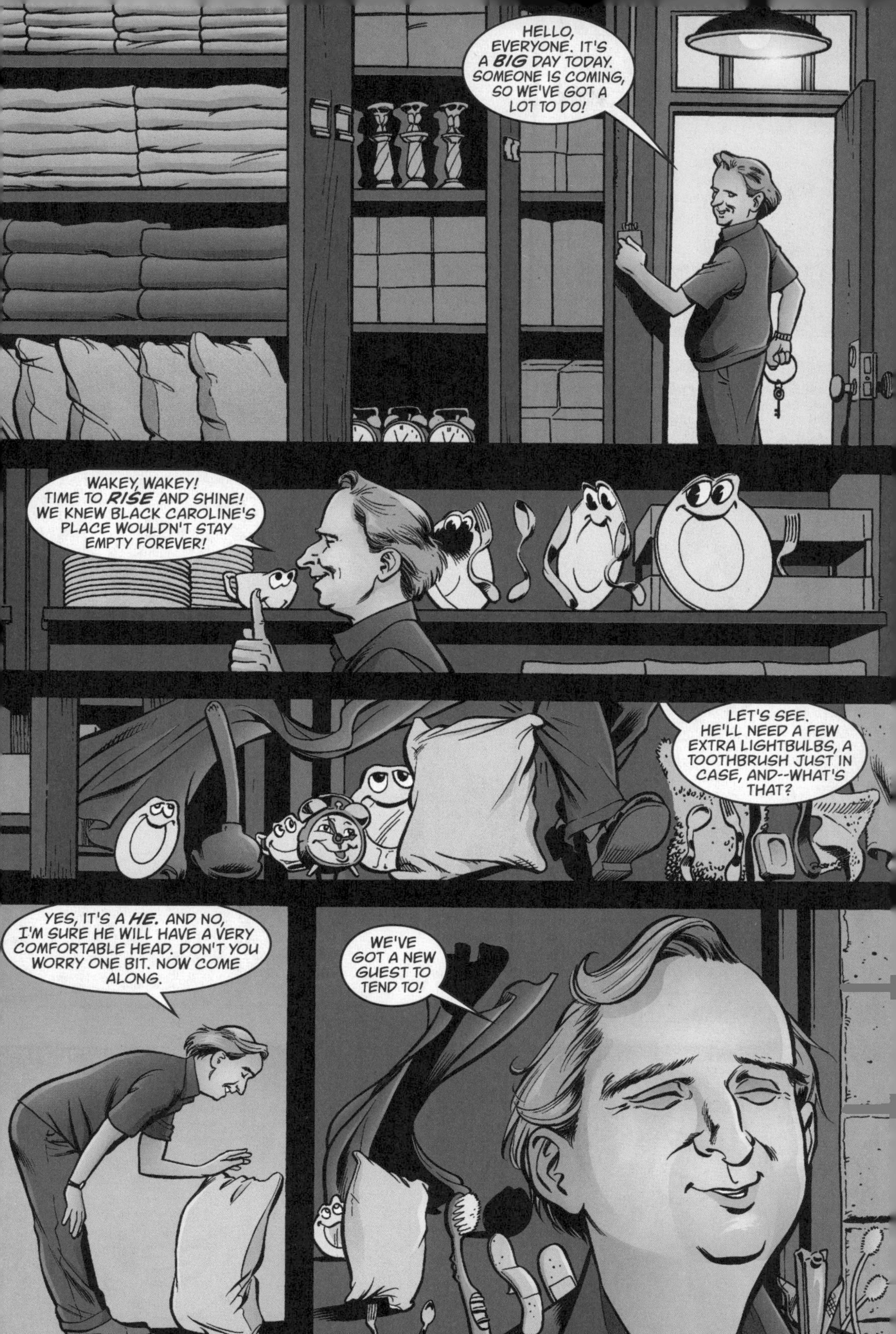
HELLO, EVERYONE. IT'S A BIG DAY TODAY. SOMEONE IS COMING, SO WE'VE GOT A LOT TO DO!
WAKEY, WAKEY! TIME TO RISE AND SHINE! WE KNEW BLACK CAROLINE'S PLACE WOULDN'T STAY EMPTY FOREVER!
LET'S SEE. HE'LL NEED A FEW EXTRA LIGHTBULBS, A TOOTHBRUSH JUST IN CASE, AND--WHAT'S THAT?
YES, IT'S A HE. AND NO, I'M SURE HE WILL HAVE A VERY COMFORTABLE HEAD. DON'T YOU WORRY ONE BIT. NOW COME ALONG.
WE'VE GOT A NEW GUEST TO TEND TO!

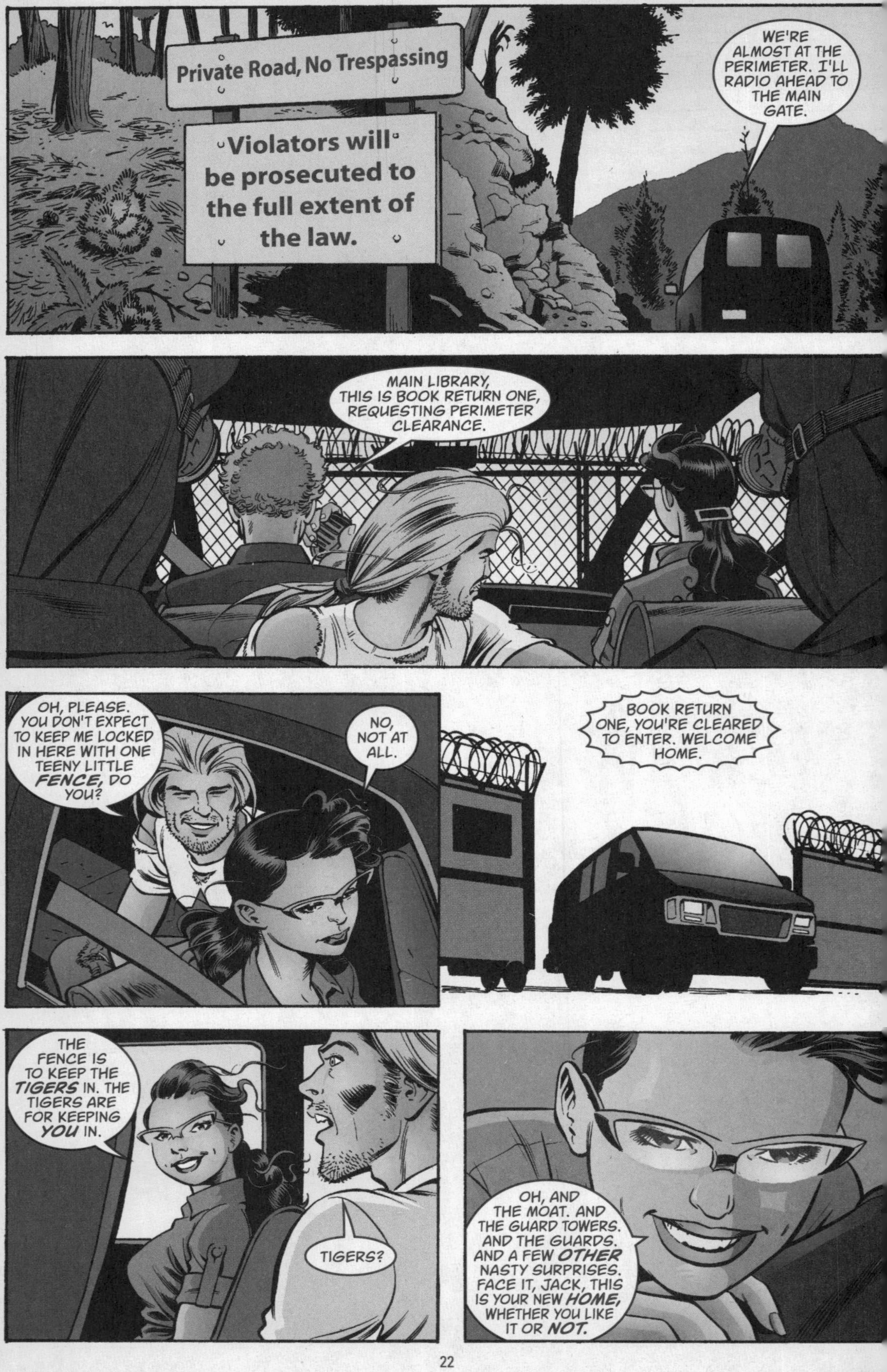

Private Road, No Trespassing
Violators will be prosecuted to the full extent of the law.
WE'RE ALMOST AT THE PERIMETER. I'LL RADIO AHEAD TO THE MAIN GATE.
MAIN LIBRARY, THIS IS BOOK RETURN ONE, REQUESTING PERIMETER CLEARANCE.
OH, PLEASE. YOU DON'T EXPECT TO KEEP ME LOCKED IN HERE WITH ONE TEENY LITTLE *FENCE,* DO YOU?
NO, NOT AT ALL.
BOOK RETURN ONE, YOU'RE CLEARED TO ENTER. WELCOME HOME.
THE FENCE IS TO KEEP THE *TIGERS* IN. THE TIGERS ARE FOR KEEPING *YOU* IN.
TIGERS?
OH, AND THE MOAT. AND THE GUARD TOWERS. AND THE GUARDS. AND A FEW *OTHER* NASTY SURPRISES. FACE IT, JACK, THIS IS YOUR NEW *HOME,* WHETHER YOU LIKE IT OR *NOT.*

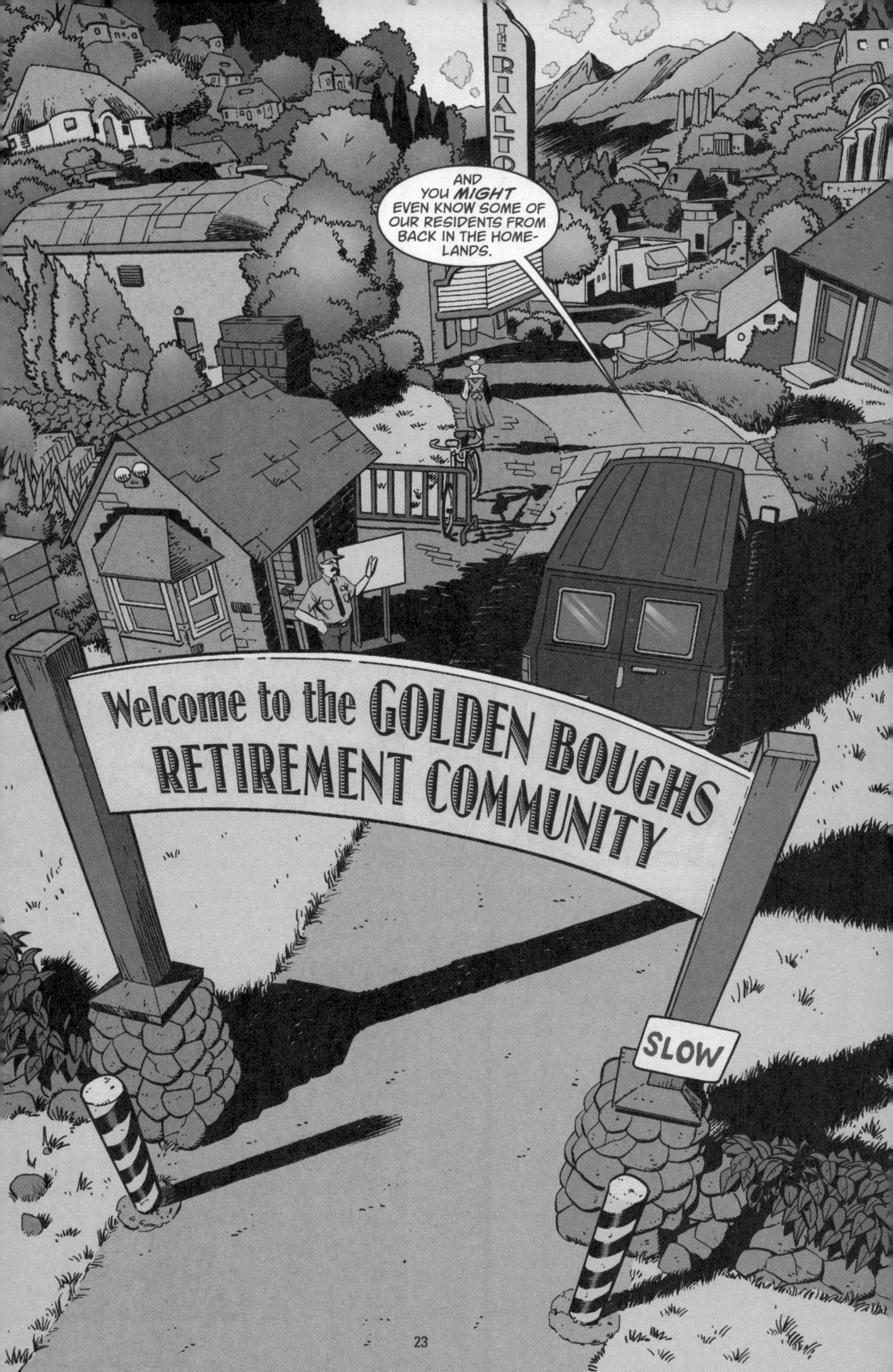
THE RIALTO
AND YOU *MIGHT* EVEN KNOW SOME OF OUR RESIDENTS FROM BACK IN THE HOME-LANDS.
Welcome to the GOLDEN BOUGHS RETIREMENT COMMUNITY
SLOW

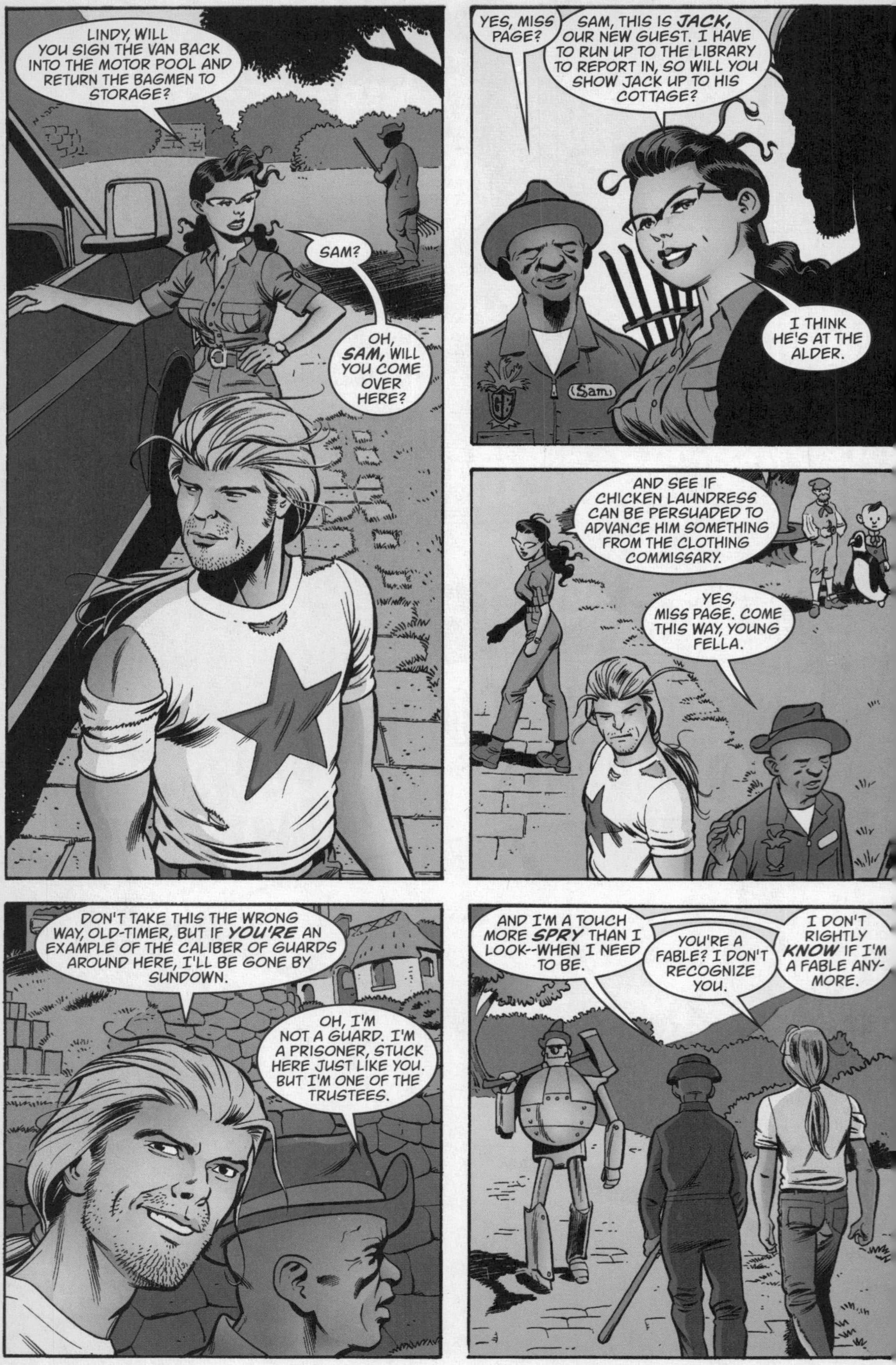
LINDY, WILL YOU SIGN THE VAN BACK INTO THE MOTOR POOL AND RETURN THE BAGMEN TO STORAGE?
SAM?
OH, SAM, WILL YOU COME OVER HERE?
YES, MISS PAGE?
SAM, THIS IS JACK, OUR NEW GUEST. I HAVE TO RUN UP TO THE LIBRARY TO REPORT IN, SO WILL YOU SHOW JACK UP TO HIS COTTAGE?
I THINK HE'S AT THE ALDER.
SAM
AND SEE IF CHICKEN LAUNDRESS CAN BE PERSUADED TO ADVANCE HIM SOMETHING FROM THE CLOTHING COMMISSARY.
YES, MISS PAGE. COME THIS WAY, YOUNG FELLA.
DON'T TAKE THIS THE WRONG WAY, OLD-TIMER, BUT IF YOU'RE AN EXAMPLE OF THE CALIBER OF GUARDS AROUND HERE, I'LL BE GONE BY SUNDOWN.
OH, I'M NOT A GUARD. I'M A PRISONER, STUCK HERE JUST LIKE YOU. BUT I'M ONE OF THE TRUSTEES.
AND I'M A TOUCH MORE SPRY THAN I LOOK--WHEN I NEED TO BE.
YOU'RE A FABLE? I DON'T RECOGNIZE YOU.
I DON'T RIGHTLY KNOW IF I'M A FABLE ANY-MORE.

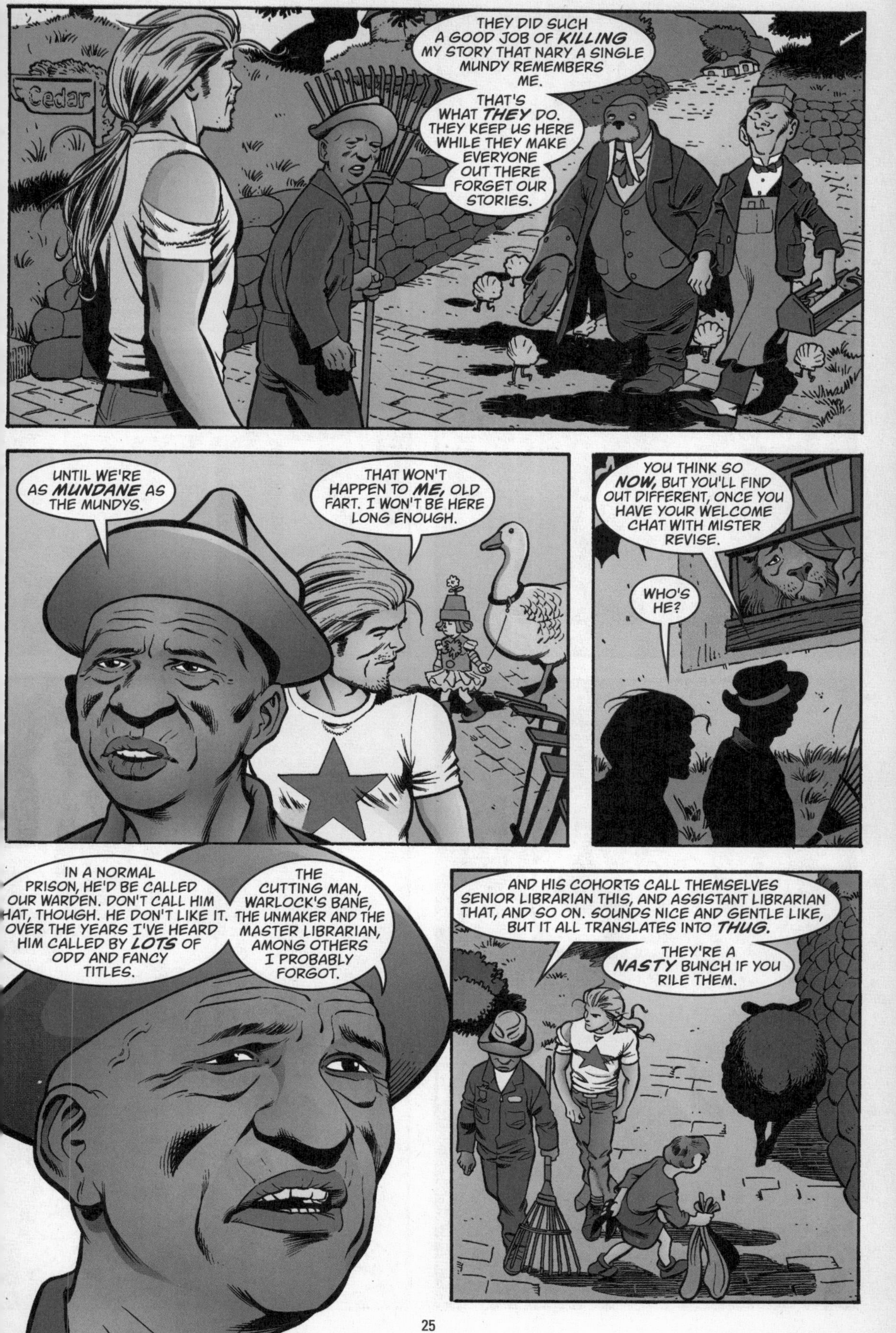
Cedar
THEY DID SUCH A GOOD JOB OF KILLING MY STORY THAT NARY A SINGLE MUNDY REMEMBERS ME.
THAT'S WHAT THEY DO. THEY KEEP US HERE WHILE THEY MAKE EVERYONE OUT THERE FORGET OUR STORIES.
UNTIL WE'RE AS MUNDANE AS THE MUNDYS.
THAT WON'T HAPPEN TO ME, OLD FART. I WON'T BE HERE LONG ENOUGH.
YOU THINK SO NOW, BUT YOU'LL FIND OUT DIFFERENT, ONCE YOU HAVE YOUR WELCOME CHAT WITH MISTER REVISE.
WHO'S HE?
IN A NORMAL PRISON, HE'D BE CALLED OUR WARDEN. DON'T CALL HIM THAT, THOUGH. HE DON'T LIKE IT. OVER THE YEARS I'VE HEARD HIM CALLED BY LOTS OF ODD AND FANCY TITLES.
THE CUTTING MAN, WARLOCK'S BANE, THE UNMAKER AND THE MASTER LIBRARIAN, AMONG OTHERS I PROBABLY FORGOT.
AND HIS COHORTS CALL THEMSELVES SENIOR LIBRARIAN THIS, AND ASSISTANT LIBRARIAN THAT, AND SO ON. SOUNDS NICE AND GENTLE LIKE, BUT IT ALL TRANSLATES INTO THUG.
THEY'RE A NASTY BUNCH IF YOU RILE THEM.

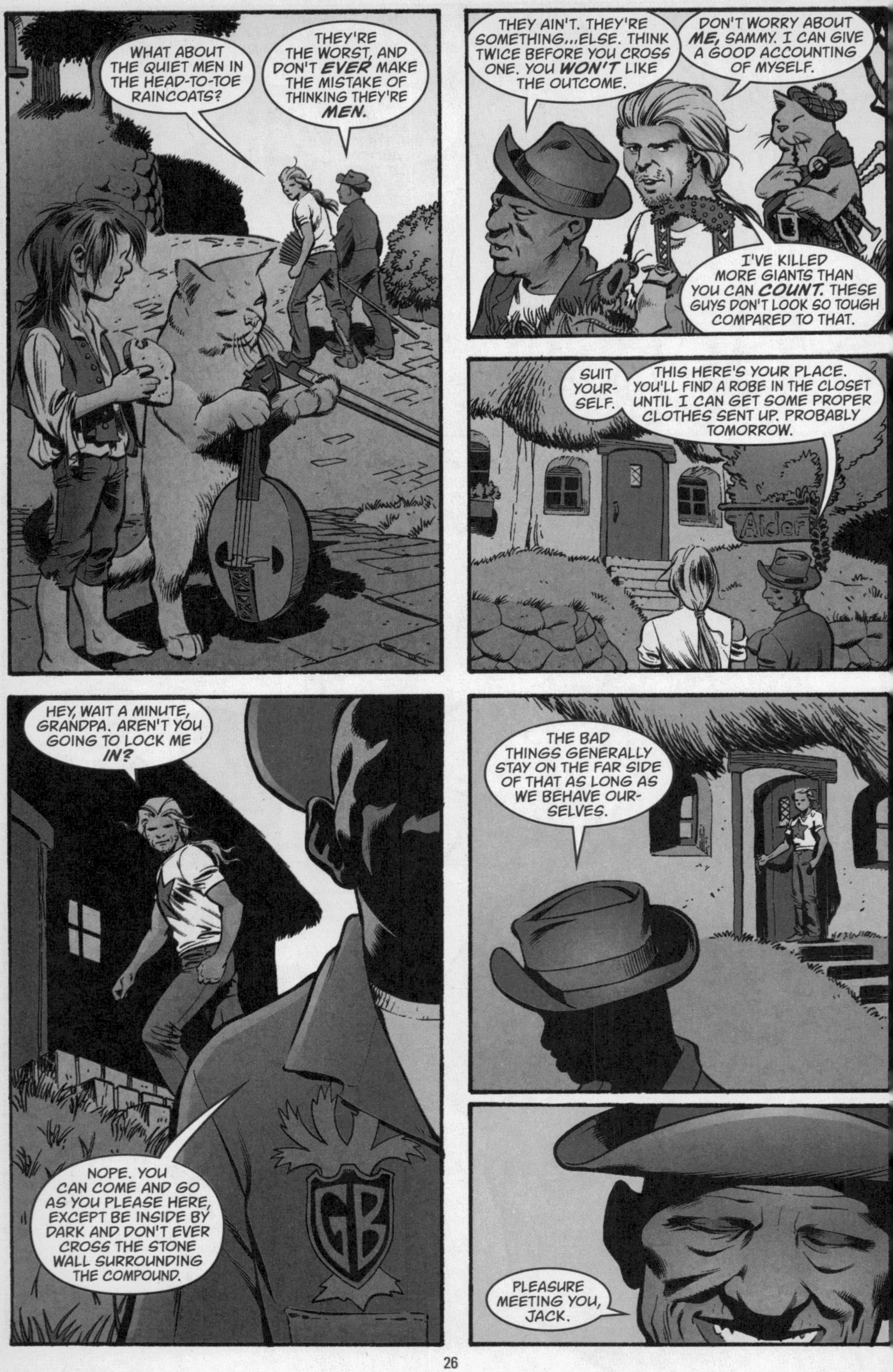
WHAT ABOUT THE QUIET MEN IN THE HEAD-TO-TOE RAINCOATS?
THEY'RE THE WORST, AND DON'T EVER MAKE THE MISTAKE OF THINKING THEY'RE MEN.
THEY AIN'T. THEY'RE SOMETHING...ELSE. THINK TWICE BEFORE YOU CROSS ONE. YOU WON'T LIKE THE OUTCOME.
DON'T WORRY ABOUT ME, SAMMY. I CAN GIVE A GOOD ACCOUNTING OF MYSELF.
I'VE KILLED MORE GIANTS THAN YOU CAN COUNT. THESE GUYS DON'T LOOK SO TOUGH COMPARED TO THAT.
SUIT YOUR-SELF.
THIS HERE'S YOUR PLACE. YOU'LL FIND A ROBE IN THE CLOSET UNTIL I CAN GET SOME PROPER CLOTHES SENT UP. PROBABLY TOMORROW.
Alder
HEY, WAIT A MINUTE, GRANDPA. AREN'T YOU GOING TO LOCK ME IN?
NOPE. YOU CAN COME AND GO AS YOU PLEASE HERE, EXCEPT BE INSIDE BY DARK AND DON'T EVER CROSS THE STONE WALL SURROUNDING THE COMPOUND.
GB
THE BAD THINGS GENERALLY STAY ON THE FAR SIDE OF THAT AS LONG AS WE BEHAVE OUR-SELVES.
PLEASURE MEETING YOU, JACK.

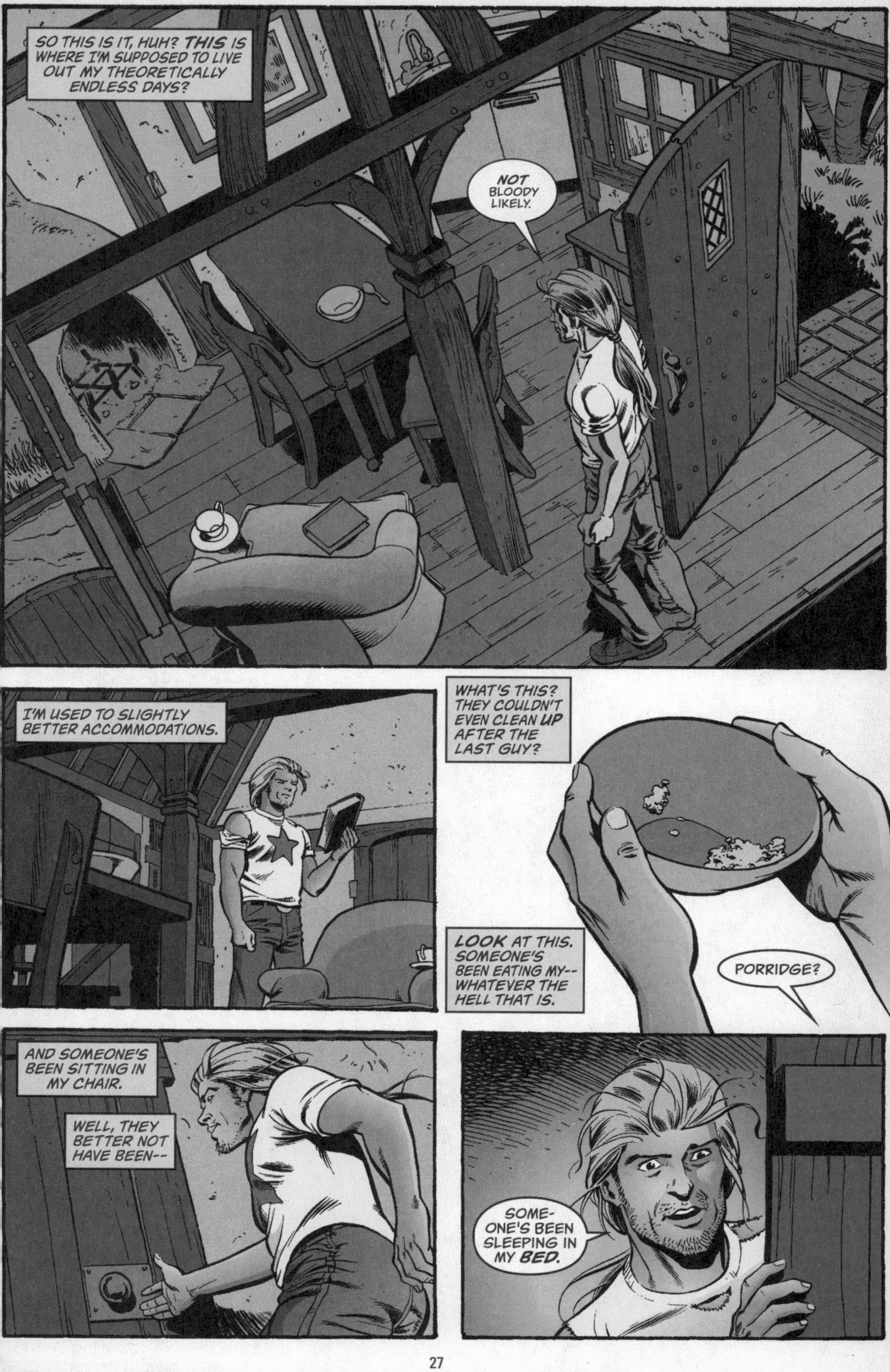
SO THIS IS IT, HUH? THIS IS WHERE I'M SUPPOSED TO LIVE OUT MY THEORETICALLY ENDLESS DAYS?
NOT BLOODY LIKELY.
I'M USED TO SLIGHTLY BETTER ACCOMMODATIONS.
WHAT'S THIS? THEY COULDN'T EVEN CLEAN UP AFTER THE LAST GUY?
LOOK AT THIS. SOMEONE'S BEEN EATING MY-- WHATEVER THE HELL THAT IS.
PORRIDGE?
AND SOMEONE'S BEEN SITTING IN MY CHAIR.
WELL, THEY BETTER NOT HAVE BEEN--
SOME-ONE'S BEEN SLEEPING IN MY BED.

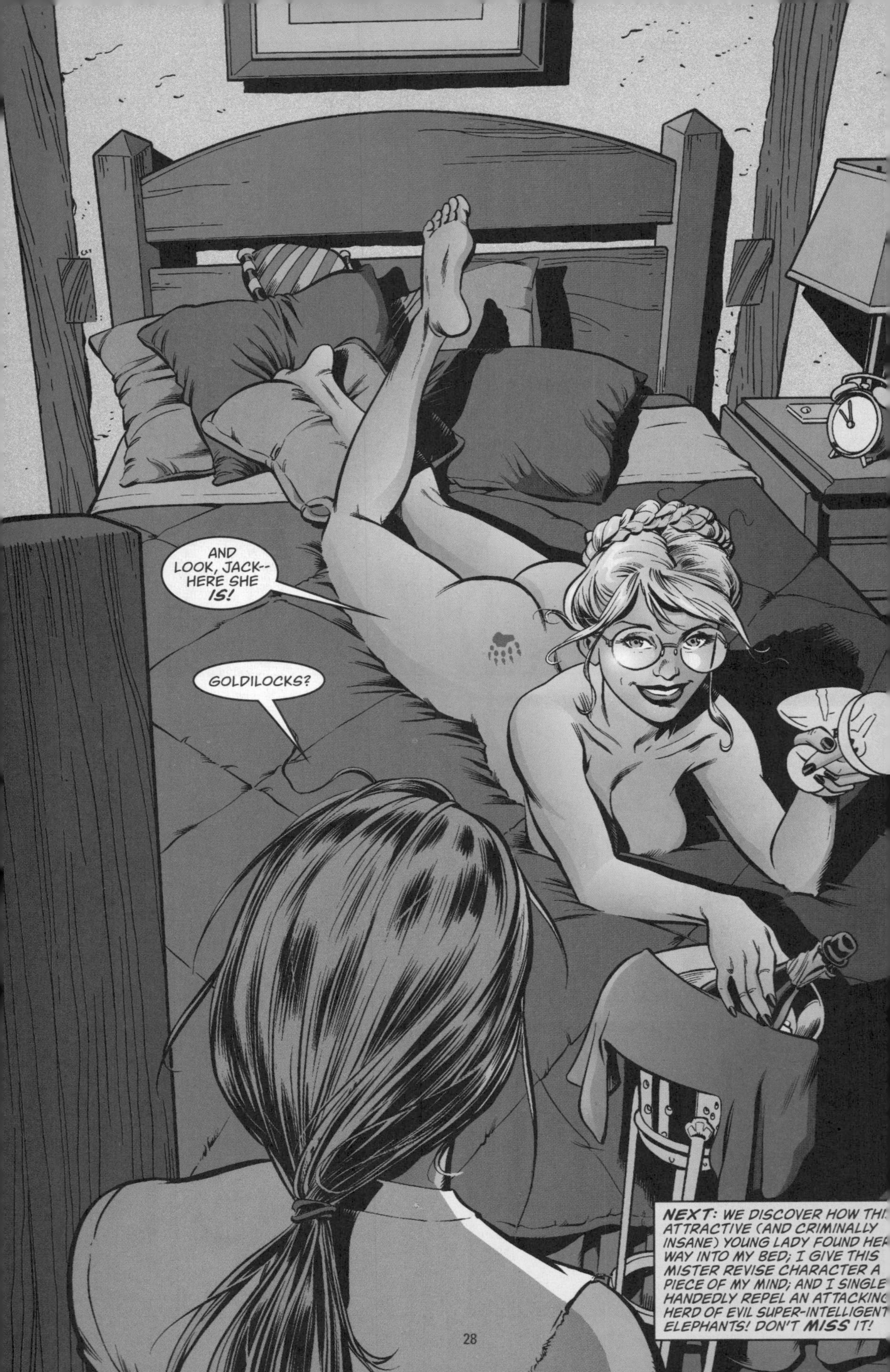
AND LOOK, JACK-- HERE SHE IS!
GOLDILOCKS?
NEXT: WE DISCOVER HOW THI ATTRACTIVE (AND CRIMINALLY INSANE) YOUNG LADY FOUND HE WAY INTO MY BED; I GIVE THIS MISTER REVISE CHARACTER A PIECE OF MY MIND; AND I SINGLE HANDEDLY REPEL AN ATTACKIN HERD OF EVIL SUPER-INTELLIGENT ELEPHANTS! DON'T MISS IT!

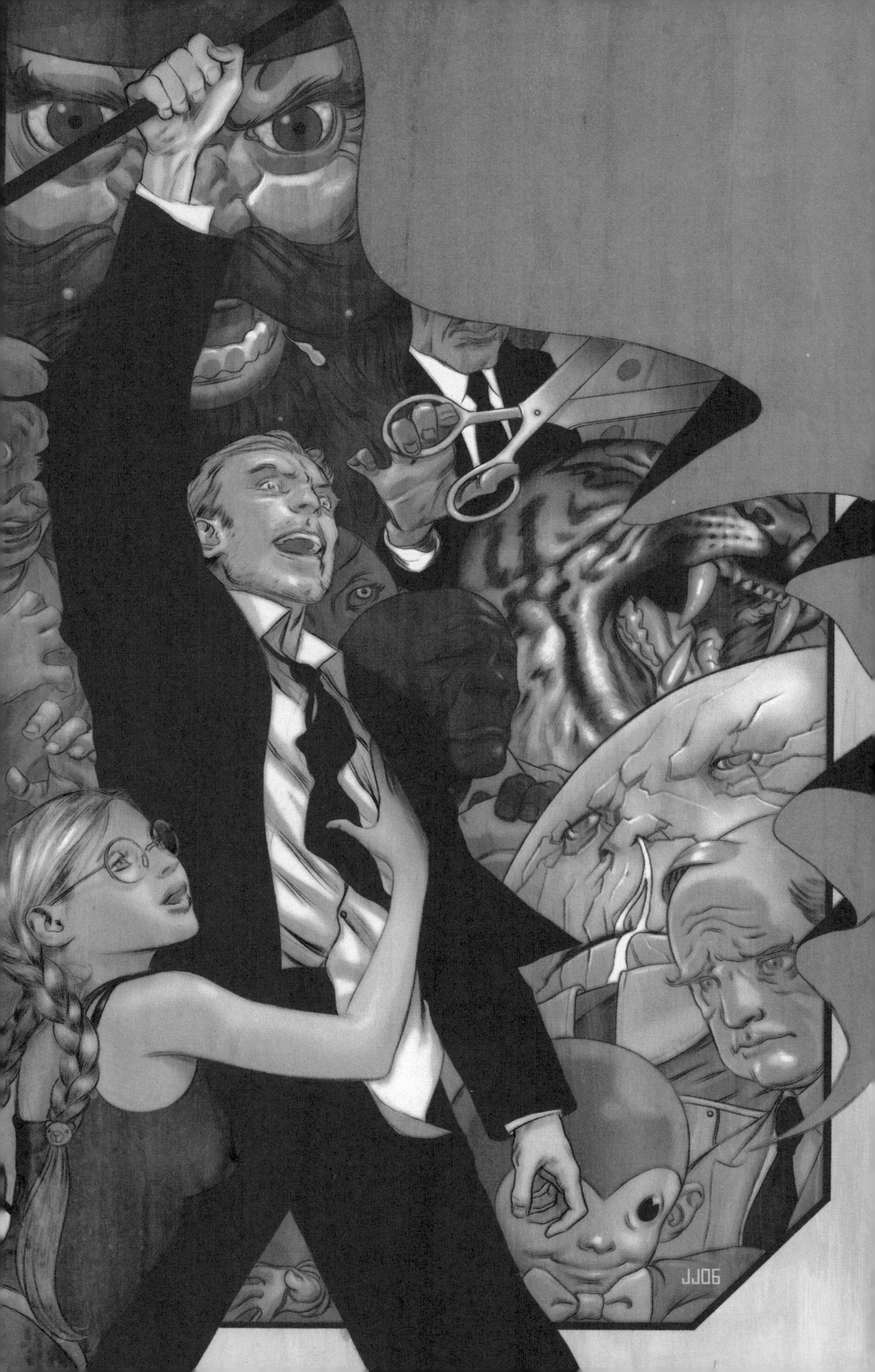
JJ06

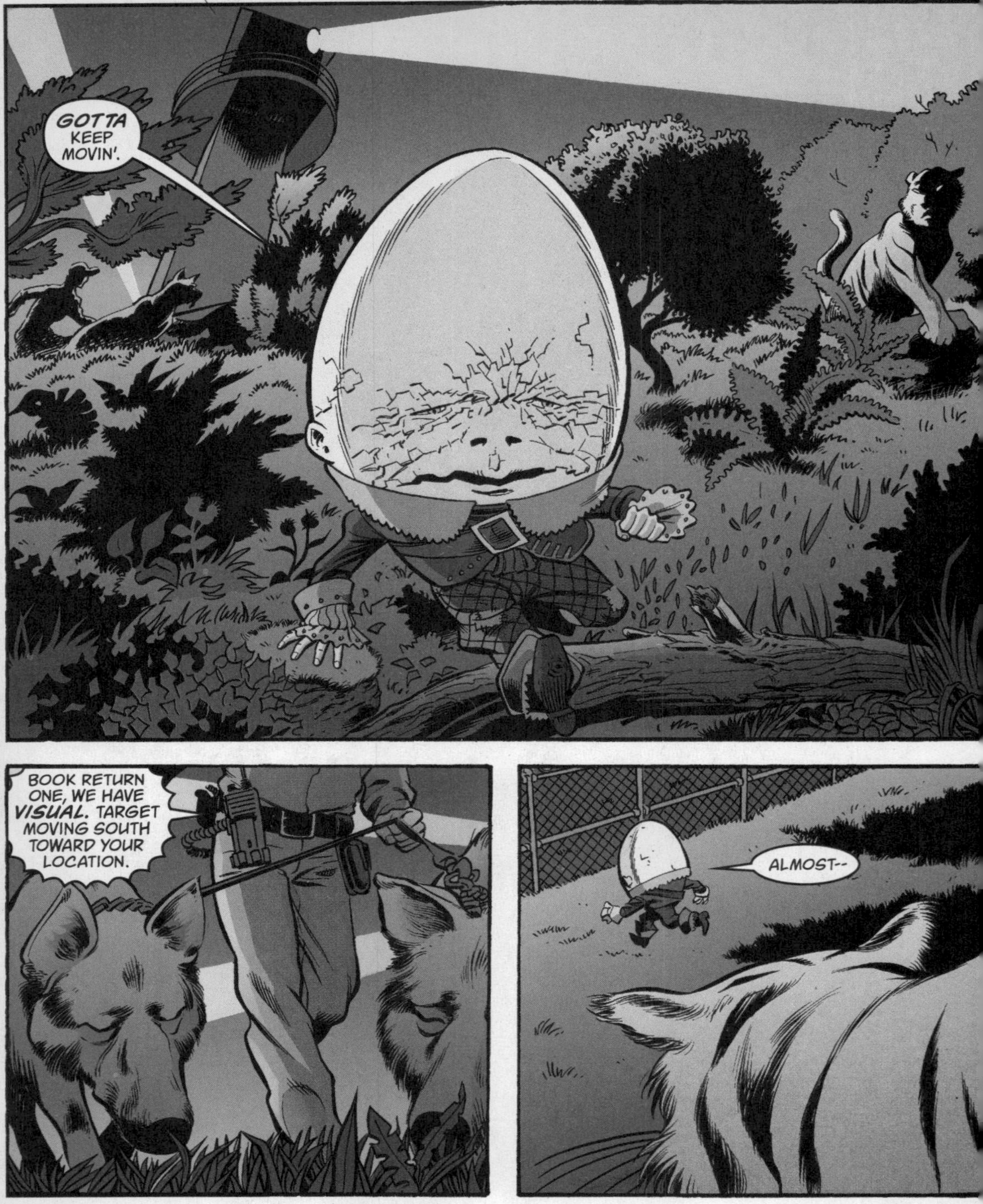
GOTTA KEEP MOVIN'.
BOOK RETURN ONE, WE HAVE VISUAL. TARGET MOVING SOUTH TOWARD YOUR LOCATION.
ALMOST--

In which our hero makes time and does time, two drunks fight in a bar, and an egg scrambles.

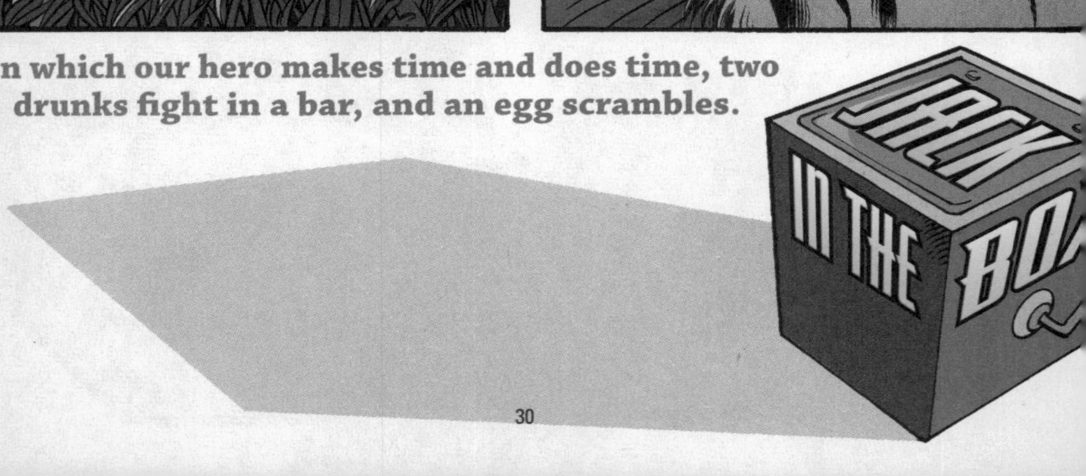
JACK
IN THE

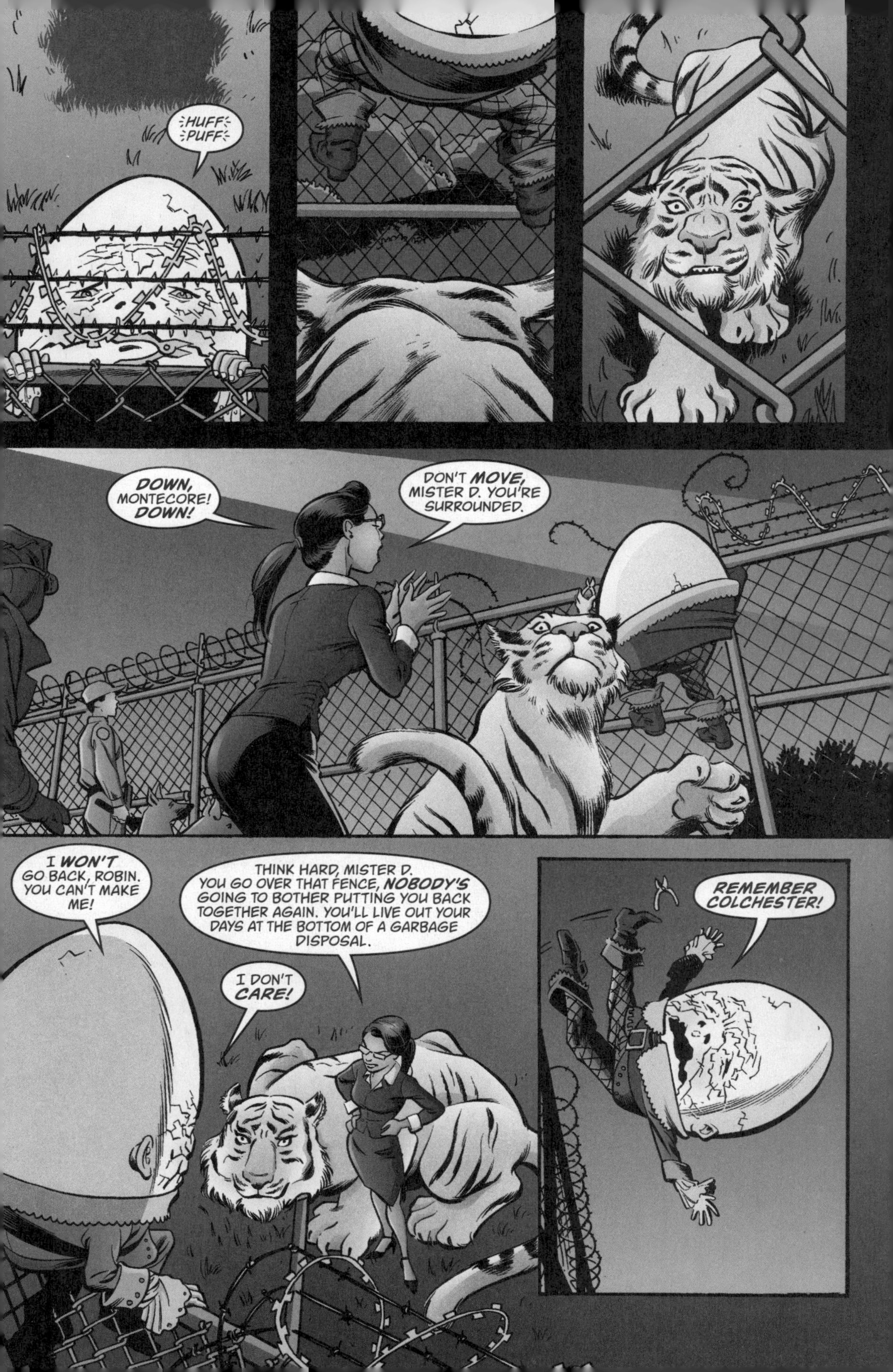
HUFF PUFF
DOWN, MONTECORE! DOWN!
DON'T MOVE, MISTER D. YOU'RE SURROUNDED.
I WON'T GO BACK, ROBIN. YOU CAN'T MAKE ME!
THINK HARD, MISTER D. YOU GO OVER THAT FENCE, NOBODY'S GOING TO BOTHER PUTTING YOU BACK TOGETHER AGAIN. YOU'LL LIVE OUT YOUR DAYS AT THE BOTTOM OF A GARBAGE DISPOSAL.
I DON'T CARE!
REMEMBER COLCHESTER!

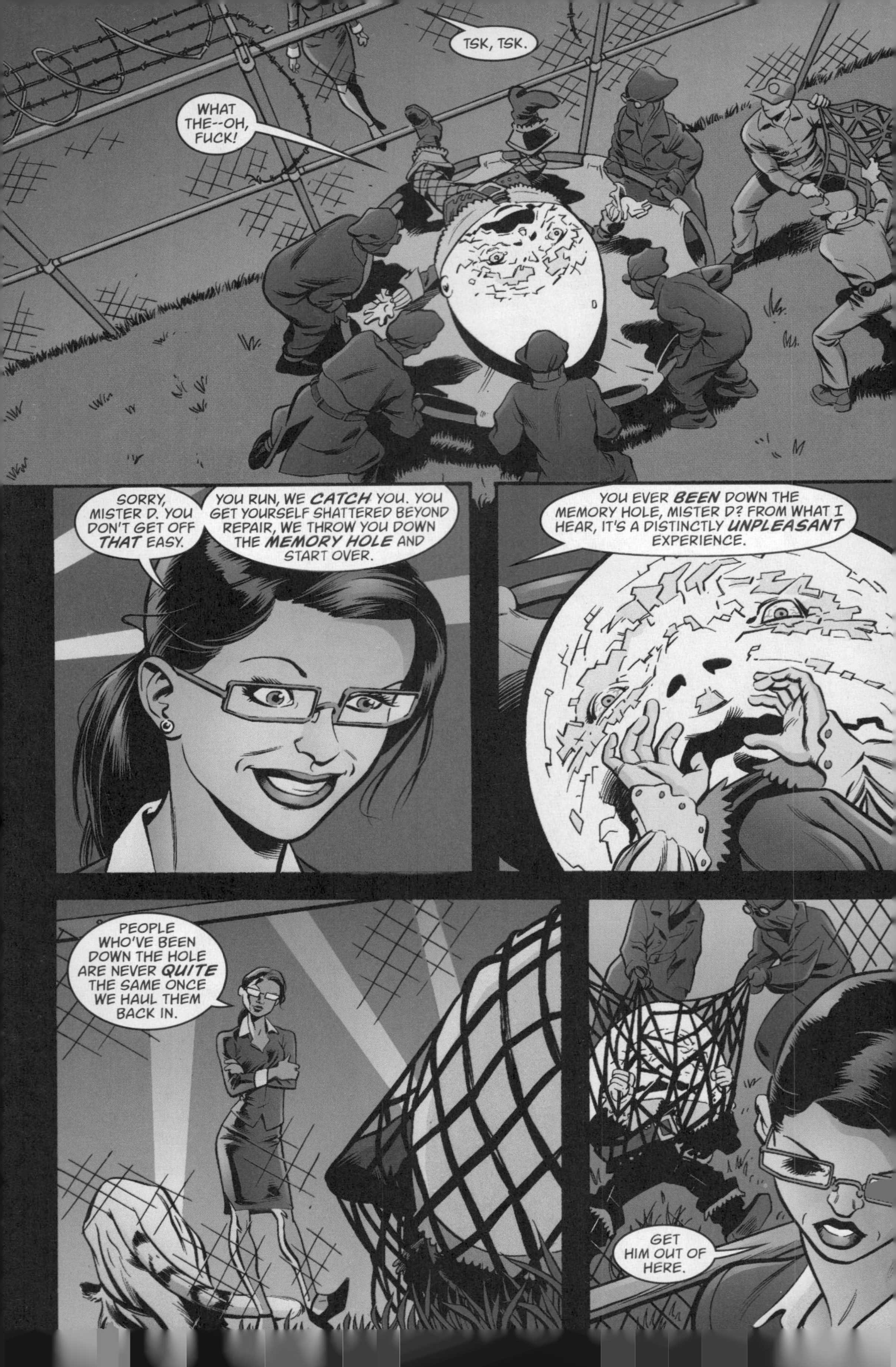
TSK, TSK.
WHAT THE--OH, FUCK!
SORRY, MISTER D. YOU DON'T GET OFF *THAT* EASY.
YOU RUN, WE *CATCH* YOU. YOU GET YOURSELF SHATTERED BEYOND REPAIR, WE THROW YOU DOWN THE *MEMORY HOLE* AND START OVER.
YOU EVER *BEEN* DOWN THE MEMORY HOLE, MISTER D? FROM WHAT I HEAR, IT'S A DISTINCTLY *UNPLEASANT* EXPERIENCE.
PEOPLE WHO'VE BEEN DOWN THE HOLE ARE NEVER *QUITE* THE SAME ONCE WE HAUL THEM BACK IN.
GET HIM OUT OF HERE.

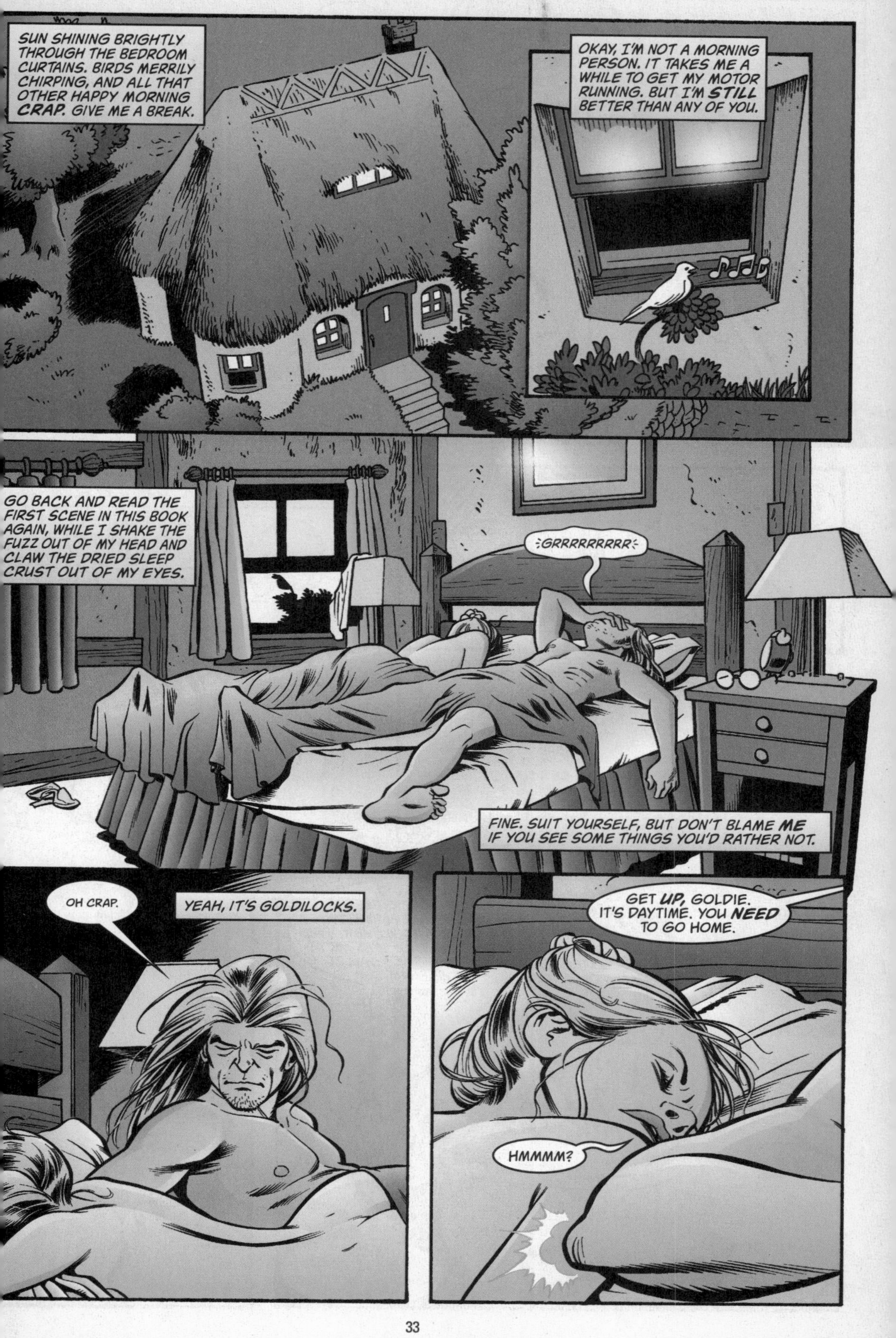
SUN SHINING BRIGHTLY THROUGH THE BEDROOM CURTAINS. BIRDS MERRILY CHIRPING, AND ALL THAT OTHER HAPPY MORNING CRAP. GIVE ME A BREAK.
OKAY, I'M NOT A MORNING PERSON. IT TAKES ME A WHILE TO GET MY MOTOR RUNNING. BUT I'M STILL BETTER THAN ANY OF YOU.
GO BACK AND READ THE FIRST SCENE IN THIS BOOK AGAIN, WHILE I SHAKE THE FUZZ OUT OF MY HEAD AND CLAW THE DRIED SLEEP CRUST OUT OF MY EYES.
GRRRRRRRRR
FINE. SUIT YOURSELF, BUT DON'T BLAME ME IF YOU SEE SOME THINGS YOU'D RATHER NOT.
OH CRAP.
YEAH, IT'S GOLDILOCKS.
GET UP, GOLDIE. IT'S DAYTIME. YOU NEED TO GO HOME.
HMMMM?

OH, GET THAT SHOCKED LOOK OFF YOUR FACE. JUST BECAUSE SHE'S AN INSANE KILLER DIDN'T MEAN I WASN'T GOING TO *SLEEP* WITH HER.

JACK? GOOD MORNING. HAND ME MY GLASSES.

LOOK AT HER. YOU WOULD'VE DONE IT TOO.

UNLESS YOU WANT TO *VIOLATE* ME AGAIN?

ERM, NO.

YOU *HAVE* TO GET OUT. I NEED MY MORNINGS ALONE. NO BREAKFAST. NO COFFEE. NO TOAST. JUST *GO*.

SURE SHE TRIED TO KILL SNOW WHITE--*TWICE*--AND THAT'S BAD. BUT SHE ALSO TRIED TO KILL BIGBY WOLF, AND THAT'S OKAY IN MY BOOK.

YOU DON'T WANT TO TALK ABOUT OLD TIMES?

YOU AND I DIDN'T *HAVE* ANY OLD TIMES.

SURE WE DID. WE WERE OPPRESSED MEMBERS OF THE FABLETOWN *PROLETARIAT* TOGETHER, EVEN IF I SPENT MOST OF MY TIME AT THE *GULAG* THEY CALLED THE FARM.

MOST OF THE FABLES HERE NEVER *SAW* FABLE-TOWN.

THEY WERE CAPTURED *CENTURIES* AGO AND HAVE LIVED HERE--UTTERLY DIS-POSSESSED--EVER SINCE.

THAT'S YOUR *FIRST* LIE OF THE DAY, GOLDIE I TRAVELED *THROUGH* HERE CENTURIES AGO AND IT WAS UNTOUCHED WILDER-NESS.

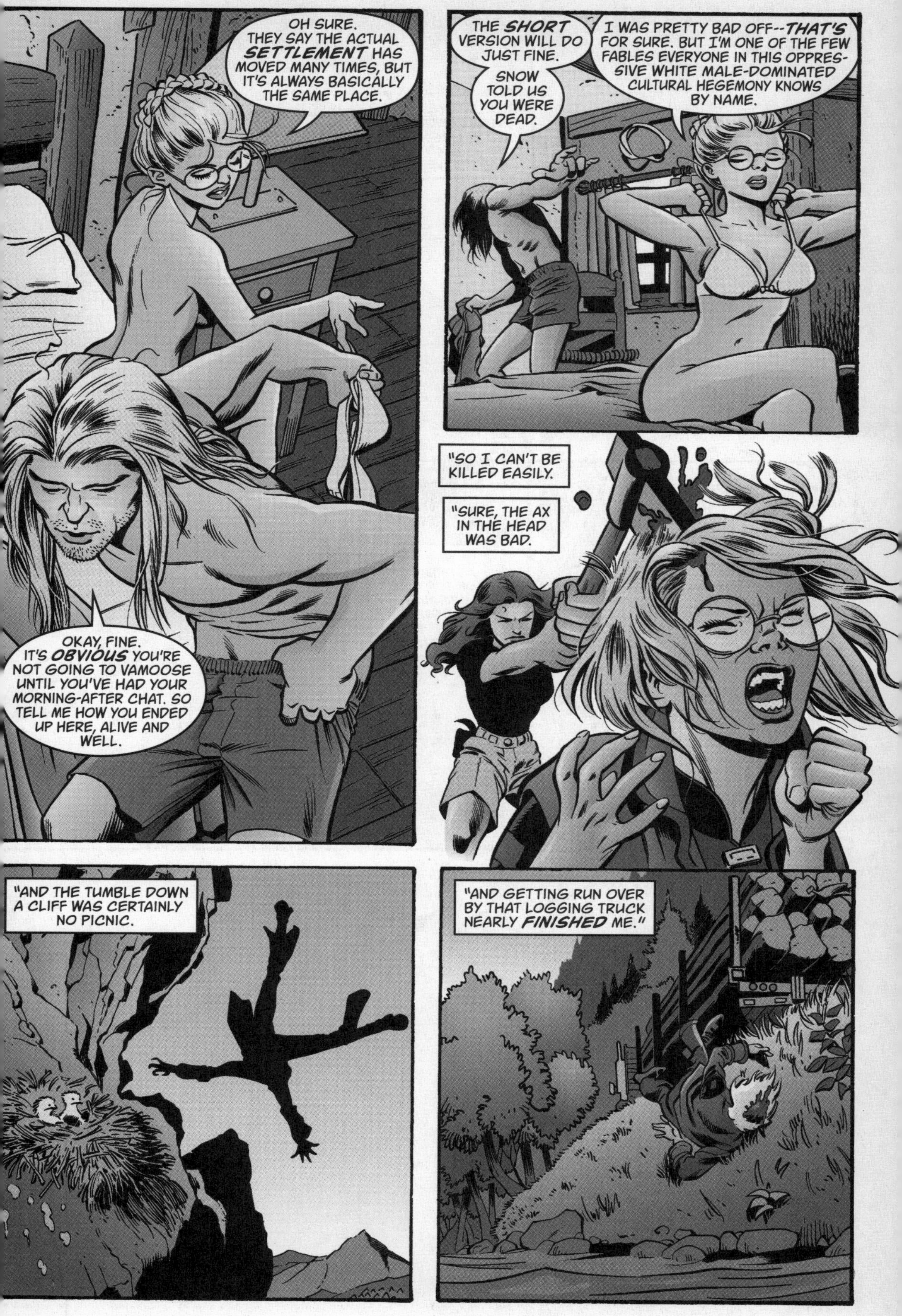
OH SURE. THEY SAY THE ACTUAL SETTLEMENT HAS MOVED MANY TIMES, BUT IT'S ALWAYS BASICALLY THE SAME PLACE.
OKAY, FINE. IT'S OBVIOUS YOU'RE NOT GOING TO VAMOOSE UNTIL YOU'VE HAD YOUR MORNING-AFTER CHAT. SO TELL ME HOW YOU ENDED UP HERE, ALIVE AND WELL.
THE SHORT VERSION WILL DO JUST FINE.
SNOW TOLD US YOU WERE DEAD.
I WAS PRETTY BAD OFF--THAT'S FOR SURE. BUT I'M ONE OF THE FEW FABLES EVERYONE IN THIS OPPRES-SIVE WHITE MALE-DOMINATED CULTURAL HEGEMONY KNOWS BY NAME.
"SO I CAN'T BE KILLED EASILY.
"SURE, THE AX IN THE HEAD WAS BAD.
"AND THE TUMBLE DOWN A CLIFF WAS CERTAINLY NO PICNIC.
"AND GETTING RUN OVER BY THAT LOGGING TRUCK NEARLY FINISHED ME."

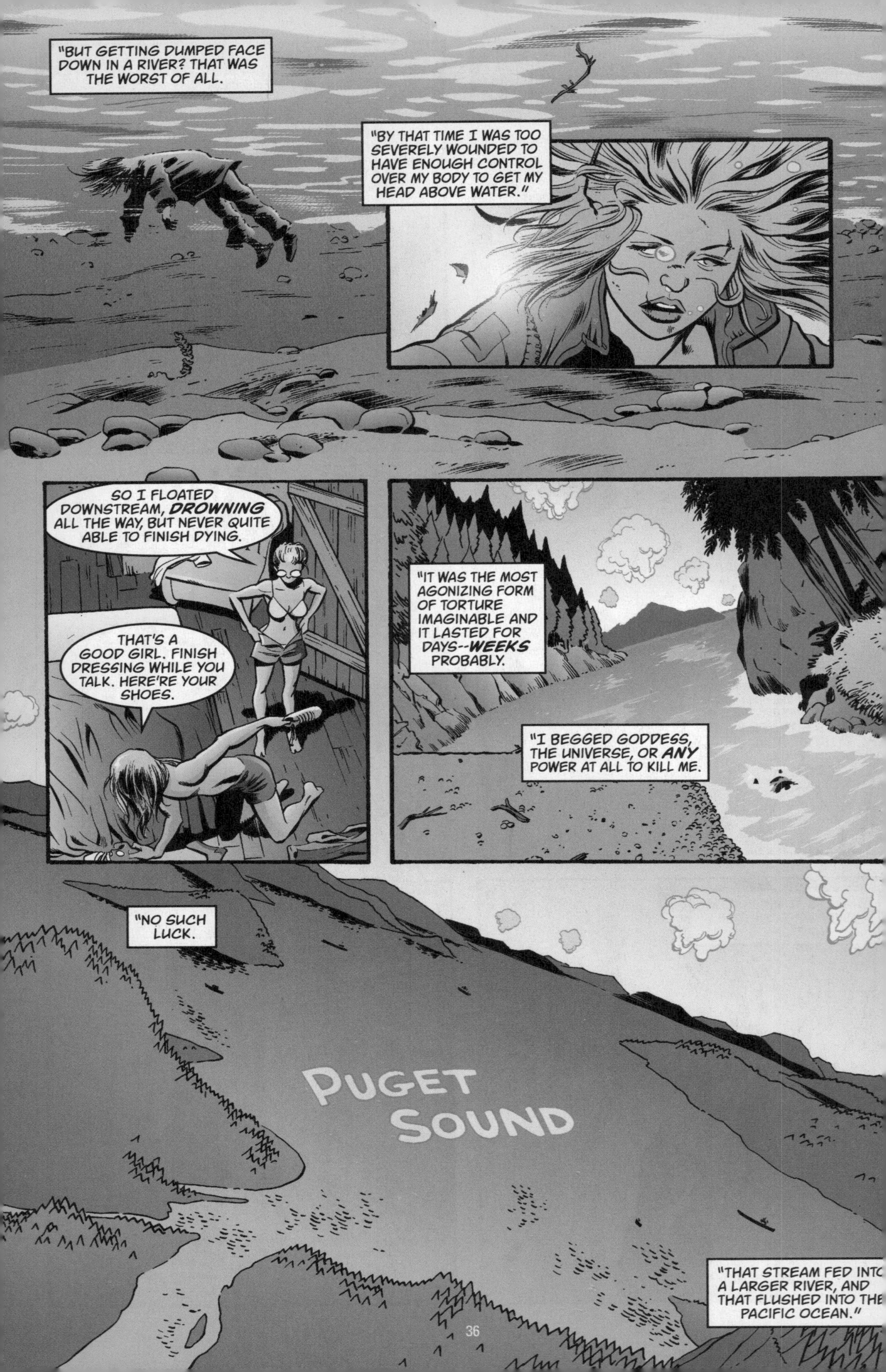
"BUT GETTING DUMPED FACE DOWN IN A RIVER? THAT WAS THE WORST OF ALL.
"BY THAT TIME I WAS TOO SEVERELY WOUNDED TO HAVE ENOUGH CONTROL OVER MY BODY TO GET MY HEAD ABOVE WATER."
SO I FLOATED DOWNSTREAM, DROWNING ALL THE WAY, BUT NEVER QUITE ABLE TO FINISH DYING.
THAT'S A GOOD GIRL. FINISH DRESSING WHILE YOU TALK. HERE'RE YOUR SHOES.
"IT WAS THE MOST AGONIZING FORM OF TORTURE IMAGINABLE AND IT LASTED FOR DAYS--WEEKS PROBABLY.
"I BEGGED GODDESS, THE UNIVERSE, OR ANY POWER AT ALL TO KILL ME.
"NO SUCH LUCK.
PUGET SOUND
"THAT STREAM FED INTO A LARGER RIVER, AND THAT FLUSHED INTO THE PACIFIC OCEAN."

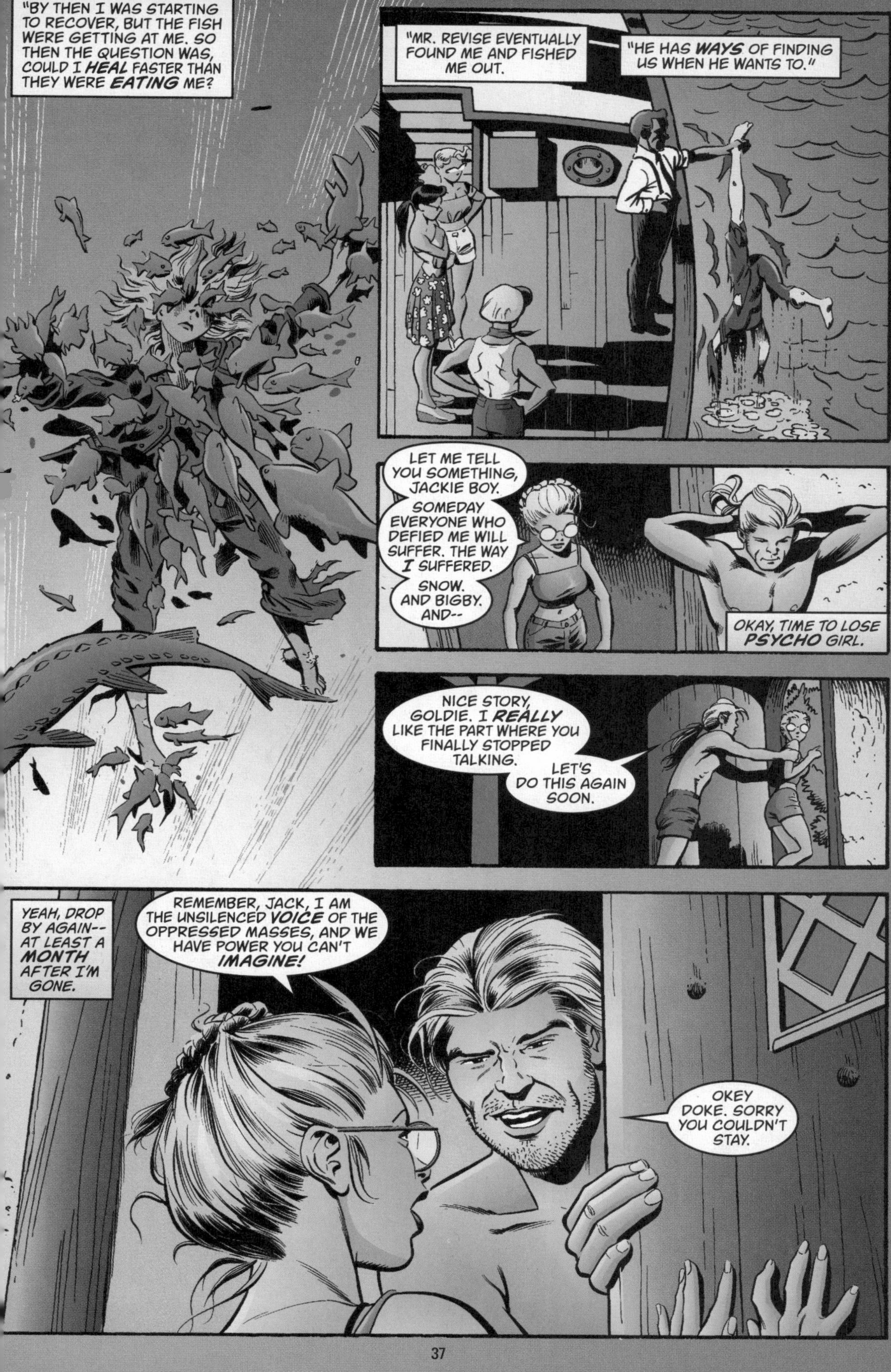
"BY THEN I WAS STARTING TO RECOVER, BUT THE FISH WERE GETTING AT ME. SO THEN THE QUESTION WAS, COULD I HEAL FASTER THAN THEY WERE EATING ME?
"MR. REVISE EVENTUALLY FOUND ME AND FISHED ME OUT.
"HE HAS WAYS OF FINDING US WHEN HE WANTS TO."
LET ME TELL YOU SOMETHING, JACKIE BOY.
SOMEDAY EVERYONE WHO DEFIED ME WILL SUFFER. THE WAY I SUFFERED.
SNOW. AND BIGBY. AND--
OKAY, TIME TO LOSE PSYCHO GIRL.
NICE STORY, GOLDIE. I REALLY LIKE THE PART WHERE YOU FINALLY STOPPED TALKING.
LET'S DO THIS AGAIN SOON.
YEAH, DROP BY AGAIN-- AT LEAST A MONTH AFTER I'M GONE.
REMEMBER, JACK, I AM THE UNSILENCED VOICE OF THE OPPRESSED MASSES, AND WE HAVE POWER YOU CAN'T IMAGINE!
OKEY DOKE. SORRY YOU COULDN'T STAY.

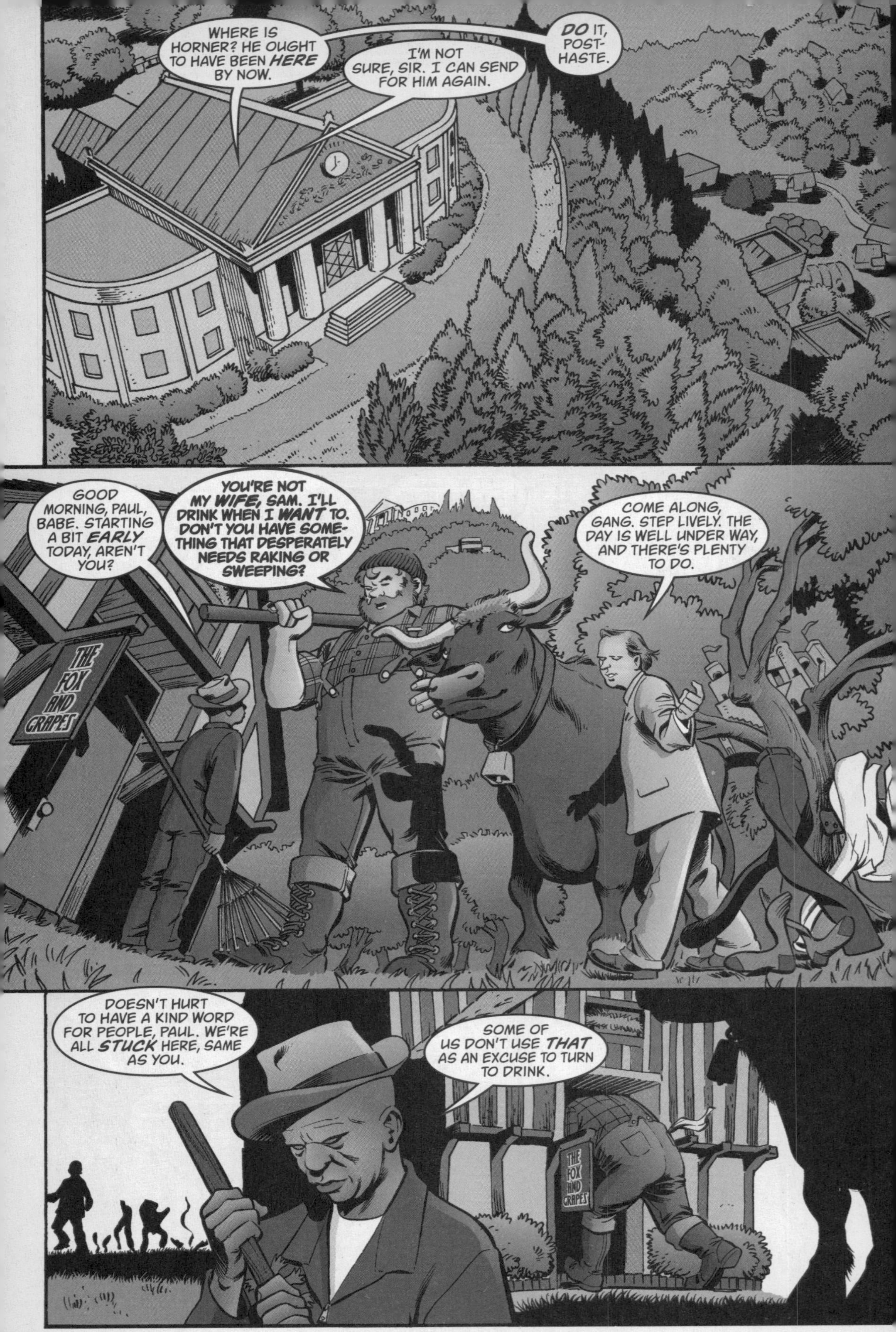
WHERE IS HORNER? HE OUGHT TO HAVE BEEN HERE BY NOW.
I'M NOT SURE, SIR. I CAN SEND FOR HIM AGAIN.
DO IT, POST-HASTE.
GOOD MORNING, PAUL, BABE. STARTING A BIT EARLY TODAY, AREN'T YOU?
YOU'RE NOT MY WIFE, SAM. I'LL DRINK WHEN I WANT TO. DON'T YOU HAVE SOMETHING THAT DESPERATELY NEEDS RAKING OR SWEEPING?
THE FOX AND GRAPES
COME ALONG, GANG. STEP LIVELY. THE DAY IS WELL UNDER WAY, AND THERE'S PLENTY TO DO.
DOESN'T HURT TO HAVE A KIND WORD FOR PEOPLE, PAUL. WE'RE ALL STUCK HERE, SAME AS YOU.
SOME OF US DON'T USE THAT AS AN EXCUSE TO TURN TO DRINK.
THE FOX AND GRAPES

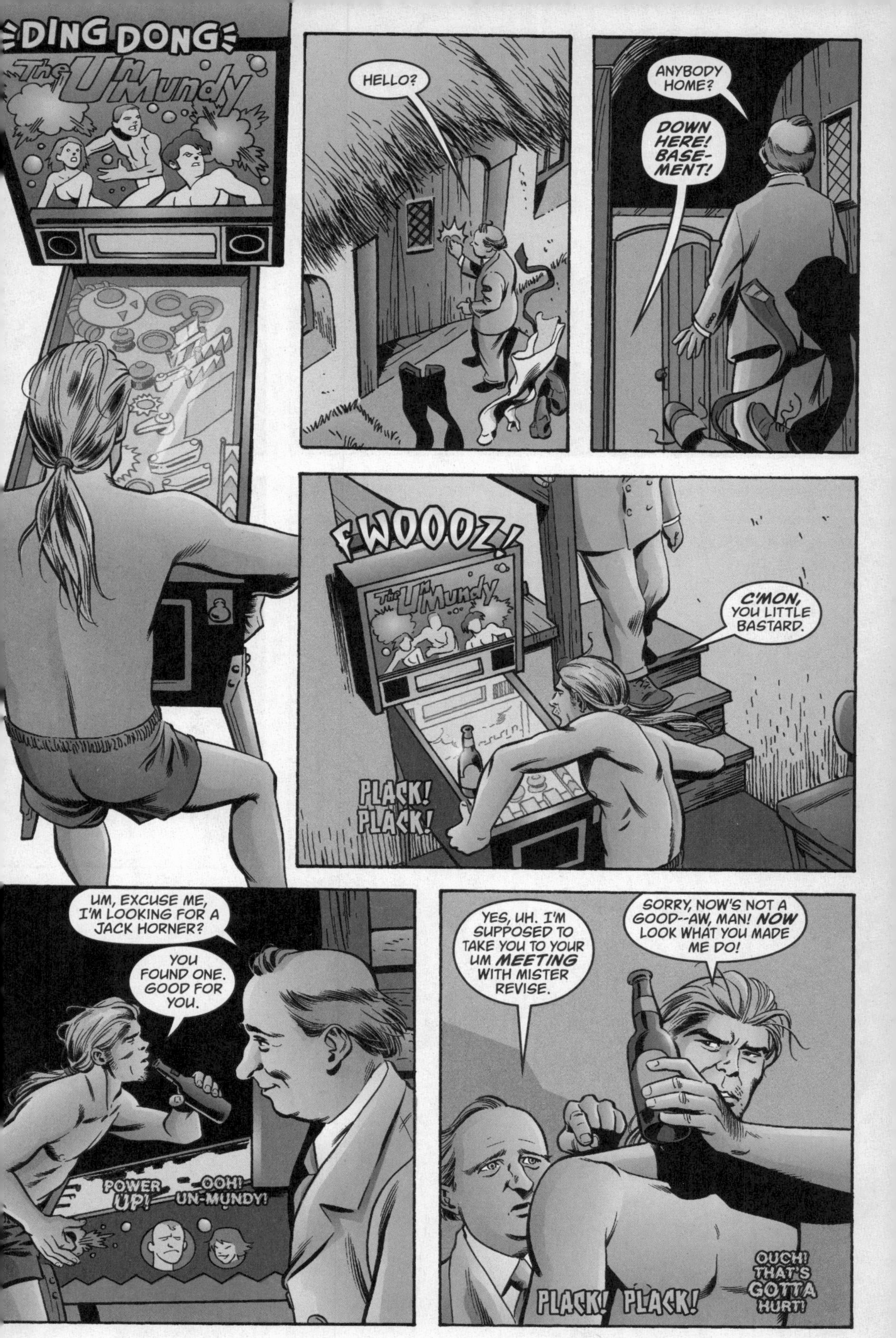
DING DONG
The Un-Mundy
HELLO?
ANYBODY HOME?
DOWN HERE! BASE-MENT!
FWOOOZ!
The Un-Mundy
C'MON, YOU LITTLE BASTARD.
PLACK! PLACK!
UM, EXCUSE ME, I'M LOOKING FOR A JACK HORNER?
YOU FOUND ONE. GOOD FOR YOU.
POWER UP!
OOH! UN-MUNDY!
YES, UH. I'M SUPPOSED TO TAKE YOU TO YOUR UM MEETING WITH MISTER REVISE.
SORRY, NOW'S NOT A GOOD--AW, MAN! NOW LOOK WHAT YOU MADE ME DO!
PLACK! PLACK!
OUCH! THAT'S GOTTA HURT!

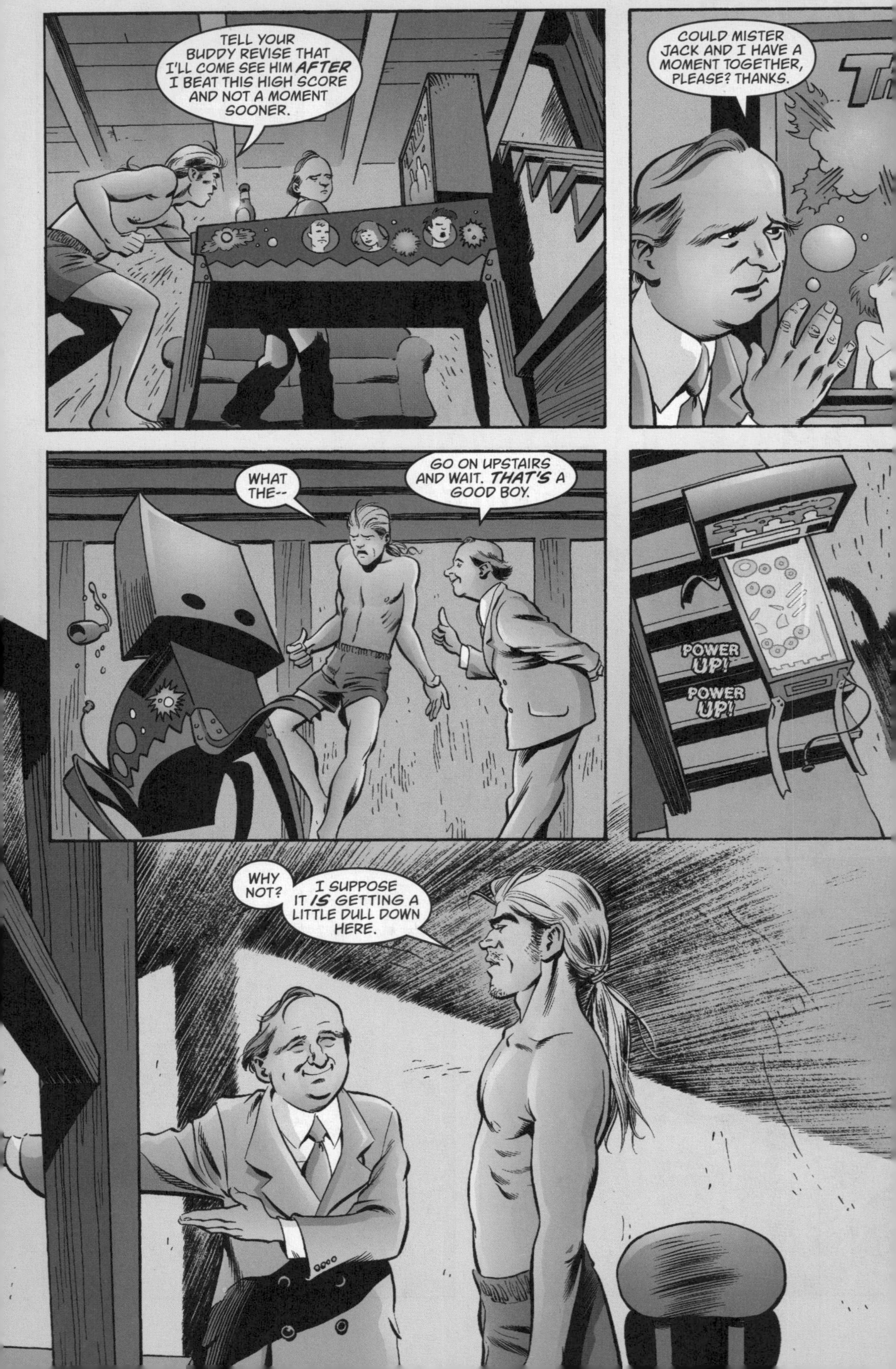
TELL YOUR BUDDY REVISE THAT I'LL COME SEE HIM *AFTER* I BEAT THIS HIGH SCORE AND NOT A MOMENT SOONER.
COULD MISTER JACK AND I HAVE A MOMENT TOGETHER, PLEASE? THANKS.
WHAT THE--
GO ON UPSTAIRS AND WAIT. *THAT'S* A GOOD BOY.
POWER UP!
POWER UP!
WHY NOT?
I SUPPOSE IT *IS* GETTING A LITTLE DULL DOWN HERE.

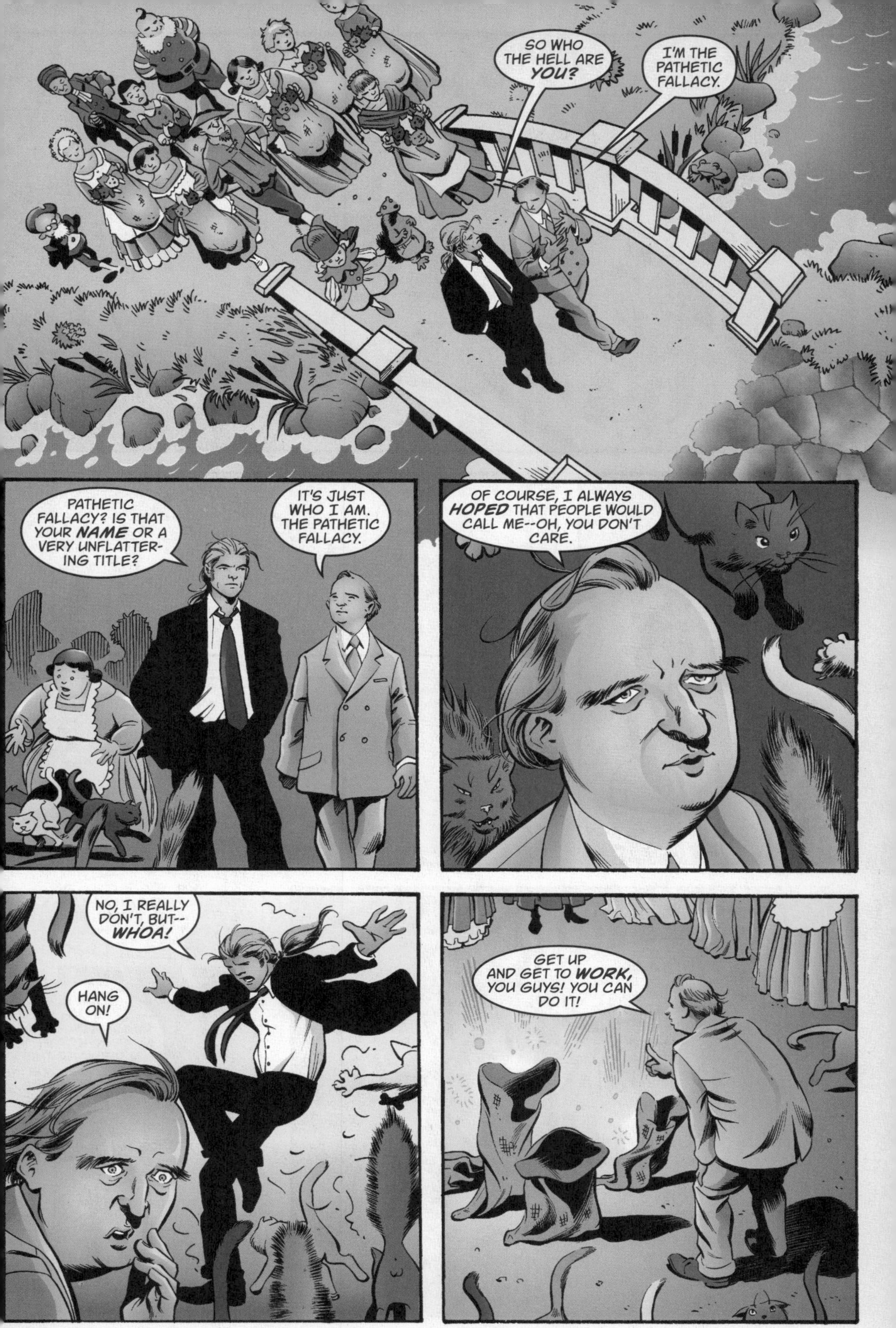
SO WHO THE HELL ARE YOU?
I'M THE PATHETIC FALLACY.
PATHETIC FALLACY? IS THAT YOUR NAME OR A VERY UNFLATTERING TITLE?
IT'S JUST WHO I AM. THE PATHETIC FALLACY.
OF COURSE, I ALWAYS HOPED THAT PEOPLE WOULD CALL ME--OH, YOU DON'T CARE.
NO, I REALLY DON'T, BUT-- WHOA!
HANG ON!
GET UP AND GET TO WORK, YOU GUYS! YOU CAN DO IT!

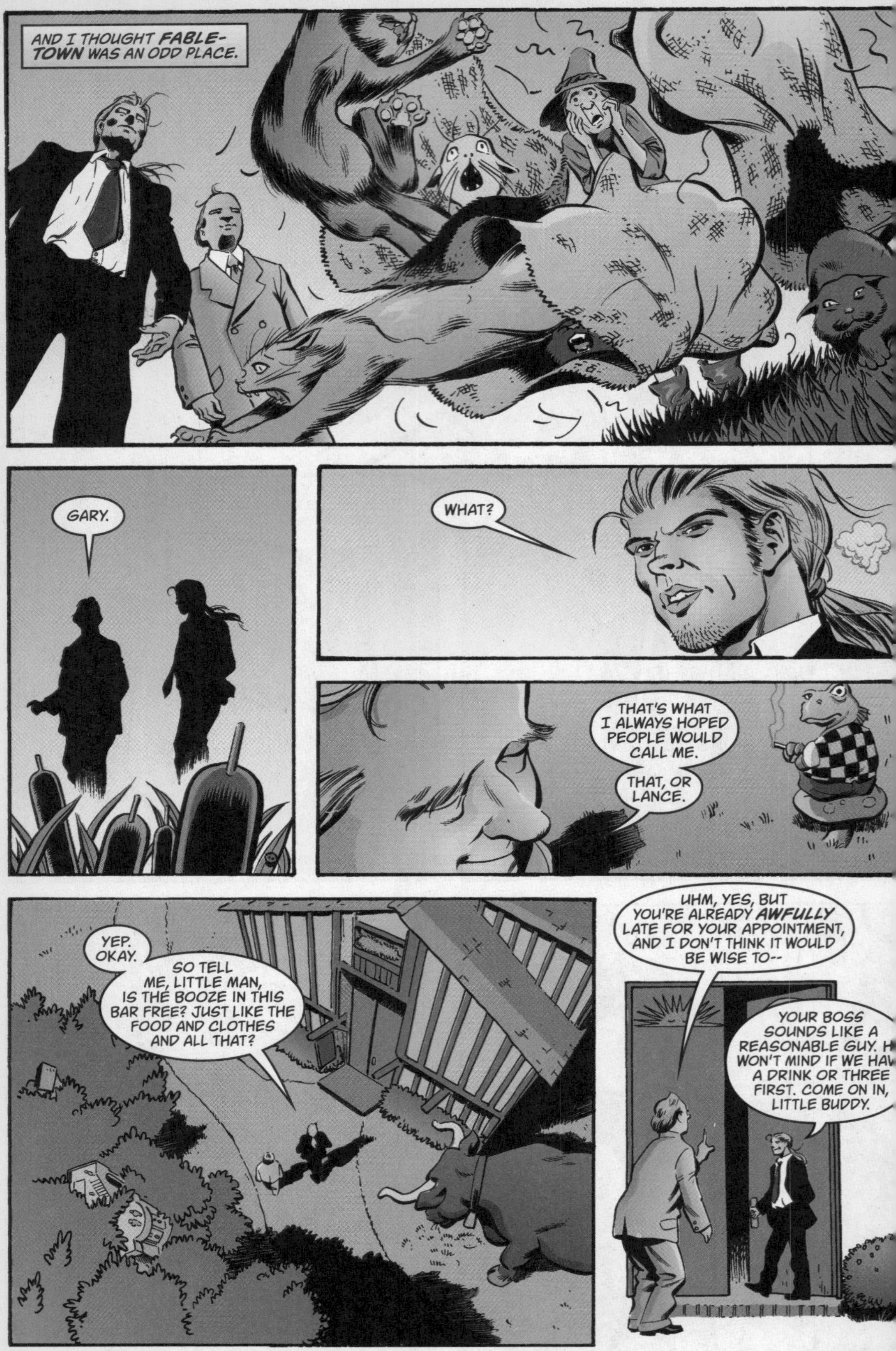
AND I THOUGHT FABLE-TOWN WAS AN ODD PLACE.
GARY.
WHAT?
THAT'S WHAT I ALWAYS HOPED PEOPLE WOULD CALL ME.
THAT, OR LANCE.
YEP. OKAY.
SO TELL ME, LITTLE MAN, IS THE BOOZE IN THIS BAR FREE? JUST LIKE THE FOOD AND CLOTHES AND ALL THAT?
UHM, YES, BUT YOU'RE ALREADY AWFULLY LATE FOR YOUR APPOINTMENT, AND I DON'T THINK IT WOULD BE WISE TO--
YOUR BOSS SOUNDS LIKE A REASONABLE GUY. H WON'T MIND IF WE HAV A DRINK OR THREE FIRST. COME ON IN, LITTLE BUDDY.

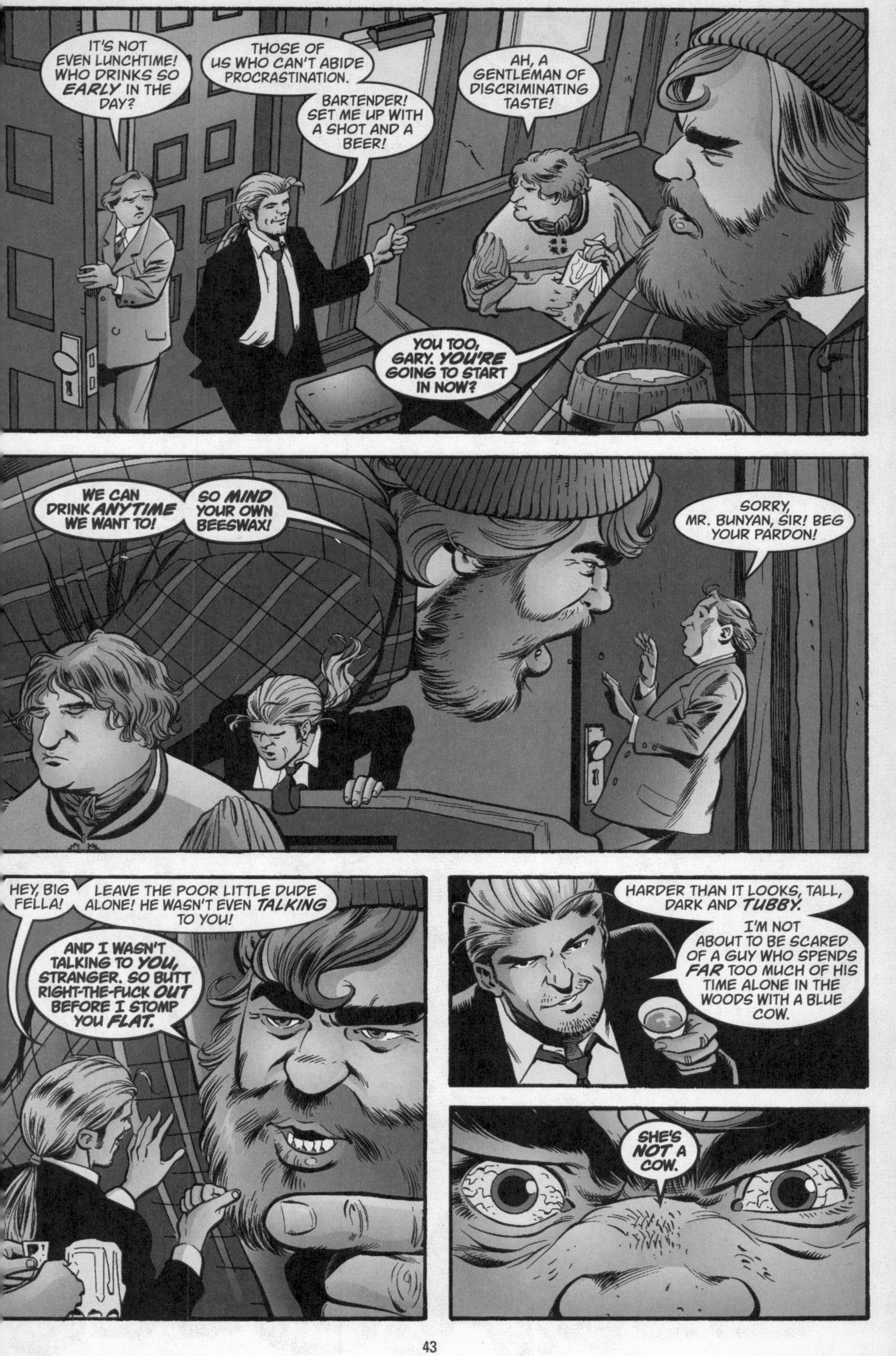
IT'S NOT EVEN LUNCHTIME! WHO DRINKS SO EARLY IN THE DAY?
THOSE OF US WHO CAN'T ABIDE PROCRASTINATION.
BARTENDER! SET ME UP WITH A SHOT AND A BEER!
AH, A GENTLEMAN OF DISCRIMINATING TASTE!
YOU TOO, GARY. YOU'RE GOING TO START IN NOW?
WE CAN DRINK ANYTIME WE WANT TO!
SO MIND YOUR OWN BEESWAX!
SORRY, MR. BUNYAN, SIR! BEG YOUR PARDON!
HEY, BIG FELLA!
LEAVE THE POOR LITTLE DUDE ALONE! HE WASN'T EVEN TALKING TO YOU!
AND I WASN'T TALKING TO YOU, STRANGER. SO BUTT RIGHT-THE-FUCK OUT BEFORE I STOMP YOU FLAT.
HARDER THAN IT LOOKS, TALL, DARK AND TUBBY.
I'M NOT ABOUT TO BE SCARED OF A GUY WHO SPENDS FAR TOO MUCH OF HIS TIME ALONE IN THE WOODS WITH A BLUE COW.
SHE'S NOT A COW.

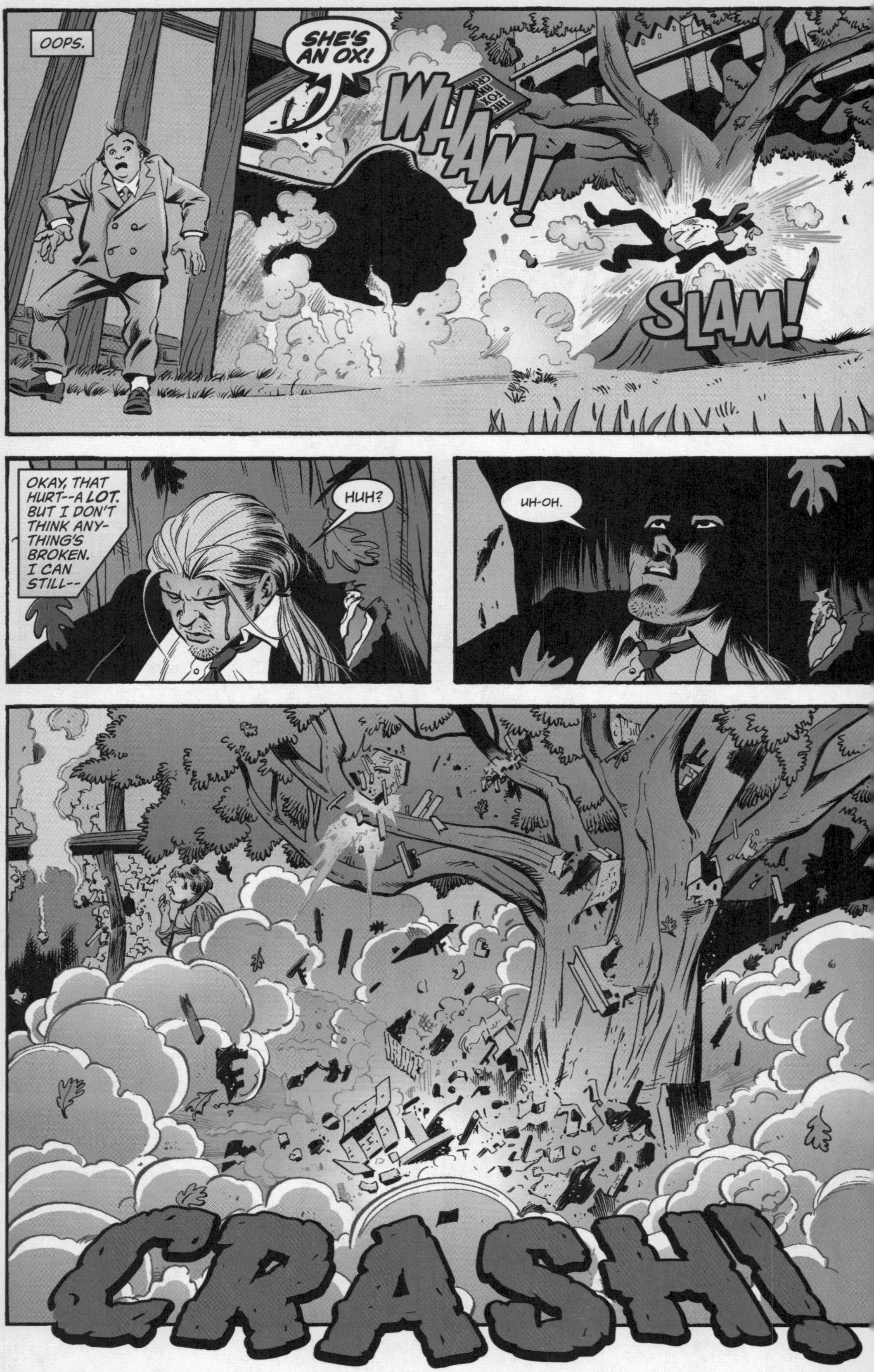
OOPS.
SHE'S AN OX!
WHAM!
SLAM!
OKAY, THAT HURT--A LOT. BUT I DON'T THINK ANYTHING'S BROKEN. I CAN STILL--
HUH?
UH-OH.
CRASH!

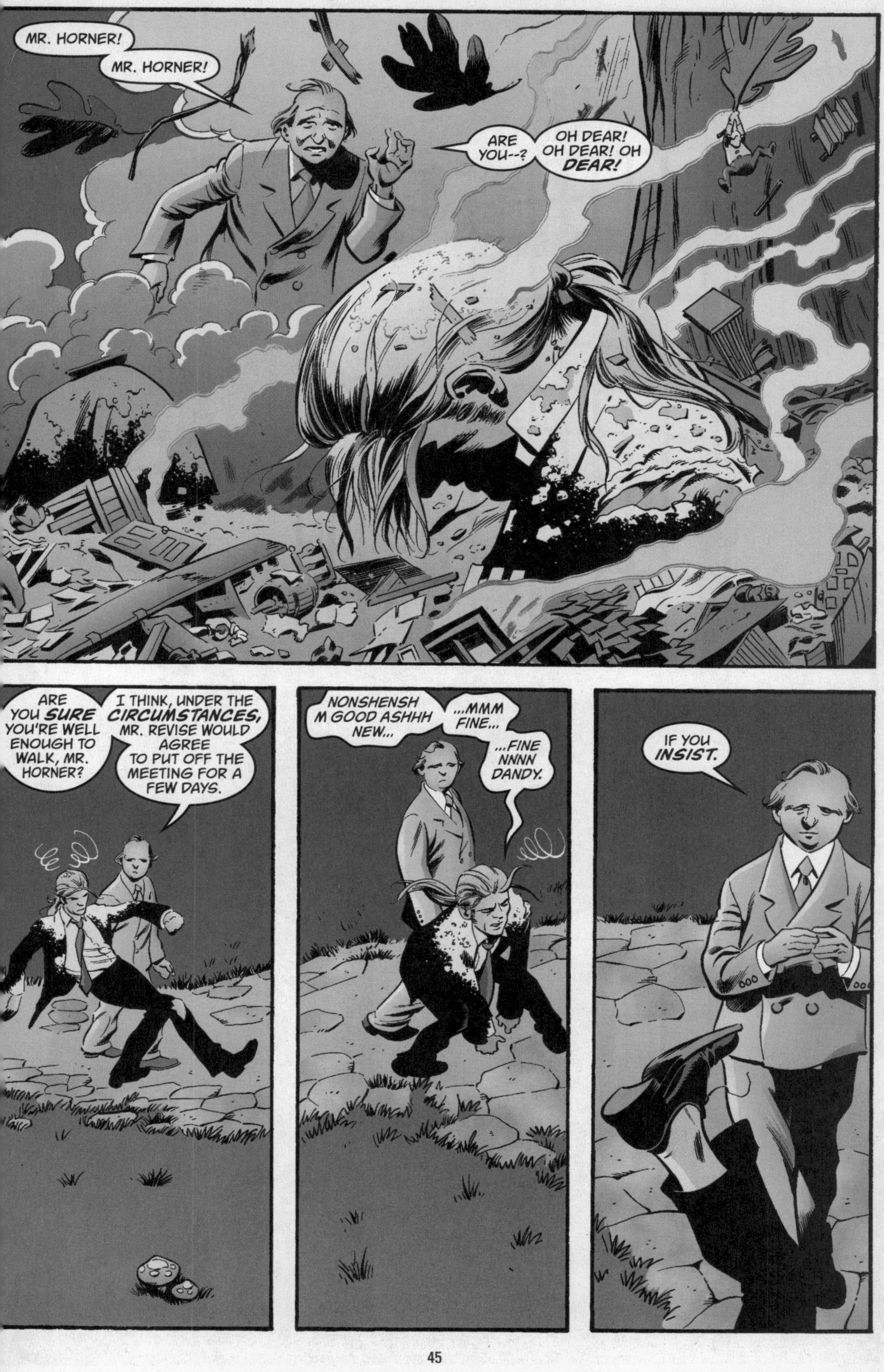
MR. HORNER!
MR. HORNER!
ARE YOU--?
OH DEAR! OH DEAR! OH DEAR!
ARE YOU SURE YOU'RE WELL ENOUGH TO WALK, MR. HORNER?
I THINK, UNDER THE CIRCUMSTANCES, MR. REVISE WOULD AGREE TO PUT OFF THE MEETING FOR A FEW DAYS.
NONSHENSH M GOOD ASHHH NEW...
...MMM FINE...
...FINE NNNN DANDY.
IF YOU INSIST.

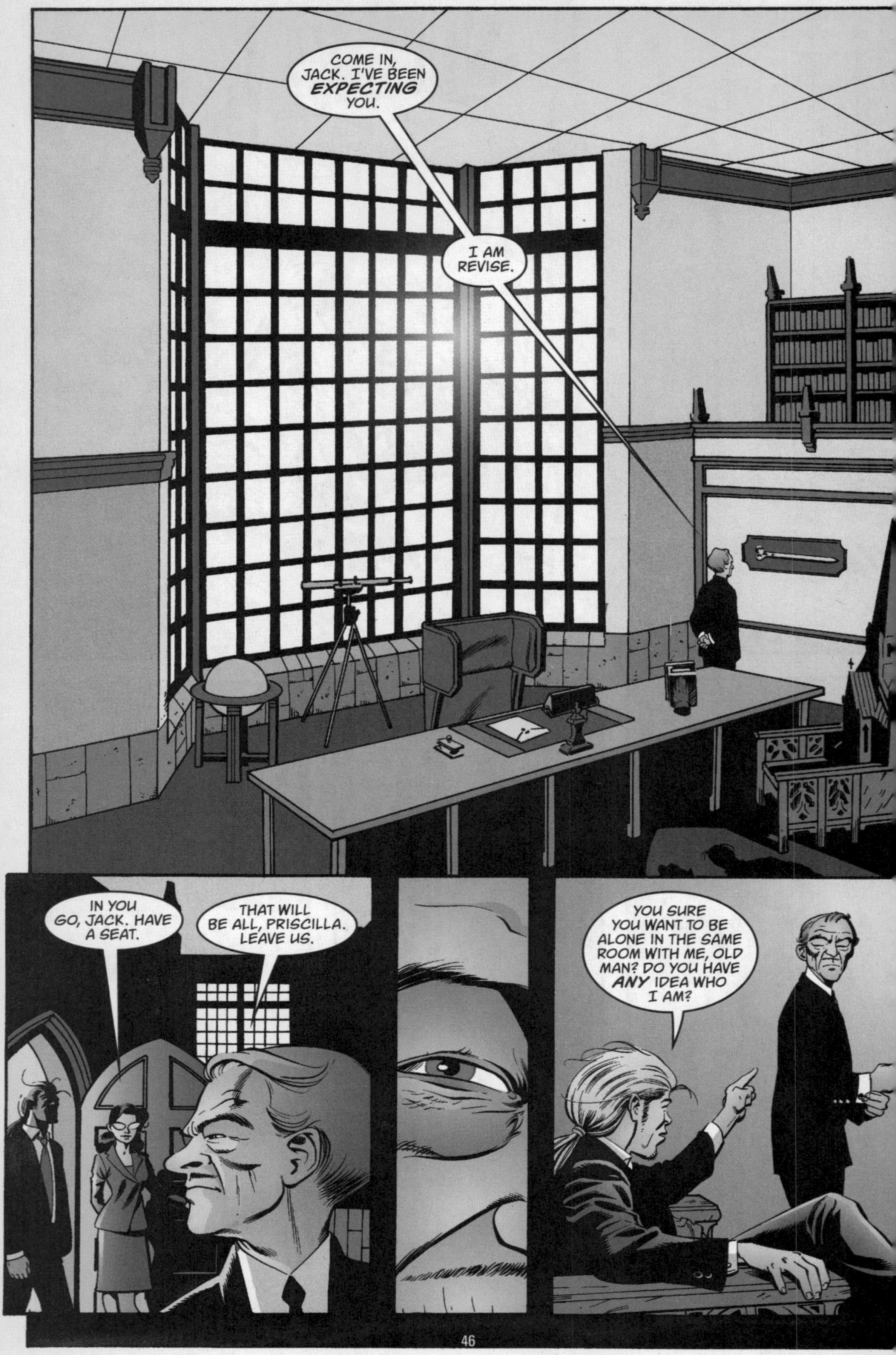
COME IN, JACK. I'VE BEEN EXPECTING YOU.
I AM REVISE.
IN YOU GO, JACK. HAVE A SEAT.
THAT WILL BE ALL, PRISCILLA. LEAVE US.
YOU SURE YOU WANT TO BE ALONE IN THE SAME ROOM WITH ME, OLD MAN? DO YOU HAVE ANY IDEA WHO I AM?

YOU ARE JACK HORNER. PSEUDONYMS INCLUDE JACK OF THE TALES, JACK B. NIMBLE, JOHN TRICK, JACK THE GIANT-KILLER. AM I LEAVING ANY OUT?

JACK FROST. BUT THAT WAS A DIFFERENT COUNTRY, AND THE SOLDIERS ARE ALL FROZEN.

THIS HAS BEEN FUN, BUT I'VE *GOT* TO GET GOING. I--

THE CHAIR YOU'RE SITTING IN DATES TO FOURTEENTH-CENTURY FRANCE. IT WAS USED BY THE PAPAL INQUISITION TO INTERROGATE CATHARS.

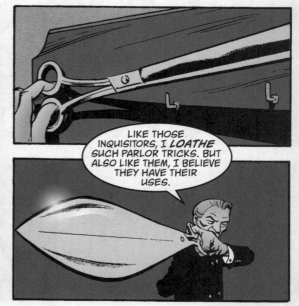

LIKE THOSE INQUISITORS, I *LOATHE* SUCH PARLOR TRICKS. BUT ALSO LIKE THEM, I BELIEVE THEY HAVE THEIR USES.

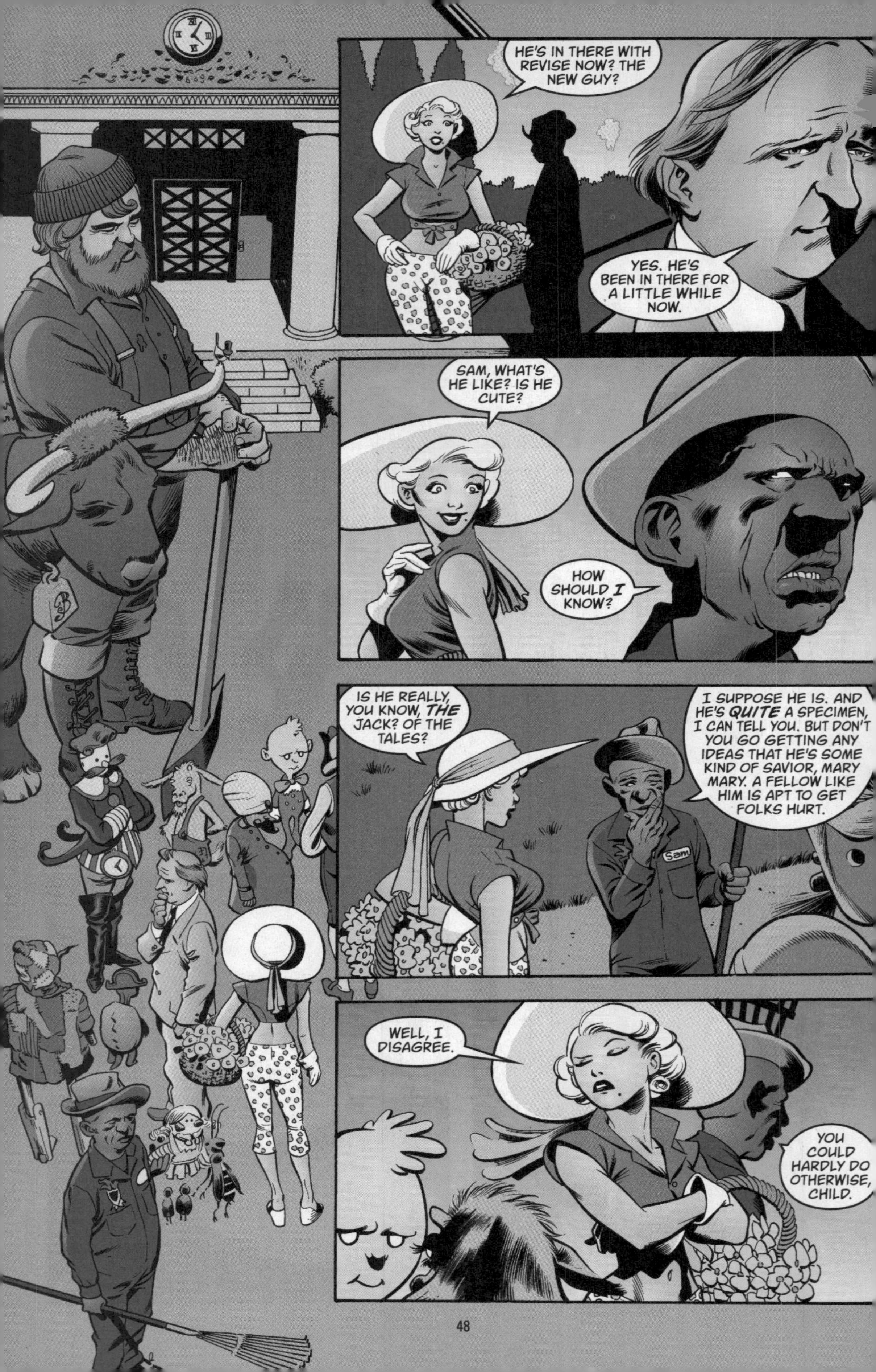
HE'S IN THERE WITH REVISE NOW? THE NEW GUY?
YES. HE'S BEEN IN THERE FOR A LITTLE WHILE NOW.
SAM, WHAT'S HE LIKE? IS HE CUTE?
HOW SHOULD *I* KNOW?
IS HE REALLY, YOU KNOW, ***THE*** JACK? OF THE TALES?
I SUPPOSE HE IS. AND HE'S ***QUITE*** A SPECIMEN, I CAN TELL YOU. BUT DON'T YOU GO GETTING ANY IDEAS THAT HE'S SOME KIND OF SAVIOR, MARY MARY. A FELLOW LIKE HIM IS APT TO GET FOLKS HURT.
WELL, I DISAGREE.
YOU COULD HARDLY DO OTHERWISE, CHILD.

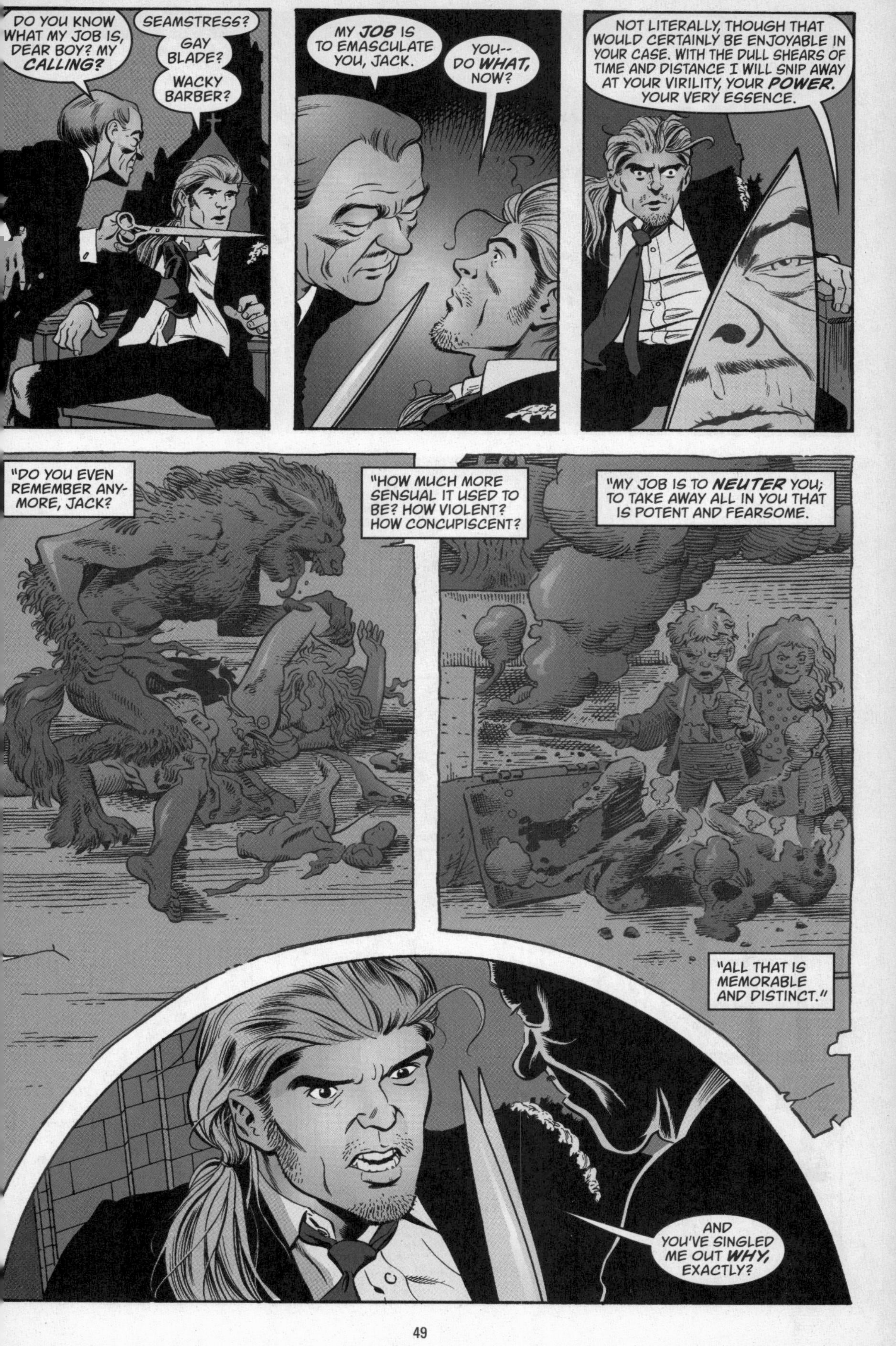
DO YOU KNOW WHAT MY JOB IS, DEAR BOY? MY CALLING?
SEAMSTRESS?
GAY BLADE?
WACKY BARBER?
MY JOB IS TO EMASCULATE YOU, JACK.
YOU-- DO WHAT, NOW?
NOT LITERALLY, THOUGH THAT WOULD CERTAINLY BE ENJOYABLE IN YOUR CASE. WITH THE DULL SHEARS OF TIME AND DISTANCE I WILL SNIP AWAY AT YOUR VIRILITY, YOUR POWER. YOUR VERY ESSENCE.
"DO YOU EVEN REMEMBER ANY-MORE, JACK?
"HOW MUCH MORE SENSUAL IT USED TO BE? HOW VIOLENT? HOW CONCUPISCENT?
"MY JOB IS TO NEUTER YOU; TO TAKE AWAY ALL IN YOU THAT IS POTENT AND FEARSOME.
"ALL THAT IS MEMORABLE AND DISTINCT."
AND YOU'VE SINGLED ME OUT WHY, EXACTLY?

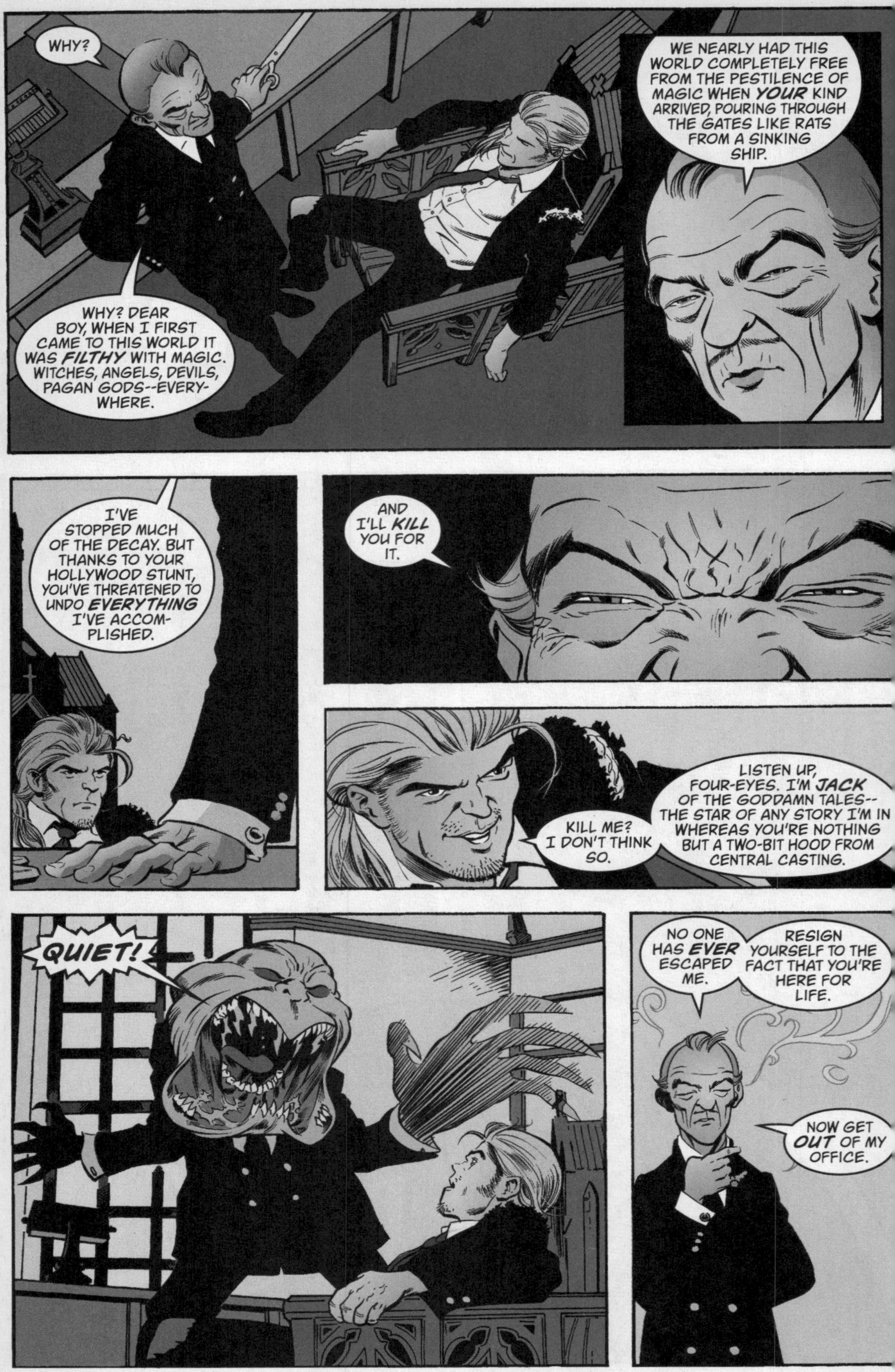
WHY?
WHY? DEAR BOY, WHEN I FIRST CAME TO THIS WORLD IT WAS **FILTHY** WITH MAGIC. WITCHES, ANGELS, DEVILS, PAGAN GODS--EVERY-WHERE.
WE NEARLY HAD THIS WORLD COMPLETELY FREE FROM THE PESTILENCE OF MAGIC WHEN **YOUR** KIND ARRIVED, POURING THROUGH THE GATES LIKE RATS FROM A SINKING SHIP.
I'VE STOPPED MUCH OF THE DECAY. BUT THANKS TO YOUR HOLLYWOOD STUNT, YOU'VE THREATENED TO UNDO **EVERYTHING** I'VE ACCOM-PLISHED.
AND I'LL **KILL** YOU FOR IT.
KILL ME? I DON'T THINK SO.
LISTEN UP, FOUR-EYES. I'M **JACK** OF THE GODDAMN TALES-- THE STAR OF ANY STORY I'M IN WHEREAS YOU'RE NOTHING BUT A TWO-BIT HOOD FROM CENTRAL CASTING.
QUIET!
NO ONE HAS **EVER** ESCAPED ME.
RESIGN YOURSELF TO THE FACT THAT YOU'RE HERE FOR LIFE.
NOW GET **OUT** OF MY OFFICE.

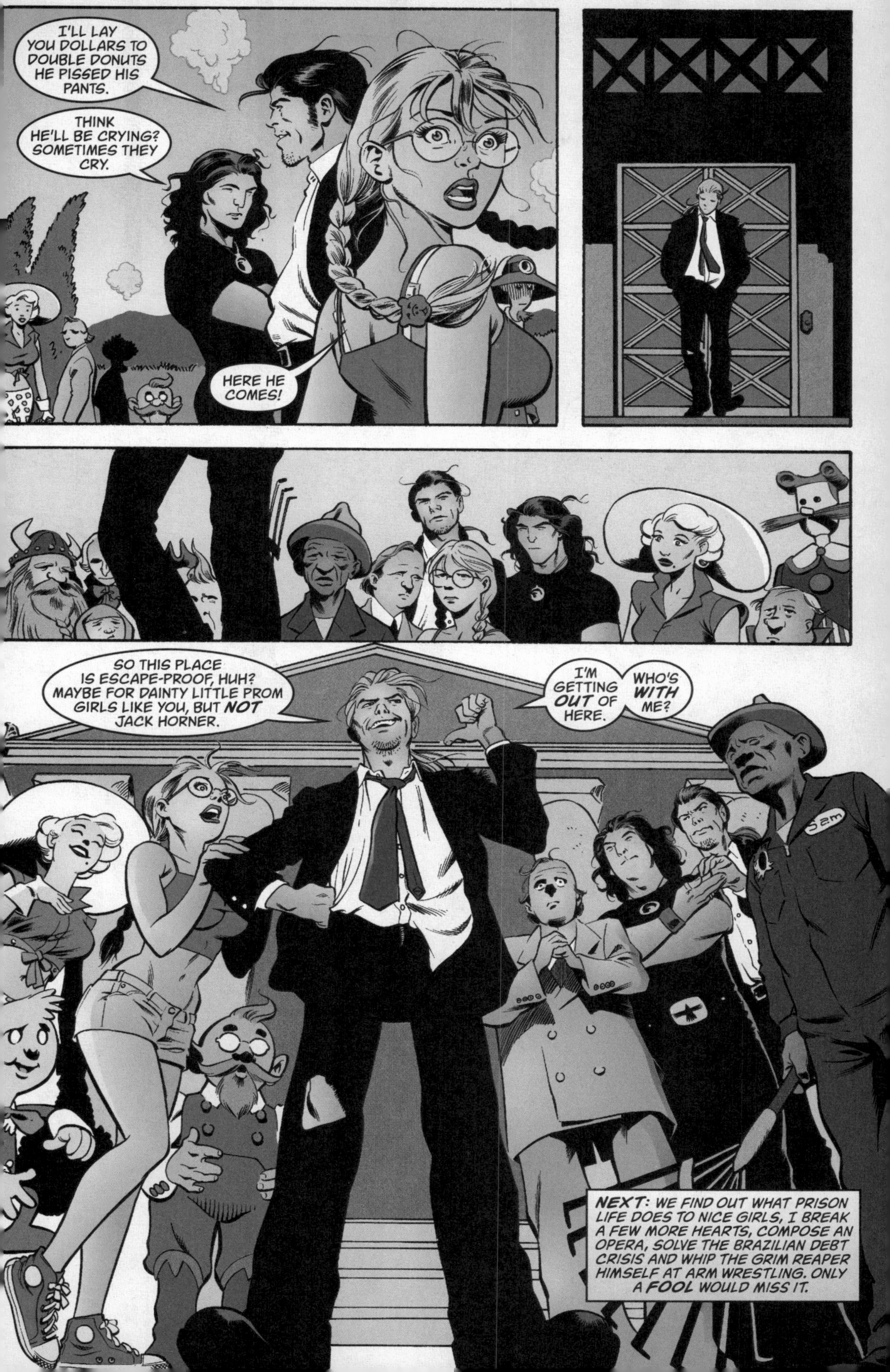
I'LL LAY YOU DOLLARS TO DOUBLE DONUTS HE PISSED HIS PANTS.
THINK HE'LL BE CRYING? SOMETIMES THEY CRY.
HERE HE COMES!
SO THIS PLACE IS ESCAPE-PROOF, HUH? MAYBE FOR DAINTY LITTLE PROM GIRLS LIKE YOU, BUT NOT JACK HORNER.
I'M GETTING OUT OF HERE.
WHO'S WITH ME?
SAM
NEXT: WE FIND OUT WHAT PRISON LIFE DOES TO NICE GIRLS, I BREAK A FEW MORE HEARTS, COMPOSE AN OPERA, SOLVE THE BRAZILIAN DEBT CRISIS AND WHIP THE GRIM REAPER HIMSELF AT ARM WRESTLING. ONLY A FOOL WOULD MISS IT.

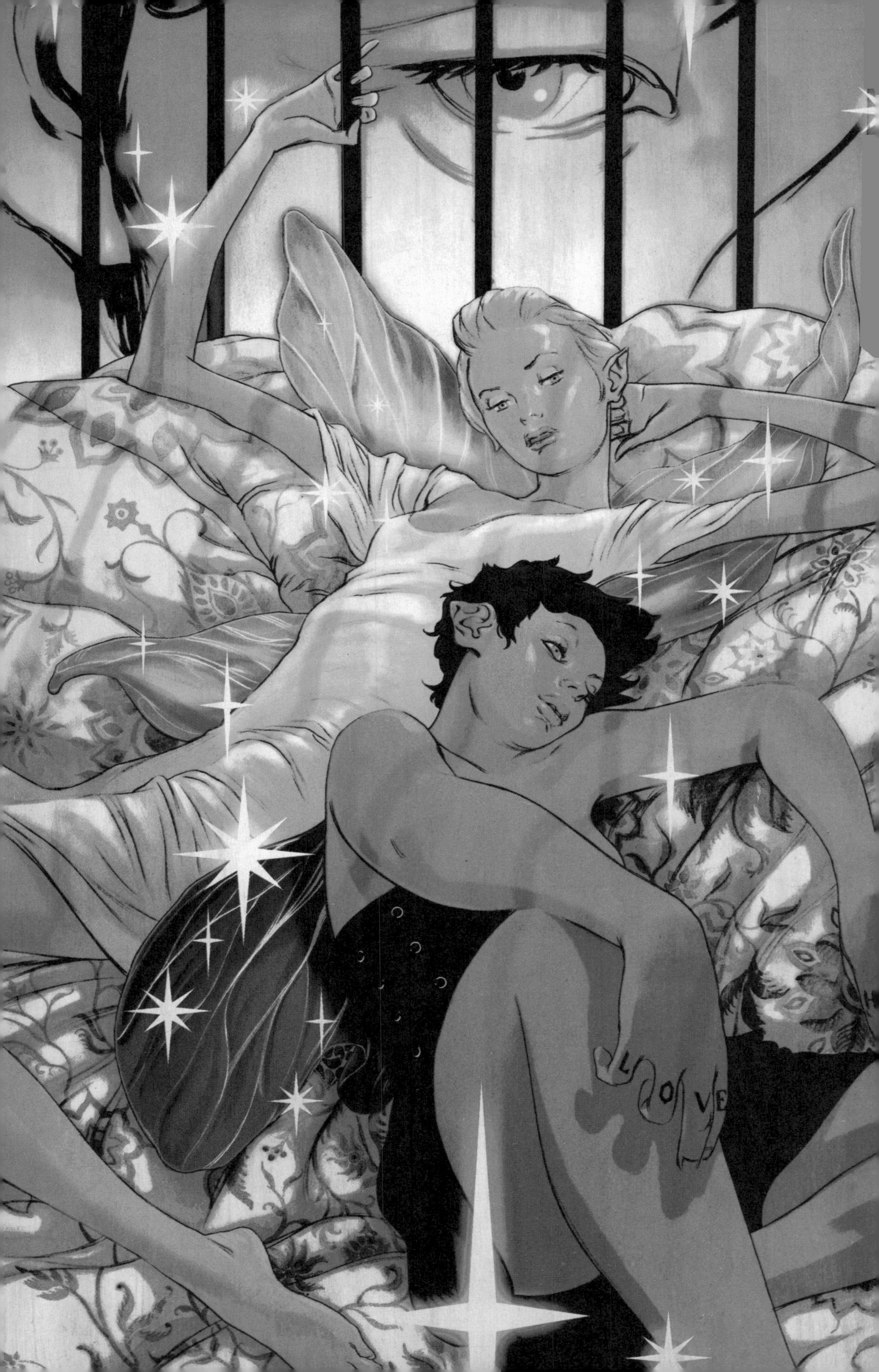
LOVE

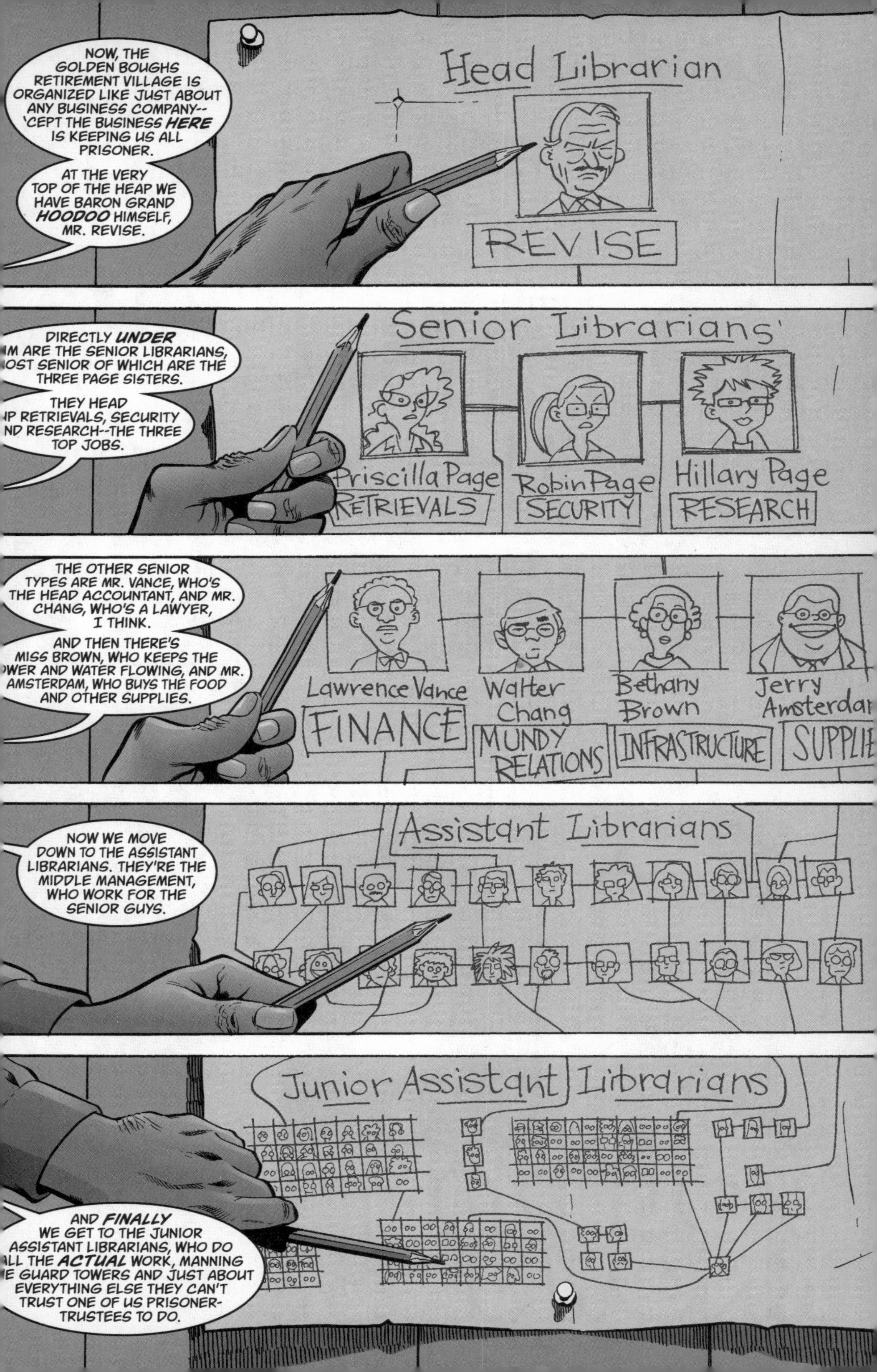
NOW, THE GOLDEN BOUGHS RETIREMENT VILLAGE IS ORGANIZED LIKE JUST ABOUT ANY BUSINESS COMPANY-- 'CEPT THE BUSINESS **HERE** IS KEEPING US ALL PRISONER.
AT THE VERY TOP OF THE HEAP WE HAVE BARON GRAND **HOODOO** HIMSELF, MR. REVISE.
Head Librarian
REVISE
DIRECTLY **UNDER** IM ARE THE SENIOR LIBRARIANS, OST SENIOR OF WHICH ARE THE THREE PAGE SISTERS.
THEY HEAD IP RETRIEVALS, SECURITY ND RESEARCH--THE THREE TOP JOBS.
Senior Librarians
Priscilla Page
RETRIEVALS
Robin Page
SECURITY
Hillary Page
RESEARCH
THE OTHER SENIOR TYPES ARE MR. VANCE, WHO'S THE HEAD ACCOUNTANT, AND MR. CHANG, WHO'S A LAWYER, I THINK.
AND THEN THERE'S MISS BROWN, WHO KEEPS THE OWER AND WATER FLOWING, AND MR. AMSTERDAM, WHO BUYS THE FOOD AND OTHER SUPPLIES.
Lawrence Vance
FINANCE
Walter Chang
MUNDY RELATIONS
Bethany Brown
INFRASTRUCTURE
Jerry Amsterdar
SUPPLIE
NOW WE MOVE DOWN TO THE ASSISTANT LIBRARIANS. THEY'RE THE MIDDLE MANAGEMENT, WHO WORK FOR THE SENIOR GUYS.
Assistant Librarians
Junior Assistant Librarians
AND **FINALLY** WE GET TO THE JUNIOR ASSISTANT LIBRARIANS, WHO DO LL THE **ACTUAL** WORK, MANNING E GUARD TOWERS AND JUST ABOUT EVERYTHING ELSE THEY CAN'T TRUST ONE OF US PRISONER-TRUSTEES TO DO.

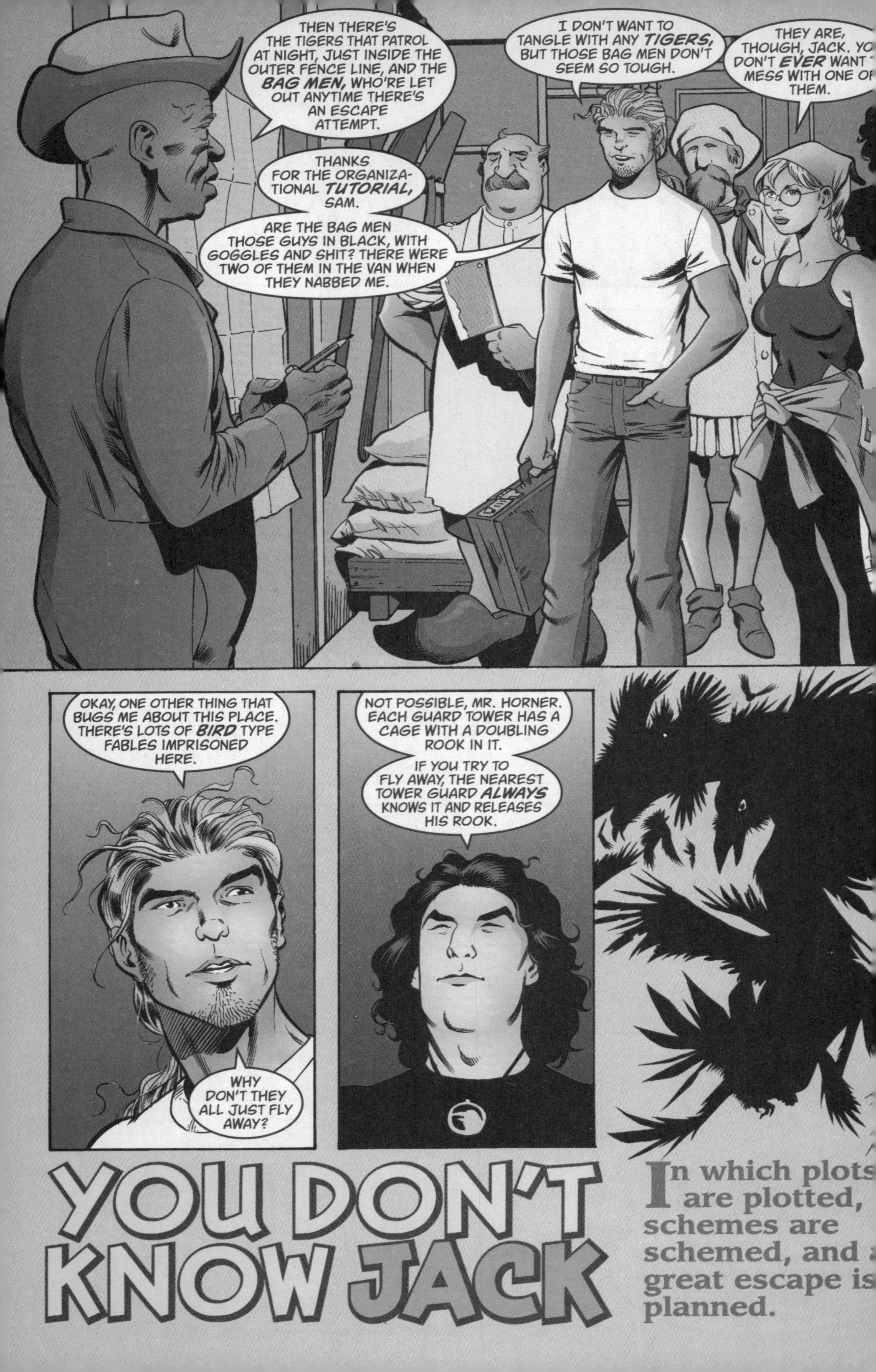
THEN THERE'S THE TIGERS THAT PATROL AT NIGHT, JUST INSIDE THE OUTER FENCE LINE, AND THE **BAG MEN,** WHO'RE LET OUT ANYTIME THERE'S AN ESCAPE ATTEMPT.
THANKS FOR THE ORGANIZATIONAL **TUTORIAL,** SAM.
ARE THE BAG MEN THOSE GUYS IN BLACK, WITH GOGGLES AND SHIT? THERE WERE TWO OF THEM IN THE VAN WHEN THEY NABBED ME.
I DON'T WANT TO TANGLE WITH ANY **TIGERS,** BUT THOSE BAG MEN DON'T SEEM SO TOUGH.
THEY ARE, THOUGH, JACK. YO DON'T **EVER** WANT T MESS WITH ONE OF THEM.
OKAY, ONE OTHER THING THAT BUGS ME ABOUT THIS PLACE. THERE'S LOTS OF **BIRD** TYPE FABLES IMPRISONED HERE.
WHY DON'T THEY ALL JUST FLY AWAY?
NOT POSSIBLE, MR. HORNER. EACH GUARD TOWER HAS A CAGE WITH A DOUBLING ROOK IN IT.
IF YOU TRY TO FLY AWAY, THE NEAREST TOWER GUARD **ALWAYS** KNOWS IT AND RELEASES HIS ROOK.
YOU DON'T KNOW JACK
In which plots are plotted, schemes are schemed, and great escape is planned.

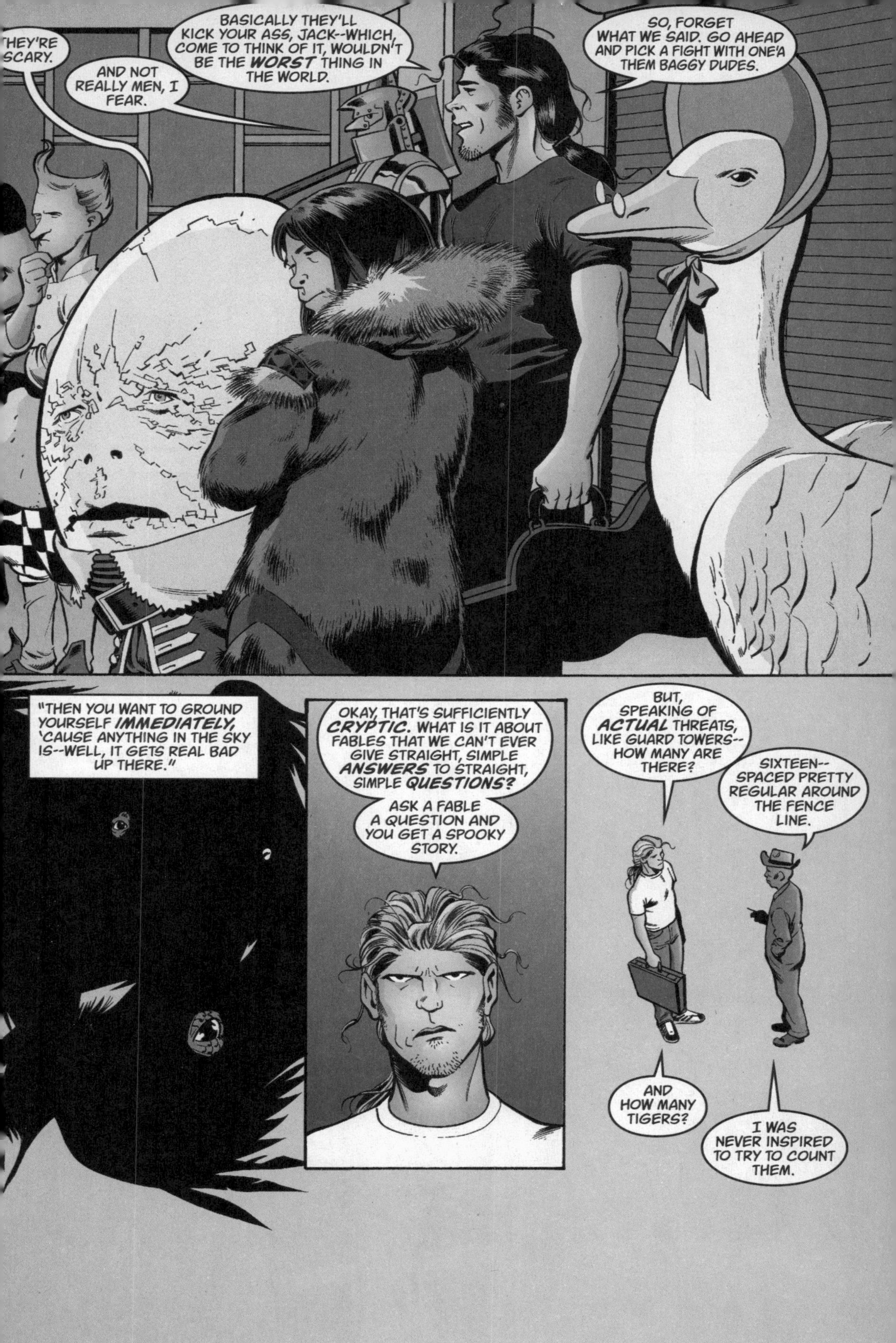
THEY'RE SCARY.
AND NOT REALLY MEN, I FEAR.
BASICALLY THEY'LL KICK YOUR ASS, JACK--WHICH, COME TO THINK OF IT, WOULDN'T BE THE WORST THING IN THE WORLD.
SO, FORGET WHAT WE SAID. GO AHEAD AND PICK A FIGHT WITH ONE'A THEM BAGGY DUDES.
"THEN YOU WANT TO GROUND YOURSELF IMMEDIATELY, 'CAUSE ANYTHING IN THE SKY IS--WELL, IT GETS REAL BAD UP THERE."
OKAY, THAT'S SUFFICIENTLY CRYPTIC. WHAT IS IT ABOUT FABLES THAT WE CAN'T EVER GIVE STRAIGHT, SIMPLE ANSWERS TO STRAIGHT, SIMPLE QUESTIONS?
ASK A FABLE A QUESTION AND YOU GET A SPOOKY STORY.
BUT, SPEAKING OF ACTUAL THREATS, LIKE GUARD TOWERS-- HOW MANY ARE THERE?
SIXTEEN-- SPACED PRETTY REGULAR AROUND THE FENCE LINE.
AND HOW MANY TIGERS?
I WAS NEVER INSPIRED TO TRY TO COUNT THEM.

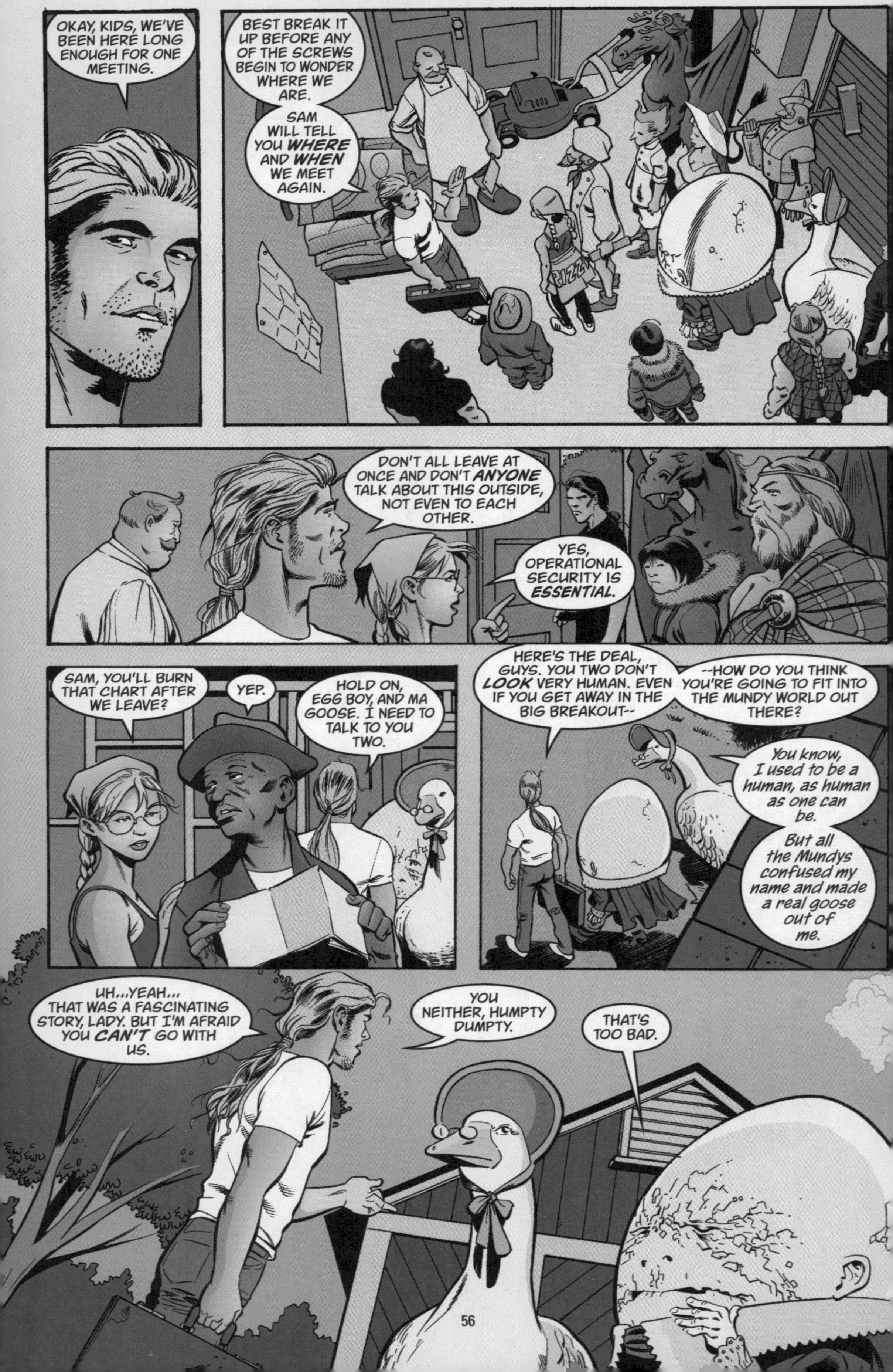
OKAY, KIDS, WE'VE BEEN HERE LONG ENOUGH FOR ONE MEETING.
BEST BREAK IT UP BEFORE ANY OF THE SCREWS BEGIN TO WONDER WHERE WE ARE.
SAM WILL TELL YOU WHERE AND WHEN WE MEET AGAIN.
RIZZY
DON'T ALL LEAVE AT ONCE AND DON'T ANYONE TALK ABOUT THIS OUTSIDE, NOT EVEN TO EACH OTHER.
YES, OPERATIONAL SECURITY IS ESSENTIAL.
SAM, YOU'LL BURN THAT CHART AFTER WE LEAVE?
YEP.
HOLD ON, EGG BOY, AND MA GOOSE. I NEED TO TALK TO YOU TWO.
HERE'S THE DEAL, GUYS. YOU TWO DON'T LOOK VERY HUMAN. EVEN IF YOU GET AWAY IN THE BIG BREAKOUT--
--HOW DO YOU THINK YOU'RE GOING TO FIT INTO THE MUNDY WORLD OUT THERE?
You know, I used to be a human, as human as one can be.
But all the Mundys confused my name and made a real goose out of me.
UH...YEAH... THAT WAS A FASCINATING STORY, LADY. BUT I'M AFRAID YOU CAN'T GO WITH US.
YOU NEITHER, HUMPTY DUMPTY.
THAT'S TOO BAD.

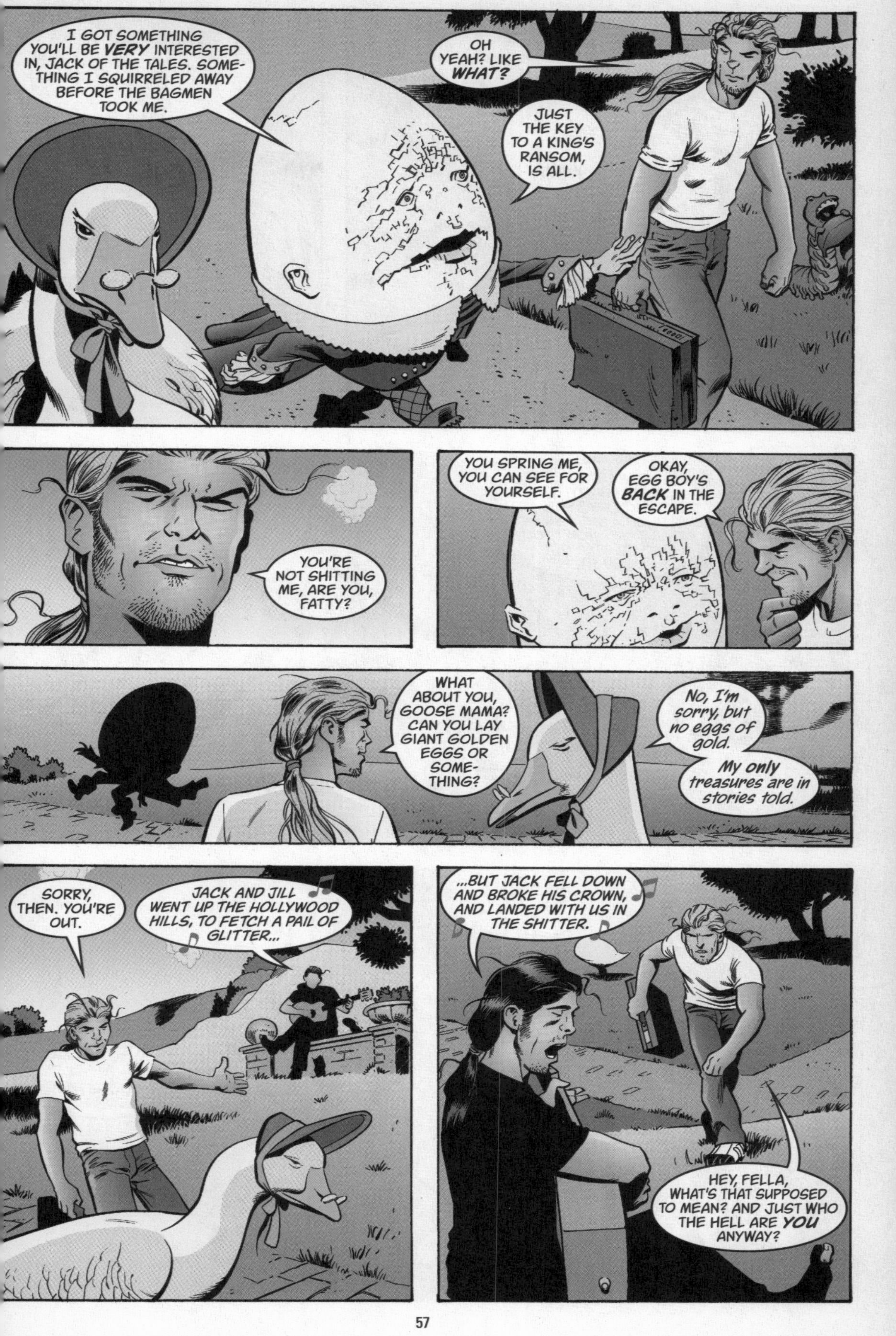
I GOT SOMETHING YOU'LL BE VERY INTERESTED IN, JACK OF THE TALES. SOMETHING I SQUIRRELED AWAY BEFORE THE BAGMEN TOOK ME.
OH YEAH? LIKE WHAT?
JUST THE KEY TO A KING'S RANSOM, IS ALL.
YOU'RE NOT SHITTING ME, ARE YOU, FATTY?
YOU SPRING ME, YOU CAN SEE FOR YOURSELF.
OKAY, EGG BOY'S BACK IN THE ESCAPE.
WHAT ABOUT YOU, GOOSE MAMA? CAN YOU LAY GIANT GOLDEN EGGS OR SOMETHING?
No, I'm sorry, but no eggs of gold.
My only treasures are in stories told.
SORRY, THEN. YOU'RE OUT.
JACK AND JILL WENT UP THE HOLLYWOOD HILLS, TO FETCH A PAIL OF GLITTER...
...BUT JACK FELL DOWN AND BROKE HIS CROWN, AND LANDED WITH US IN THE SHITTER.
HEY, FELLA, WHAT'S THAT SUPPOSED TO MEAN? AND JUST WHO THE HELL ARE YOU ANYWAY?

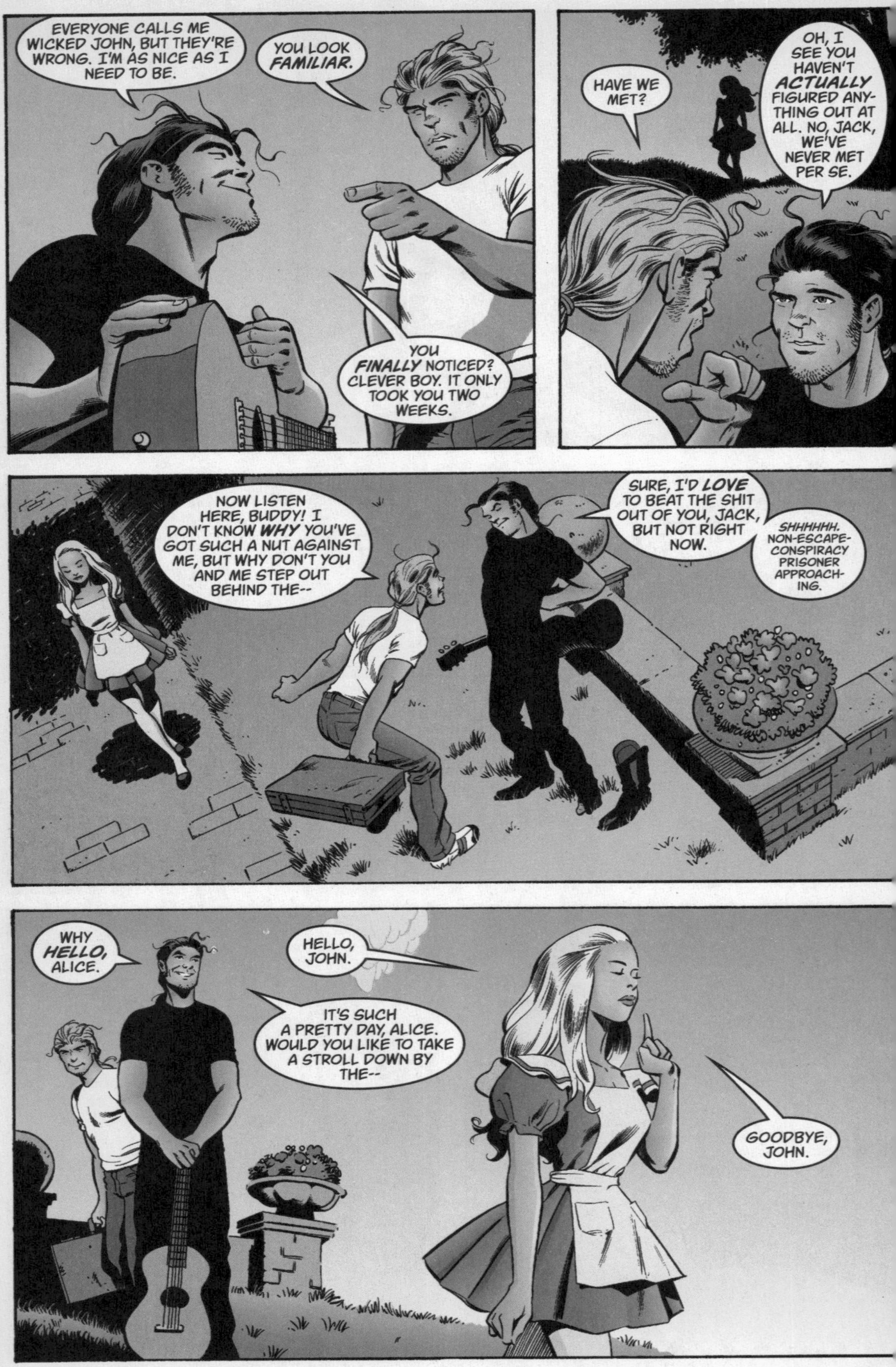
EVERYONE CALLS ME WICKED JOHN, BUT THEY'RE WRONG. I'M AS NICE AS I NEED TO BE.
YOU LOOK *FAMILIAR.*
YOU *FINALLY* NOTICED? CLEVER BOY. IT ONLY TOOK YOU TWO WEEKS.
HAVE WE MET?
OH, I SEE YOU HAVEN'T *ACTUALLY* FIGURED ANYTHING OUT AT ALL. NO, JACK, WE'VE NEVER MET PER SE.
NOW LISTEN HERE, BUDDY! I DON'T KNOW *WHY* YOU'VE GOT SUCH A NUT AGAINST ME, BUT WHY DON'T YOU AND ME STEP OUT BEHIND THE--
SURE, I'D *LOVE* TO BEAT THE SHIT OUT OF YOU, JACK, BUT NOT RIGHT NOW.
SHHHHHH. NON-ESCAPE-CONSPIRACY PRISONER APPROACHING.
WHY *HELLO,* ALICE.
HELLO, JOHN.
IT'S SUCH A PRETTY DAY, ALICE. WOULD YOU LIKE TO TAKE A STROLL DOWN BY THE--
GOODBYE, JOHN.

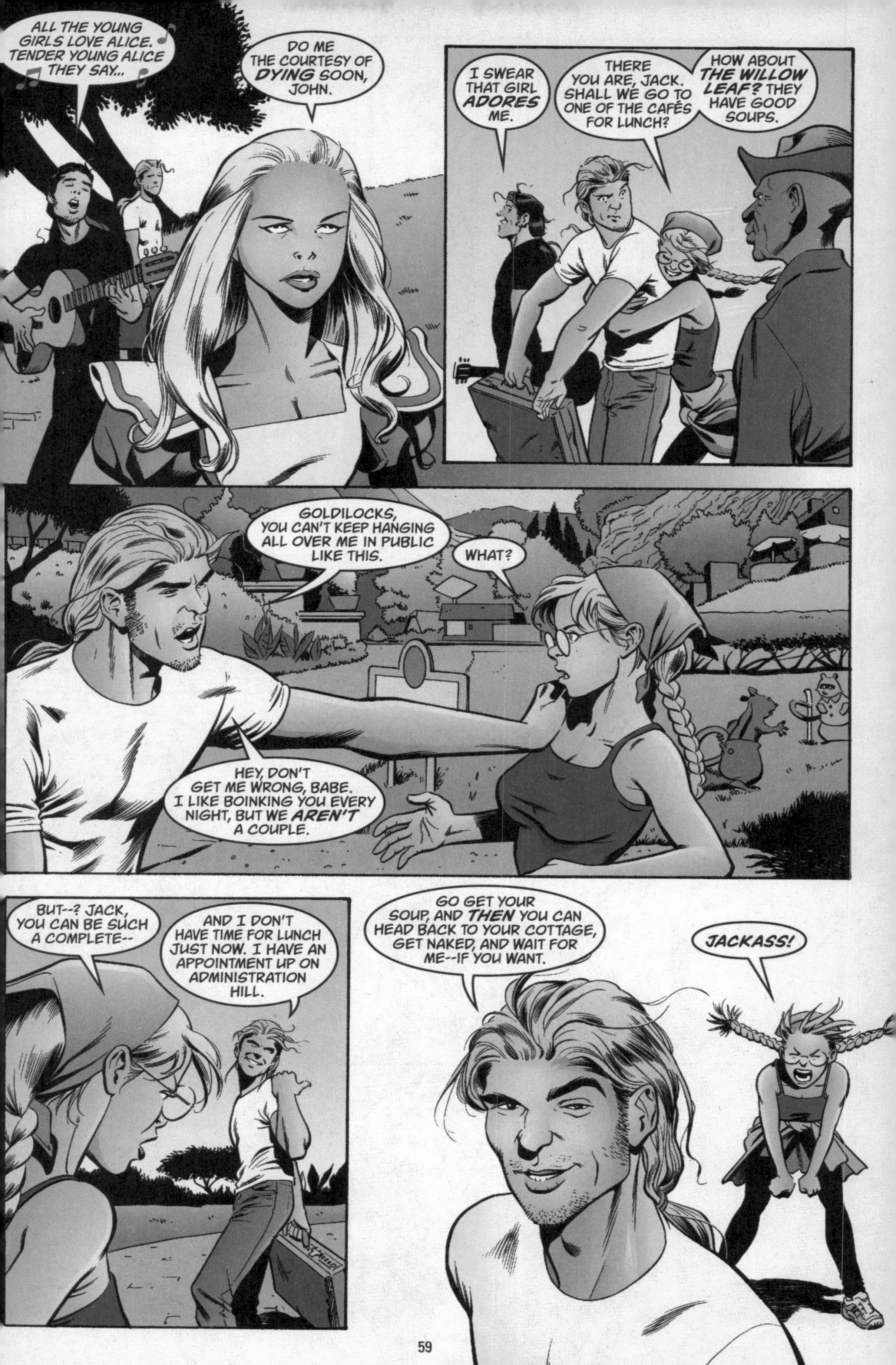
ALL THE YOUNG GIRLS LOVE ALICE. TENDER YOUNG ALICE THEY SAY...
DO ME THE COURTESY OF DYING SOON, JOHN.
I SWEAR THAT GIRL ADORES ME.
THERE YOU ARE, JACK. SHALL WE GO TO ONE OF THE CAFÉS FOR LUNCH?
HOW ABOUT THE WILLOW LEAF? THEY HAVE GOOD SOUPS.
GOLDILOCKS, YOU CAN'T KEEP HANGING ALL OVER ME IN PUBLIC LIKE THIS.
WHAT?
HEY, DON'T GET ME WRONG, BABE. I LIKE BOINKING YOU EVERY NIGHT, BUT WE AREN'T A COUPLE.
BUT--? JACK, YOU CAN BE SUCH A COMPLETE--
AND I DON'T HAVE TIME FOR LUNCH JUST NOW. I HAVE AN APPOINTMENT UP ON ADMINISTRATION HILL.
GO GET YOUR SOUP, AND THEN YOU CAN HEAD BACK TO YOUR COTTAGE, GET NAKED, AND WAIT FOR ME--IF YOU WANT.
JACKASS!

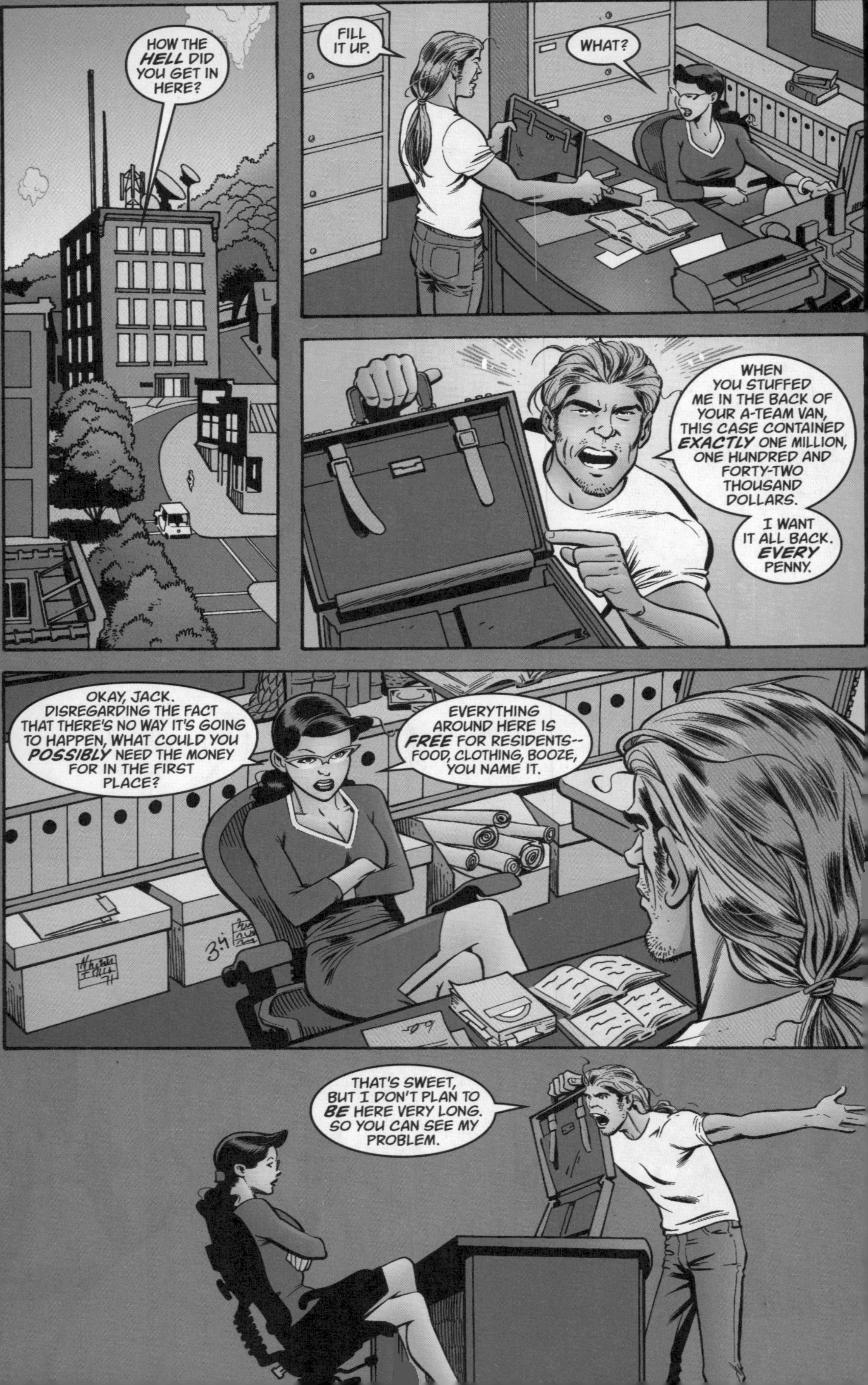
HOW THE HELL DID YOU GET IN HERE?
FILL IT UP.
WHAT?
WHEN YOU STUFFED ME IN THE BACK OF YOUR A-TEAM VAN, THIS CASE CONTAINED EXACTLY ONE MILLION, ONE HUNDRED AND FORTY-TWO THOUSAND DOLLARS.
I WANT IT ALL BACK. EVERY PENNY.
OKAY, JACK. DISREGARDING THE FACT THAT THERE'S NO WAY IT'S GOING TO HAPPEN, WHAT COULD YOU POSSIBLY NEED THE MONEY FOR IN THE FIRST PLACE?
EVERYTHING AROUND HERE IS FREE FOR RESIDENTS-- FOOD, CLOTHING, BOOZE, YOU NAME IT.
THAT'S SWEET, BUT I DON'T PLAN TO BE HERE VERY LONG. SO YOU CAN SEE MY PROBLEM.

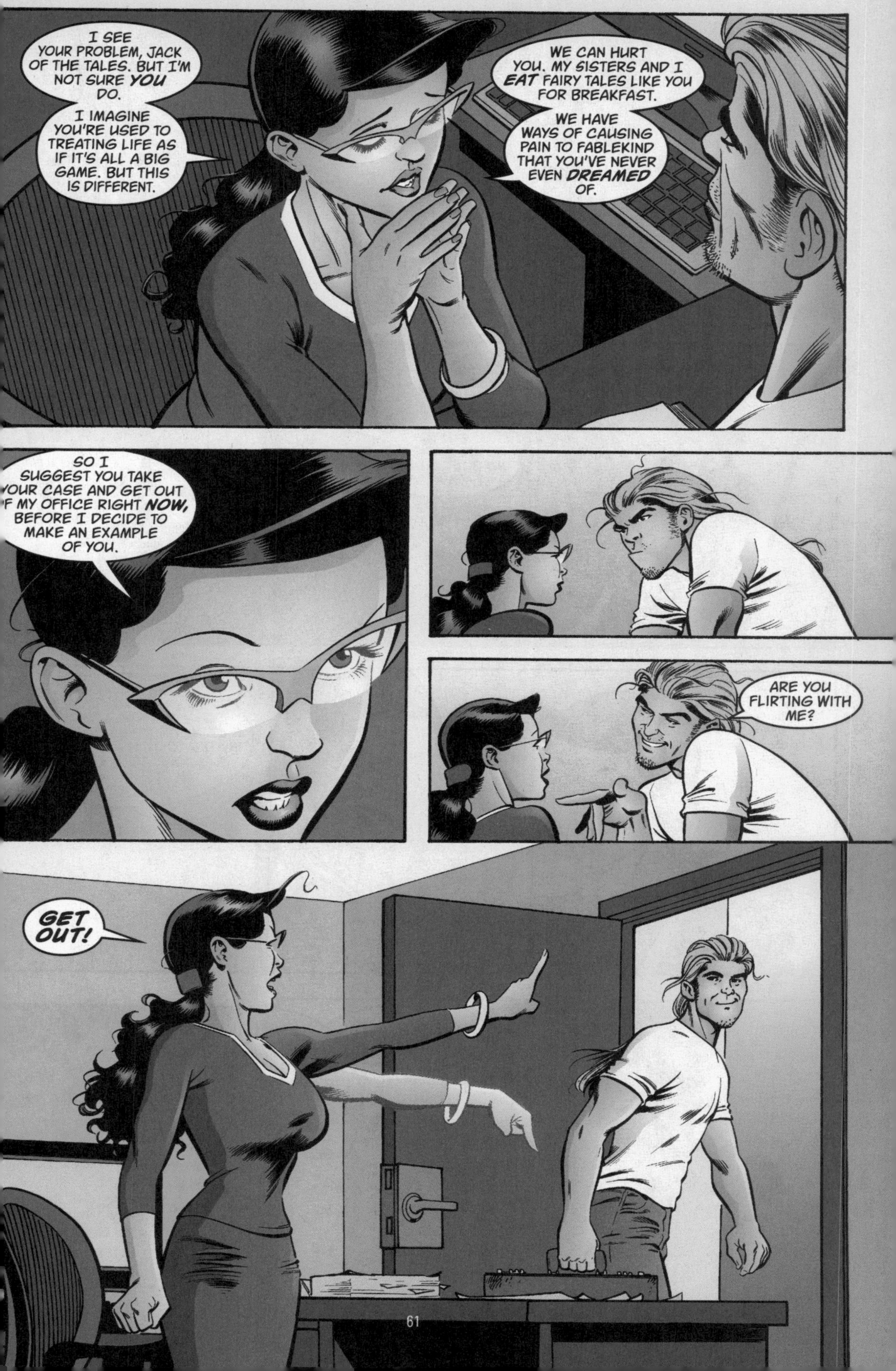
I SEE YOUR PROBLEM, JACK OF THE TALES. BUT I'M NOT SURE YOU DO.
I IMAGINE YOU'RE USED TO TREATING LIFE AS IF IT'S ALL A BIG GAME. BUT THIS IS DIFFERENT.
WE CAN HURT YOU. MY SISTERS AND I EAT FAIRY TALES LIKE YOU FOR BREAKFAST.
WE HAVE WAYS OF CAUSING PAIN TO FABLEKIND THAT YOU'VE NEVER EVEN DREAMED OF.
SO I SUGGEST YOU TAKE YOUR CASE AND GET OUT OF MY OFFICE RIGHT NOW, BEFORE I DECIDE TO MAKE AN EXAMPLE OF YOU.
ARE YOU FLIRTING WITH ME?
GET OUT!

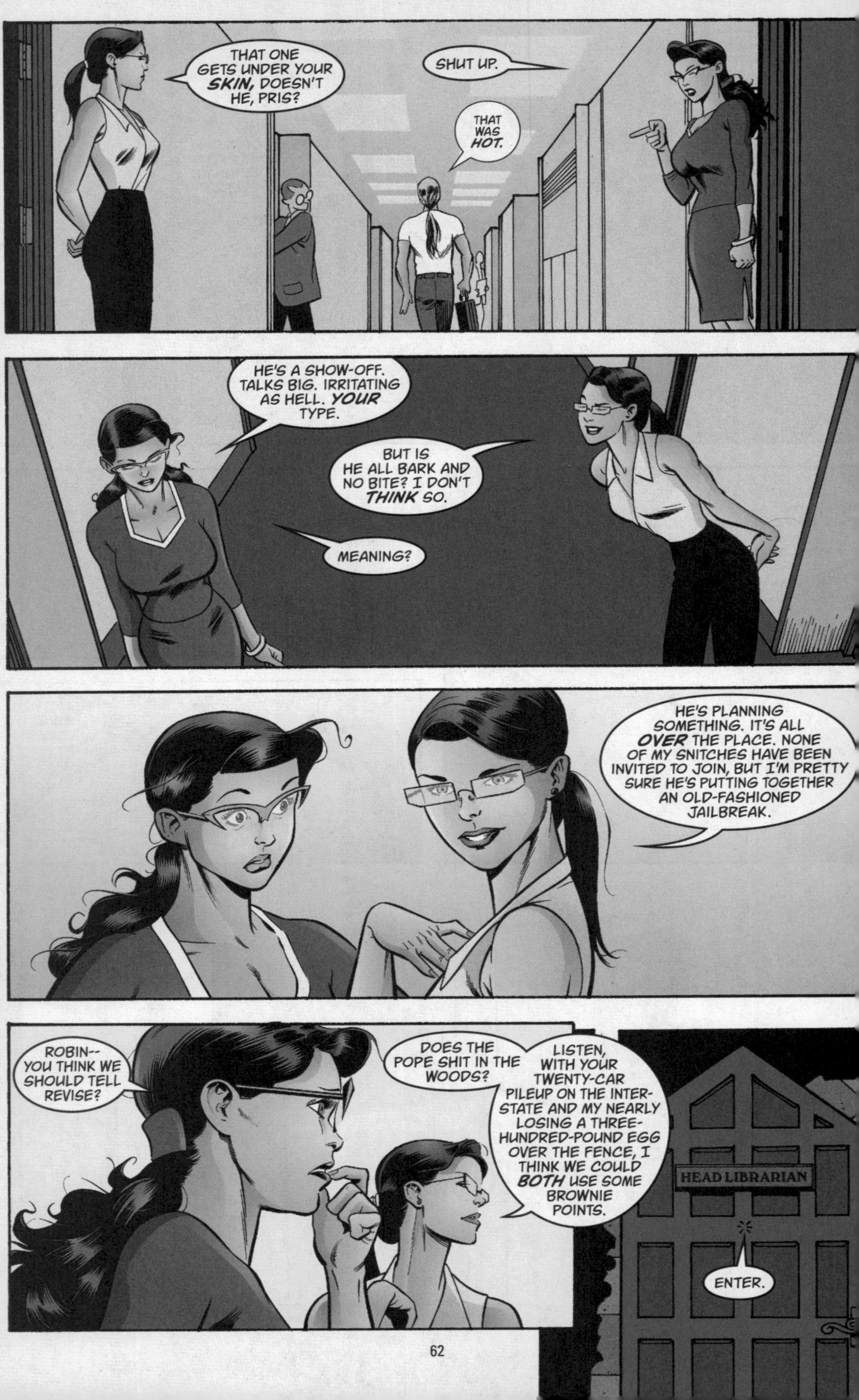

THAT ONE GETS UNDER YOUR SKIN, DOESN'T HE, PRIS?
SHUT UP.
THAT WAS HOT.
HE'S A SHOW-OFF. TALKS BIG. IRRITATING AS HELL. YOUR TYPE.
BUT IS HE ALL BARK AND NO BITE? I DON'T THINK SO.
MEANING?
HE'S PLANNING SOMETHING. IT'S ALL OVER THE PLACE. NONE OF MY SNITCHES HAVE BEEN INVITED TO JOIN, BUT I'M PRETTY SURE HE'S PUTTING TOGETHER AN OLD-FASHIONED JAILBREAK.
ROBIN-- YOU THINK WE SHOULD TELL REVISE?
DOES THE POPE SHIT IN THE WOODS?
LISTEN, WITH YOUR TWENTY-CAR PILEUP ON THE INTER-STATE AND MY NEARLY LOSING A THREE-HUNDRED-POUND EGG OVER THE FENCE, I THINK WE COULD BOTH USE SOME BROWNIE POINTS.
HEAD LIBRARIAN
ENTER.

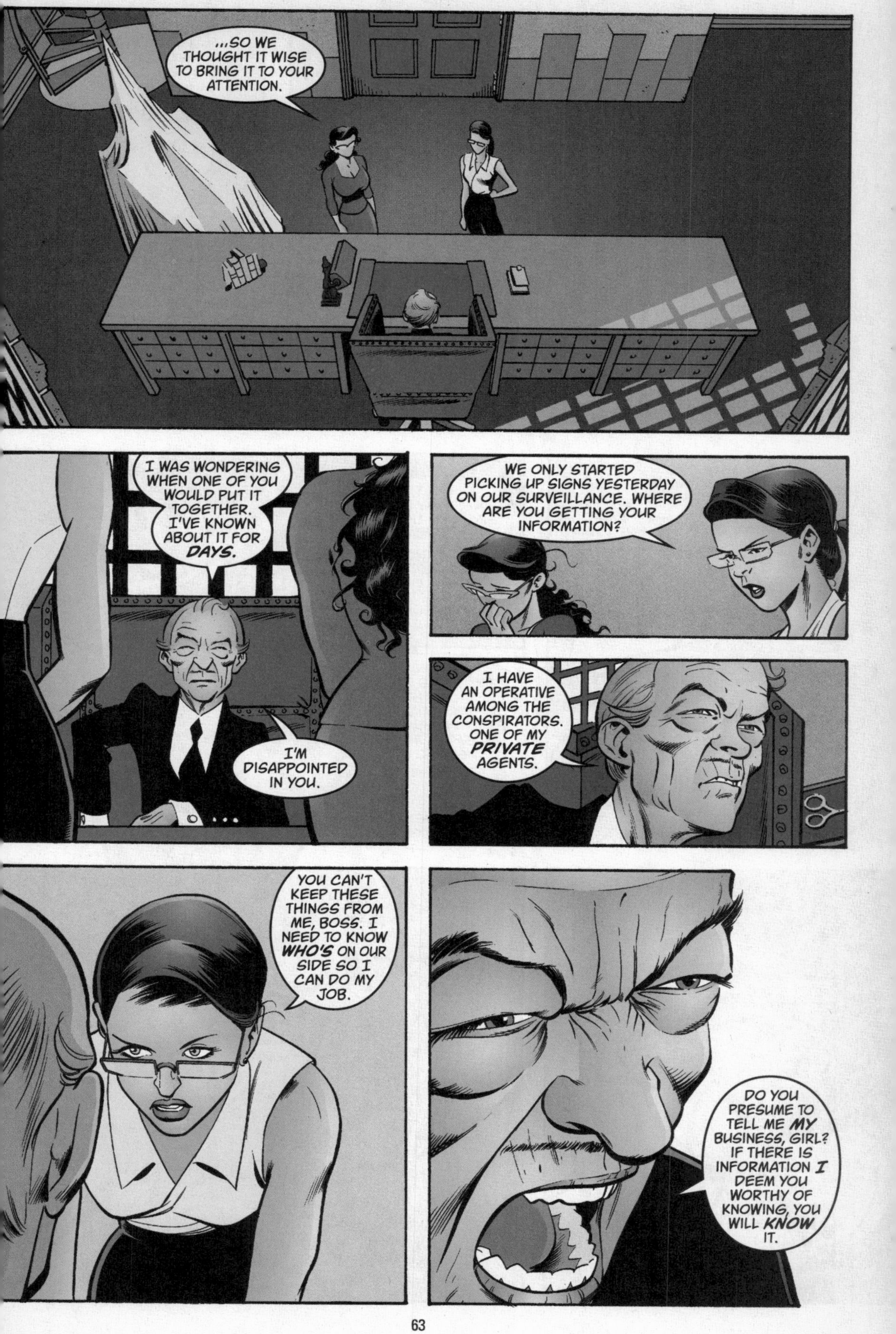
...SO WE THOUGHT IT WISE TO BRING IT TO YOUR ATTENTION.
I WAS WONDERING WHEN ONE OF YOU WOULD PUT IT TOGETHER. I'VE KNOWN ABOUT IT FOR DAYS.
I'M DISAPPOINTED IN YOU.
WE ONLY STARTED PICKING UP SIGNS YESTERDAY ON OUR SURVEILLANCE. WHERE ARE YOU GETTING YOUR INFORMATION?
I HAVE AN OPERATIVE AMONG THE CONSPIRATORS. ONE OF MY PRIVATE AGENTS.
YOU CAN'T KEEP THESE THINGS FROM ME, BOSS. I NEED TO KNOW WHO'S ON OUR SIDE SO I CAN DO MY JOB.
DO YOU PRESUME TO TELL ME MY BUSINESS, GIRL? IF THERE IS INFORMATION I DEEM YOU WORTHY OF KNOWING, YOU WILL KNOW IT.

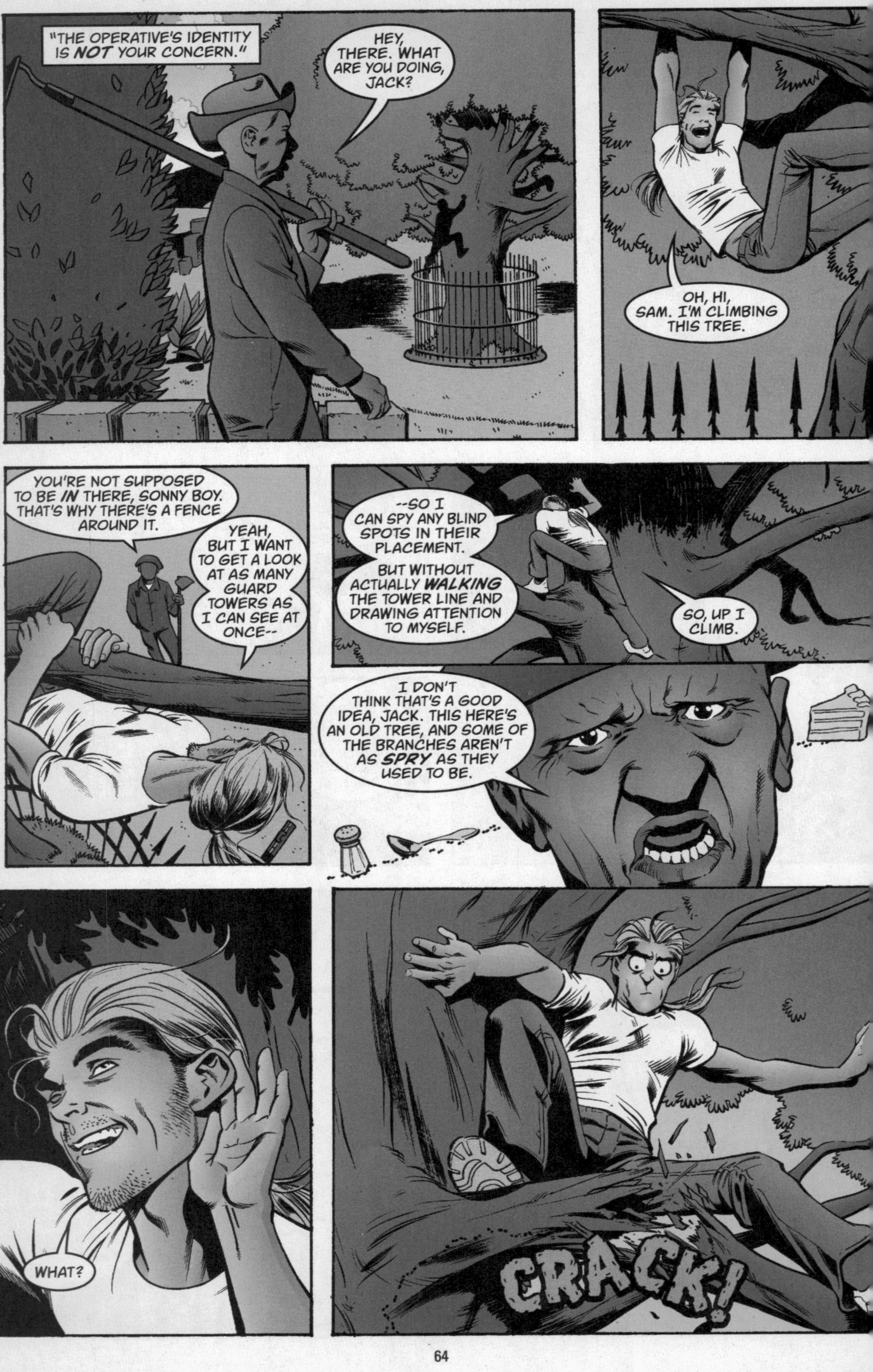
"THE OPERATIVE'S IDENTITY IS NOT YOUR CONCERN."
HEY, THERE. WHAT ARE YOU DOING, JACK?
OH, HI, SAM. I'M CLIMBING THIS TREE.
YOU'RE NOT SUPPOSED TO BE IN THERE, SONNY BOY. THAT'S WHY THERE'S A FENCE AROUND IT.
YEAH, BUT I WANT TO GET A LOOK AT AS MANY GUARD TOWERS AS I CAN SEE AT ONCE--
--SO I CAN SPY ANY BLIND SPOTS IN THEIR PLACEMENT.
BUT WITHOUT ACTUALLY WALKING THE TOWER LINE AND DRAWING ATTENTION TO MYSELF.
SO, UP I CLIMB.
I DON'T THINK THAT'S A GOOD IDEA, JACK. THIS HERE'S AN OLD TREE, AND SOME OF THE BRANCHES AREN'T AS SPRY AS THEY USED TO BE.
WHAT?
CRACK!

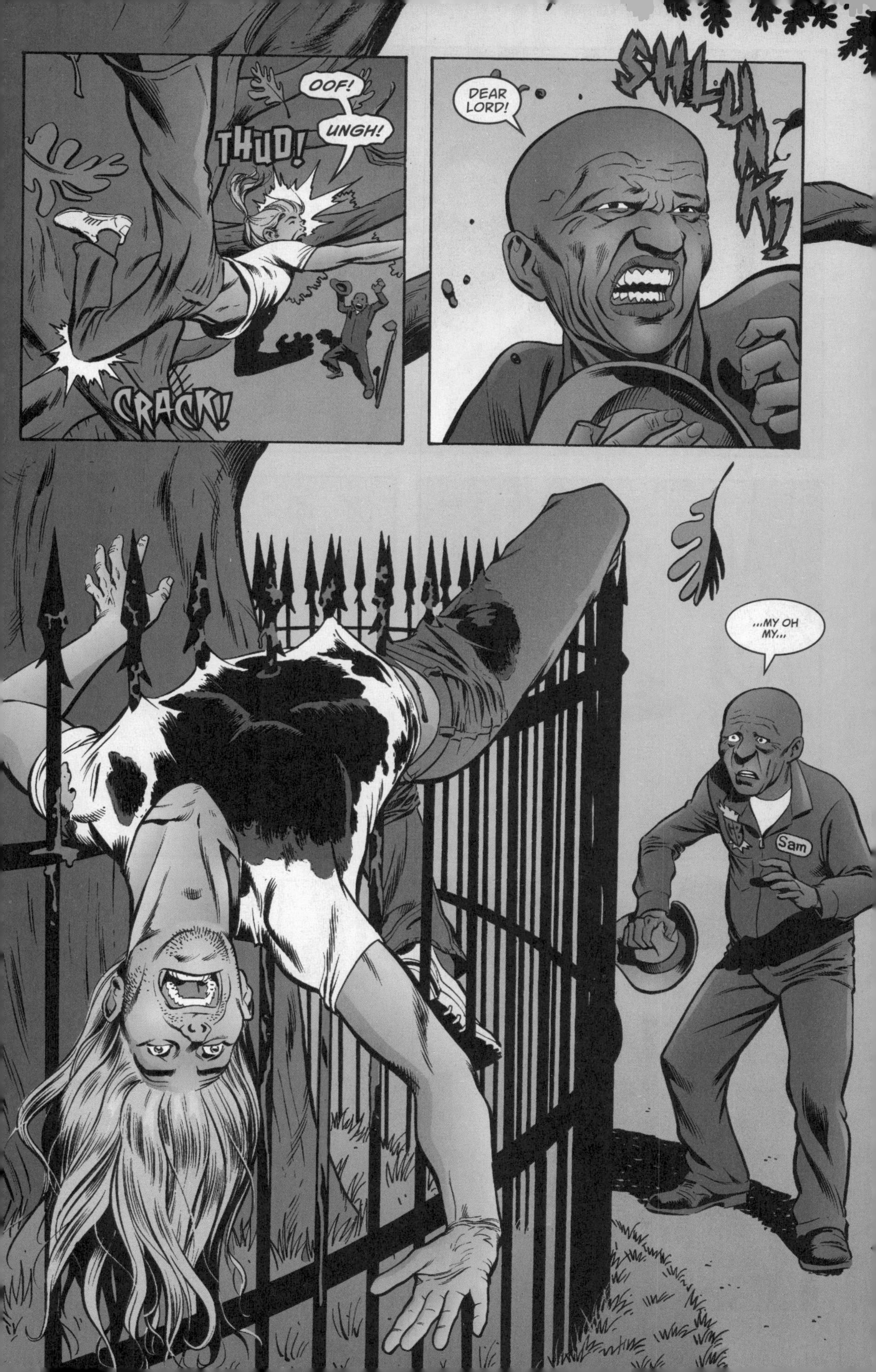
OOF!
UNGH!
THUD!
CRACK!
SHLUNK!
DEAR LORD!
...MY OH MY...
Sam

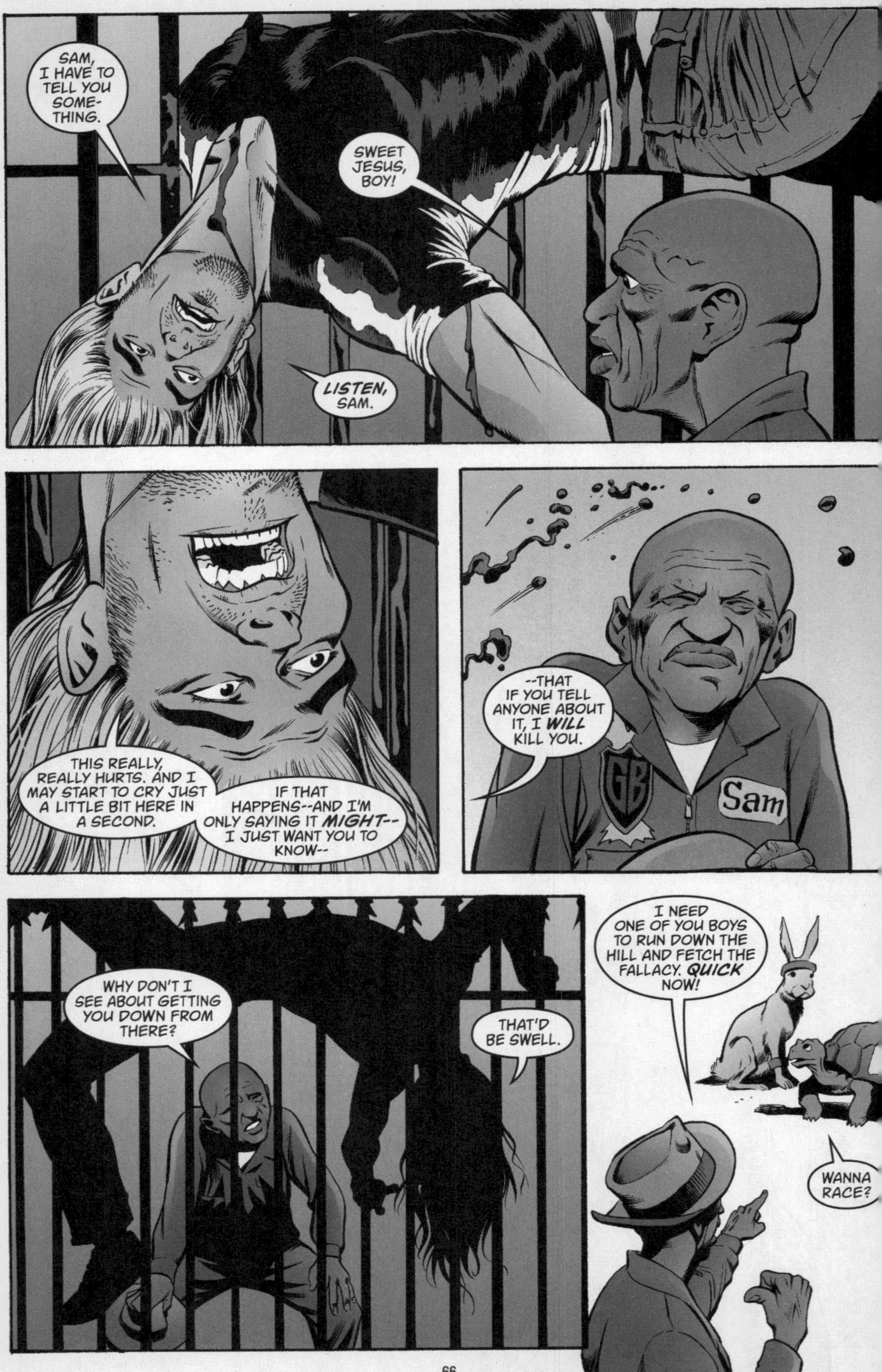
SAM, I HAVE TO TELL YOU SOME-THING.
SWEET JESUS, BOY!
LISTEN, SAM.
THIS REALLY, REALLY HURTS. AND I MAY START TO CRY JUST A LITTLE BIT HERE IN A SECOND.
IF THAT HAPPENS--AND I'M ONLY SAYING IT MIGHT-- I JUST WANT YOU TO KNOW--
--THAT IF YOU TELL ANYONE ABOUT IT, I WILL KILL YOU.
GB
Sam
WHY DON'T I SEE ABOUT GETTING YOU DOWN FROM THERE?
THAT'D BE SWELL.
I NEED ONE OF YOU BOYS TO RUN DOWN THE HILL AND FETCH THE FALLACY. QUICK NOW!
WANNA RACE?

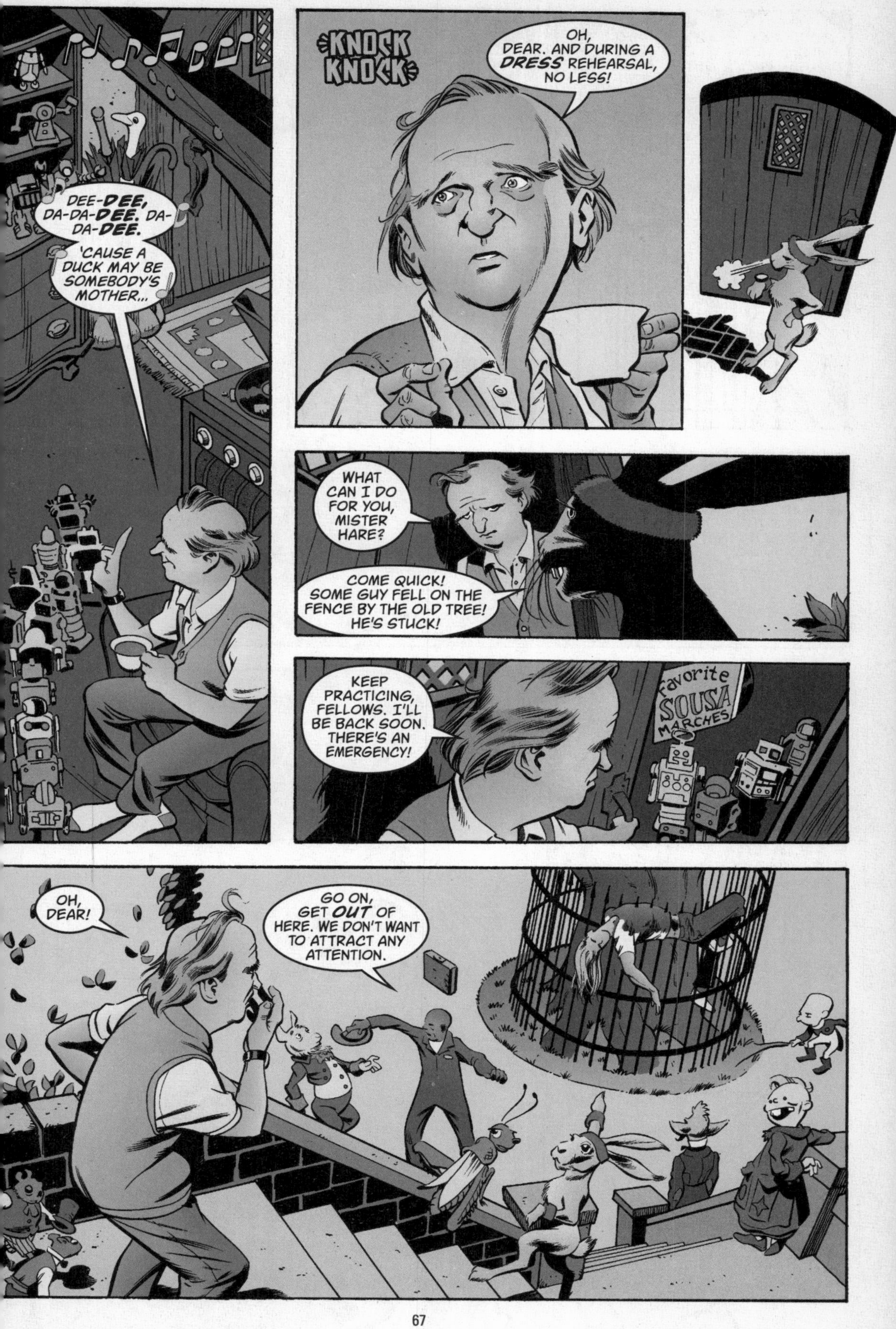
DEE-DEE, DA-DA-DEE. DA-DA-DEE.
'CAUSE A DUCK MAY BE SOMEBODY'S MOTHER...
KNOCK KNOCK
OH, DEAR. AND DURING A DRESS REHEARSAL, NO LESS!
WHAT CAN I DO FOR YOU, MISTER HARE?
COME QUICK! SOME GUY FELL ON THE FENCE BY THE OLD TREE! HE'S STUCK!
KEEP PRACTICING, FELLOWS. I'LL BE BACK SOON. THERE'S AN EMERGENCY!
Favorite SOUSA MARCHES
OH, DEAR!
GO ON, GET OUT OF HERE. WE DON'T WANT TO ATTRACT ANY ATTENTION.

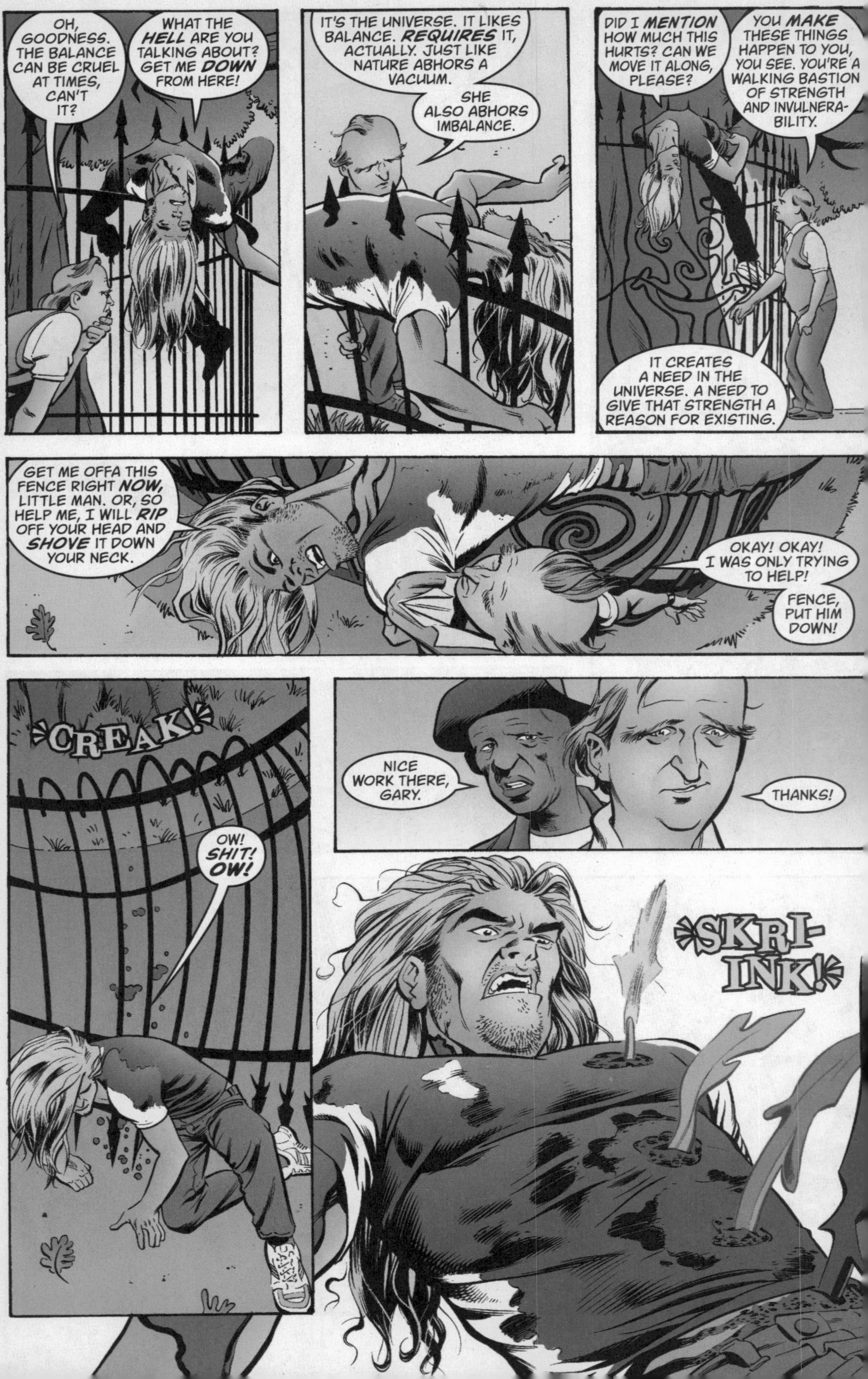
OH, GOODNESS. THE BALANCE CAN BE CRUEL AT TIMES, CAN'T IT?
WHAT THE HELL ARE YOU TALKING ABOUT? GET ME DOWN FROM HERE!
IT'S THE UNIVERSE. IT LIKES BALANCE. REQUIRES IT, ACTUALLY. JUST LIKE NATURE ABHORS A VACUUM.
SHE ALSO ABHORS IMBALANCE.
DID I MENTION HOW MUCH THIS HURTS? CAN WE MOVE IT ALONG, PLEASE?
YOU MAKE THESE THINGS HAPPEN TO YOU, YOU SEE. YOU'RE A WALKING BASTION OF STRENGTH AND INVULNERA-BILITY.
IT CREATES A NEED IN THE UNIVERSE. A NEED TO GIVE THAT STRENGTH A REASON FOR EXISTING.
GET ME OFFA THIS FENCE RIGHT NOW, LITTLE MAN. OR, SO HELP ME, I WILL RIP OFF YOUR HEAD AND SHOVE IT DOWN YOUR NECK.
OKAY! OKAY! I WAS ONLY TRYING TO HELP!
FENCE, PUT HIM DOWN!
CREAK!
OW! SHIT! OW!
NICE WORK THERE, GARY.
THANKS!
SKRI-INK!

HOW DO YOU FEEL, SON?

LIKE I JUST GOT *IMPALED* ON A FENCE. YOU?

GREAT WORK, FENCE. TOP DRAWER.

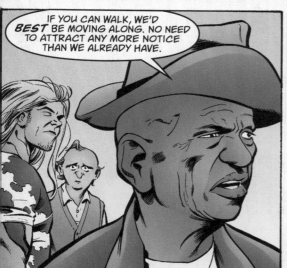

IF YOU CAN WALK, WE'D *BEST* BE MOVING ALONG. NO NEED TO ATTRACT ANY MORE NOTICE THAN WE ALREADY HAVE.

I PROBABLY SHOULDN'T TELL YOU THIS, BECAUSE YOU'RE *NOT* A VERY NICE PERSON, AND I COULD GET IN TROUBLE.

BUT I WANT TO *HELP* YOU AND SAM.

OKAY, I'M LISTENING.

YOU'RE CONCERNED ABOUT AN AIR ESCAPE. I HAD AN IDEA...

HOW DID *YOU*--?

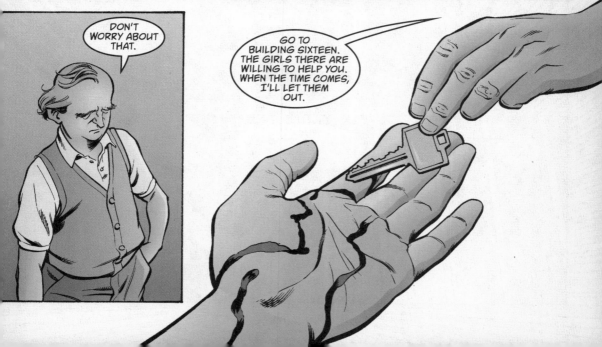

DON'T WORRY ABOUT THAT.

GO TO BUILDING SIXTEEN. THE GIRLS THERE ARE WILLING TO HELP YOU. WHEN THE TIME COMES, I'LL LET THEM OUT.

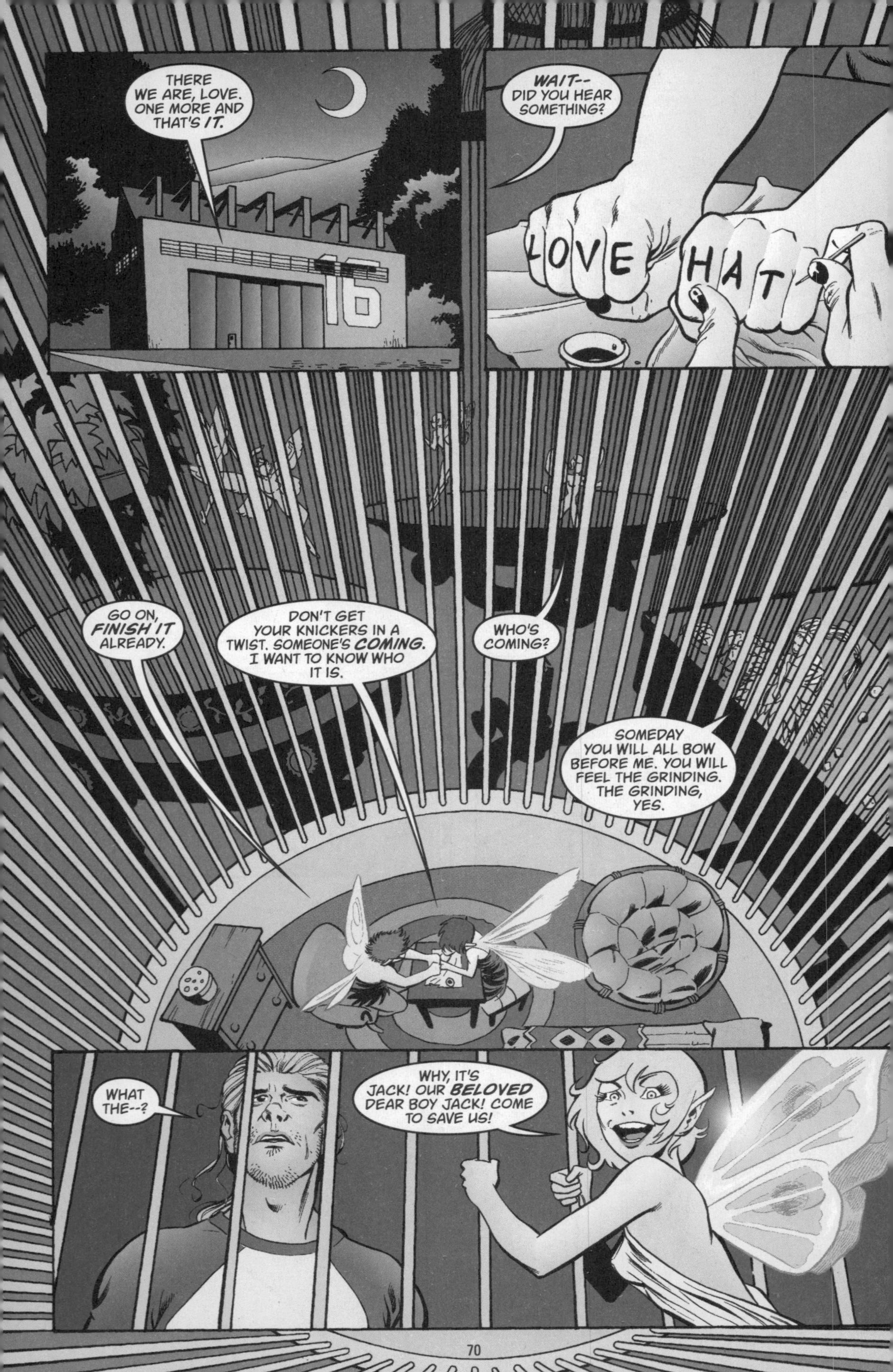
THERE WE ARE, LOVE. ONE MORE AND THAT'S *IT.*
16
WAIT-- DID YOU HEAR SOMETHING?
LOVE HAT
GO ON, *FINISH IT* ALREADY.
DON'T GET YOUR KNICKERS IN A TWIST. SOMEONE'S *COMING.* I WANT TO KNOW WHO IT IS.
WHO'S COMING?
SOMEDAY YOU WILL ALL BOW BEFORE ME. YOU WILL FEEL THE GRINDING. THE GRINDING, YES.
WHAT THE--?
WHY, IT'S JACK! OUR *BELOVED* DEAR BOY JACK! COME TO SAVE US!

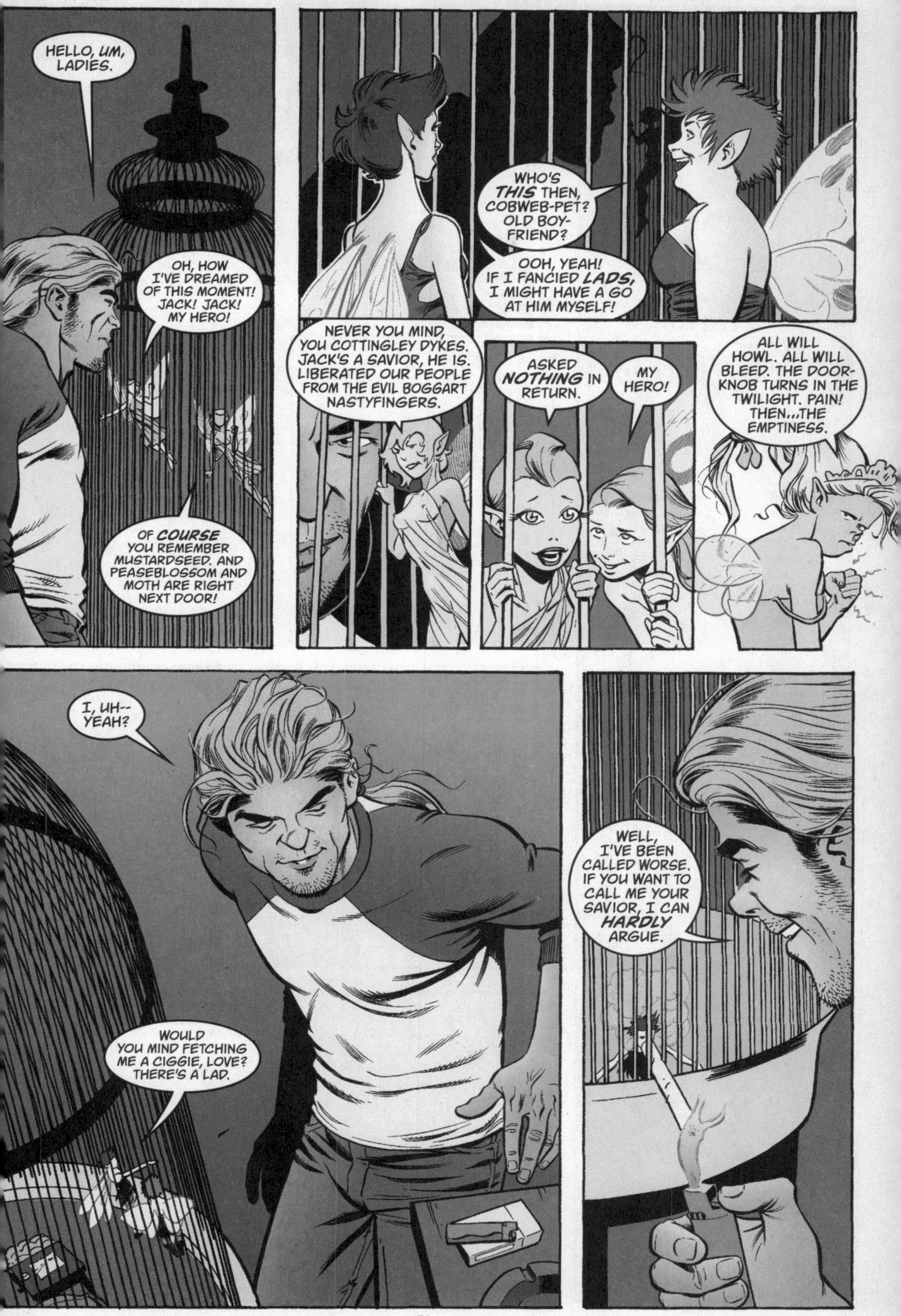
HELLO, UM, LADIES.
WHO'S THIS THEN, COBWEB-PET? OLD BOY-FRIEND?
OOH, YEAH! IF I FANCIED LADS, I MIGHT HAVE A GO AT HIM MYSELF!
OH, HOW I'VE DREAMED OF THIS MOMENT! JACK! JACK! MY HERO!
OF COURSE YOU REMEMBER MUSTARDSEED. AND PEASEBLOSSOM AND MOTH ARE RIGHT NEXT DOOR!
NEVER YOU MIND, YOU COTTINGLEY DYKES. JACK'S A SAVIOR, HE IS. LIBERATED OUR PEOPLE FROM THE EVIL BOGGART NASTYFINGERS.
ASKED NOTHING IN RETURN.
MY HERO!
ALL WILL HOWL. ALL WILL BLEED. THE DOOR-KNOB TURNS IN THE TWILIGHT. PAIN! THEN...THE EMPTINESS.
I, UH-- YEAH?
WOULD YOU MIND FETCHING ME A CIGGIE, LOVE? THERE'S A LAD.
WELL, I'VE BEEN CALLED WORSE. IF YOU WANT TO CALL ME YOUR SAVIOR, I CAN HARDLY ARGUE.

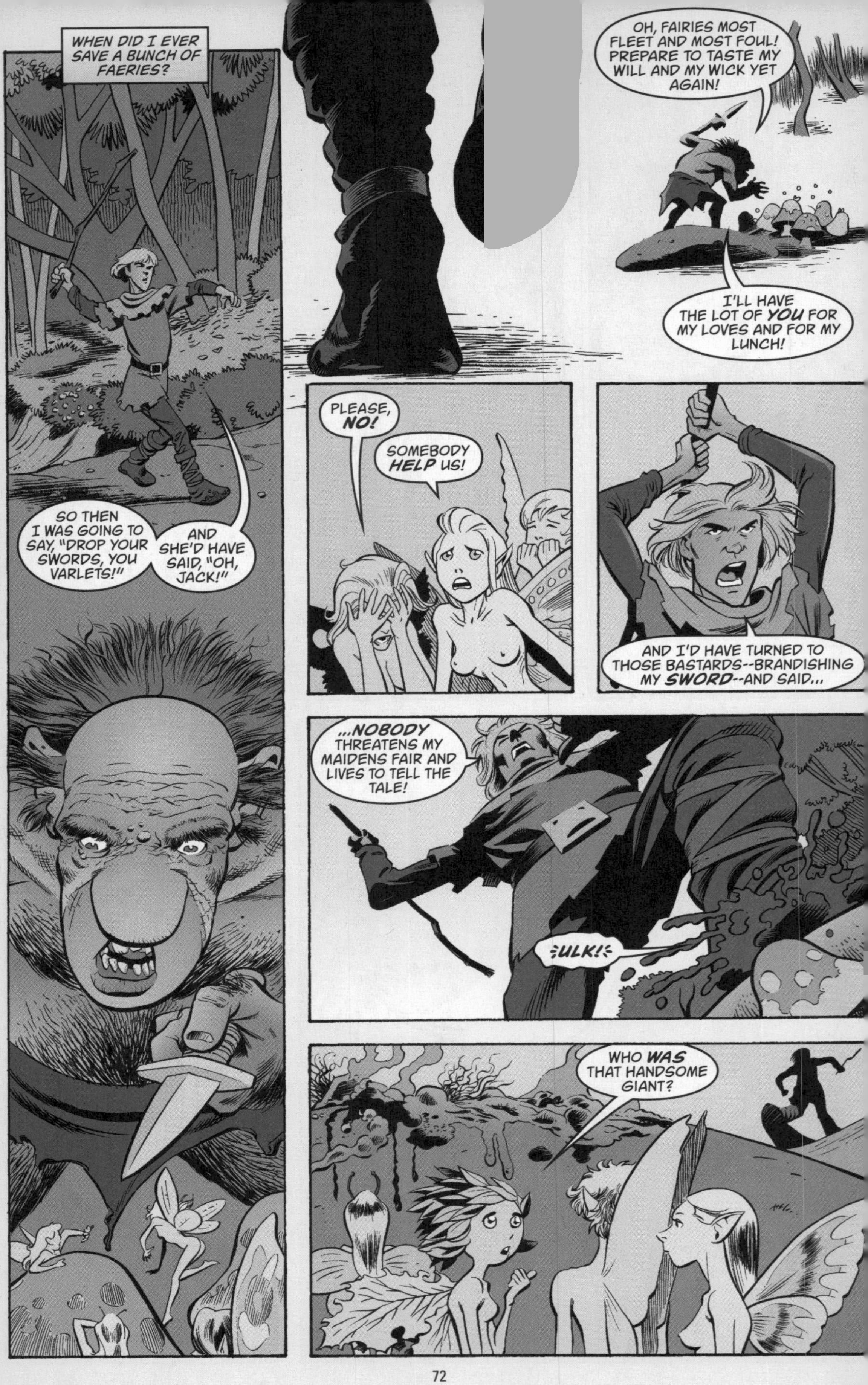

WHEN DID I EVER SAVE A BUNCH OF FAERIES?
OH, FAIRIES MOST FLEET AND MOST FOUL! PREPARE TO TASTE MY WILL AND MY WICK YET AGAIN!
I'LL HAVE THE LOT OF YOU FOR MY LOVES AND FOR MY LUNCH!
SO THEN I WAS GOING TO SAY, "DROP YOUR SWORDS, YOU VARLETS!"
AND SHE'D HAVE SAID, "OH, JACK!"
PLEASE, NO!
SOMEBODY HELP US!
AND I'D HAVE TURNED TO THOSE BASTARDS--BRANDISHING MY SWORD--AND SAID...
...NOBODY THREATENS MY MAIDENS FAIR AND LIVES TO TELL THE TALE!
ULK!
WHO WAS THAT HANDSOME GIANT?

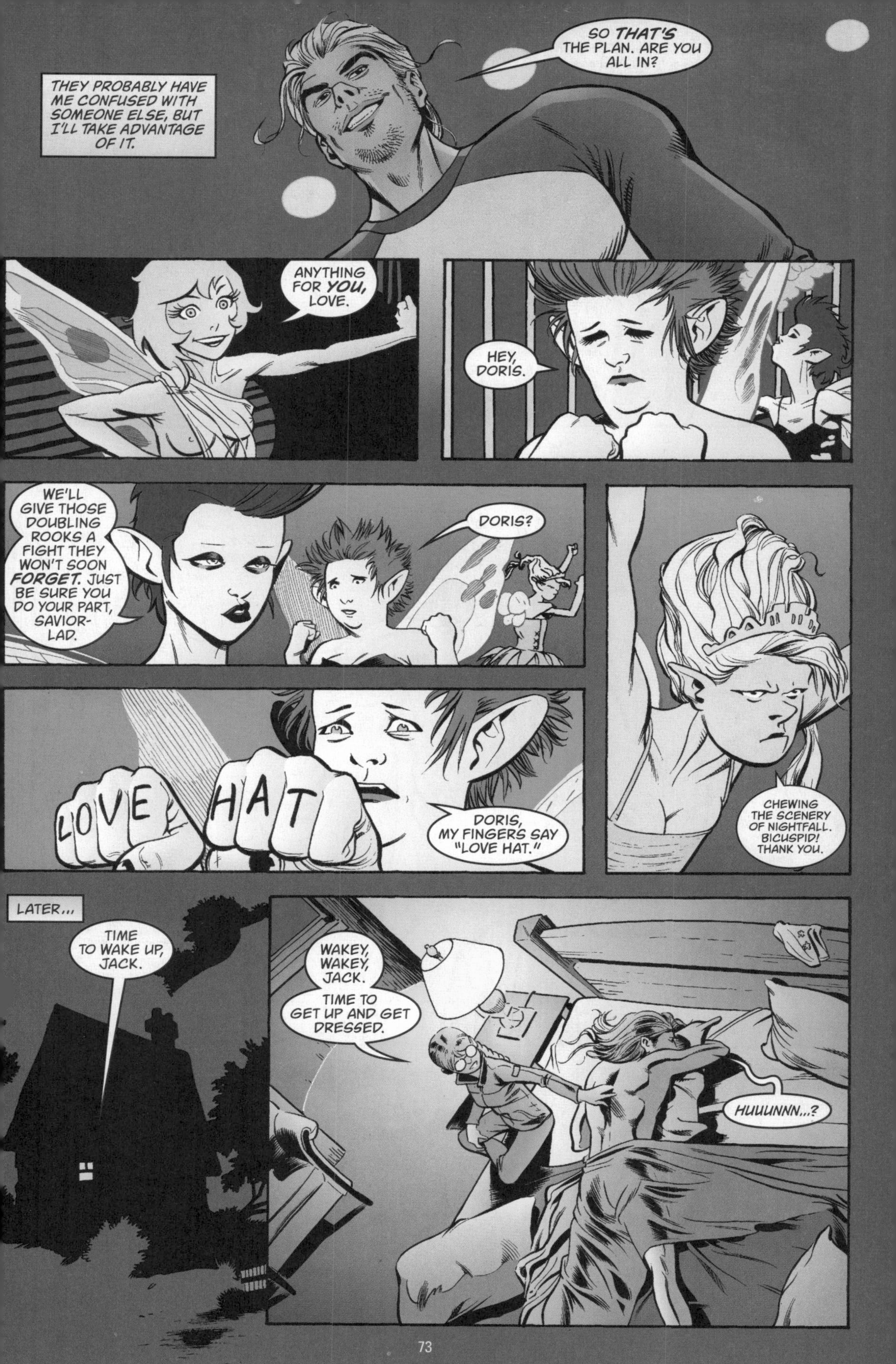
SO THAT'S THE PLAN. ARE YOU ALL IN?
THEY PROBABLY HAVE ME CONFUSED WITH SOMEONE ELSE, BUT I'LL TAKE ADVANTAGE OF IT.
ANYTHING FOR YOU, LOVE.
HEY, DORIS.
WE'LL GIVE THOSE DOUBLING ROOKS A FIGHT THEY WON'T SOON FORGET. JUST BE SURE YOU DO YOUR PART, SAVIOR-LAD.
DORIS?
LOVE HAT
DORIS, MY FINGERS SAY "LOVE HAT."
CHEWING THE SCENERY OF NIGHTFALL. BICUSPID! THANK YOU.
LATER...
TIME TO WAKE UP, JACK.
WAKEY, WAKEY, JACK. TIME TO GET UP AND GET DRESSED.
HUUUNNN...?

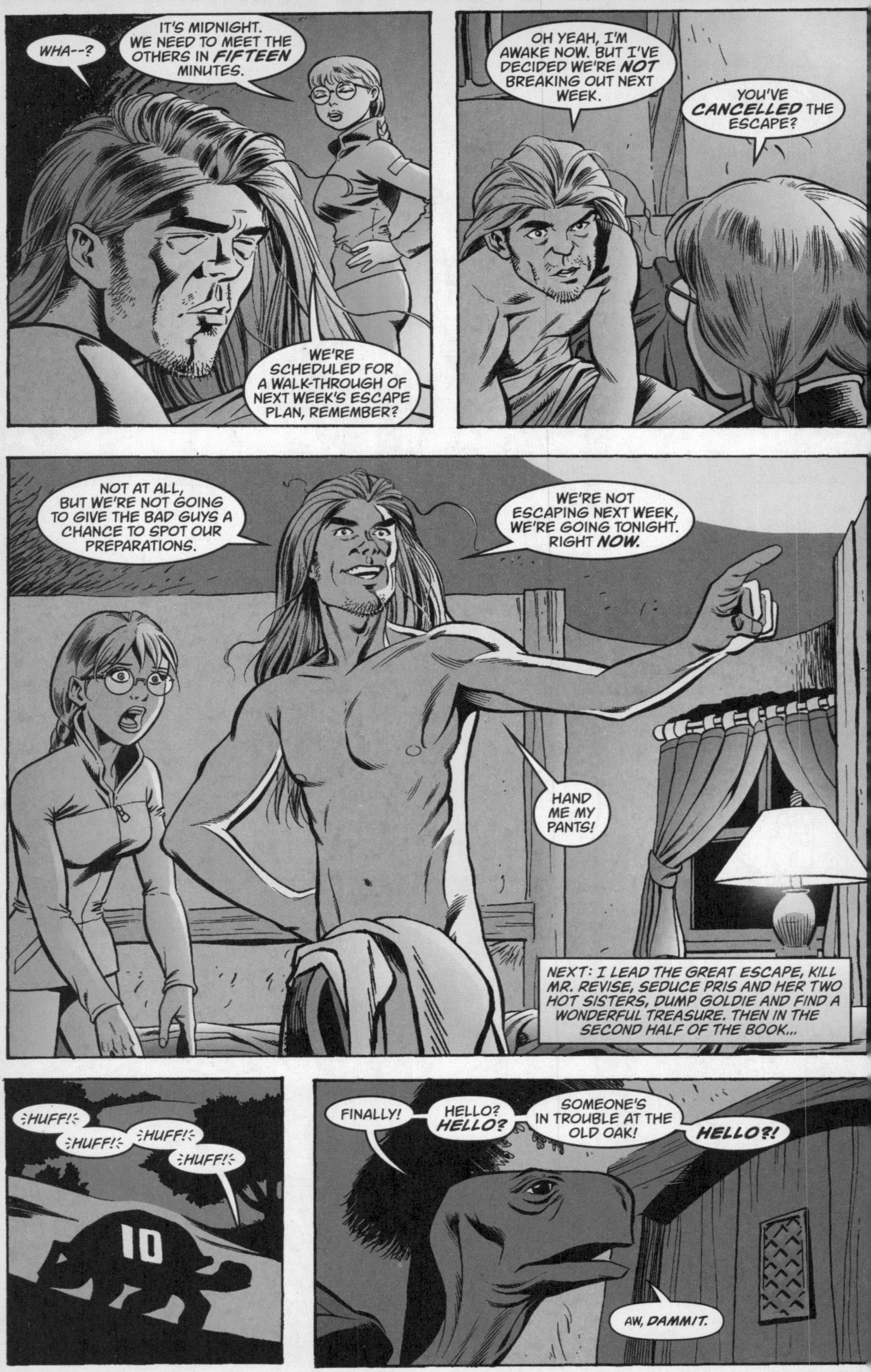
WHA--?
IT'S MIDNIGHT. WE NEED TO MEET THE OTHERS IN FIFTEEN MINUTES.
WE'RE SCHEDULED FOR A WALK-THROUGH OF NEXT WEEK'S ESCAPE PLAN, REMEMBER?
OH YEAH, I'M AWAKE NOW. BUT I'VE DECIDED WE'RE NOT BREAKING OUT NEXT WEEK.
YOU'VE CANCELLED THE ESCAPE?
NOT AT ALL, BUT WE'RE NOT GOING TO GIVE THE BAD GUYS A CHANCE TO SPOT OUR PREPARATIONS.
WE'RE NOT ESCAPING NEXT WEEK, WE'RE GOING TONIGHT. RIGHT NOW.
HAND ME MY PANTS!
NEXT: I LEAD THE GREAT ESCAPE, KILL MR. REVISE, SEDUCE PRIS AND HER TWO HOT SISTERS, DUMP GOLDIE AND FIND A WONDERFUL TREASURE. THEN IN THE SECOND HALF OF THE BOOK...
HUFF!
HUFF!
HUFF!
HUFF!
10
FINALLY!
HELLO? HELLO?
SOMEONE'S IN TROUBLE AT THE OLD OAK!
HELLO?!
AW, DAMMIT.

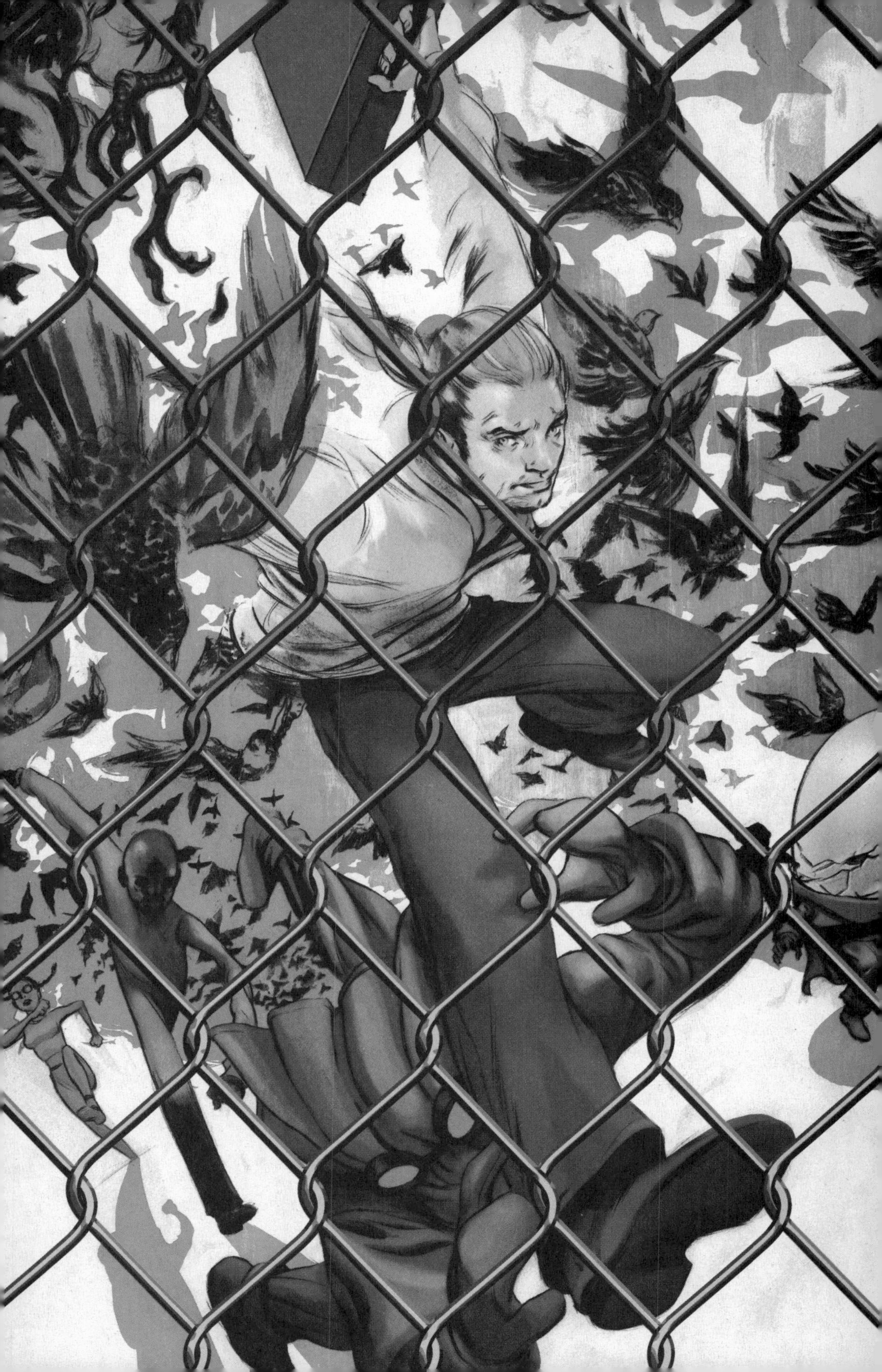

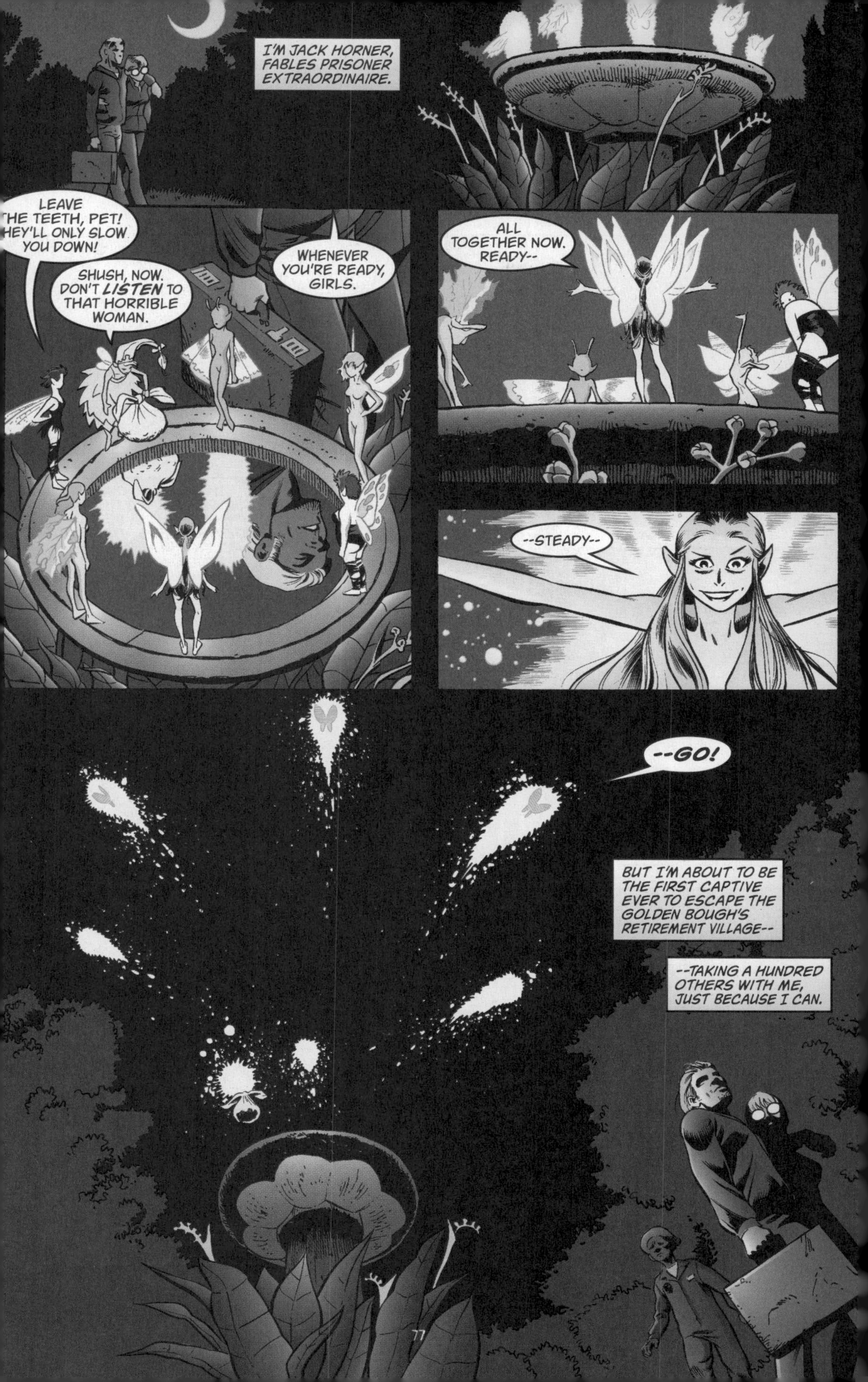

I'M JACK HORNER, FABLES PRISONER EXTRAORDINAIRE.
LEAVE THE TEETH, PET! THEY'LL ONLY SLOW YOU DOWN!
SHUSH, NOW. DON'T LISTEN TO THAT HORRIBLE WOMAN.
WHENEVER YOU'RE READY, GIRLS.
ALL TOGETHER NOW. READY--
--STEADY--
--GO!
BUT I'M ABOUT TO BE THE FIRST CAPTIVE EVER TO ESCAPE THE GOLDEN BOUGH'S RETIREMENT VILLAGE--
--TAKING A HUNDRED OTHERS WITH ME, JUST BECAUSE I CAN.

JACKRABBIT

In which the Great Escape gets underway.

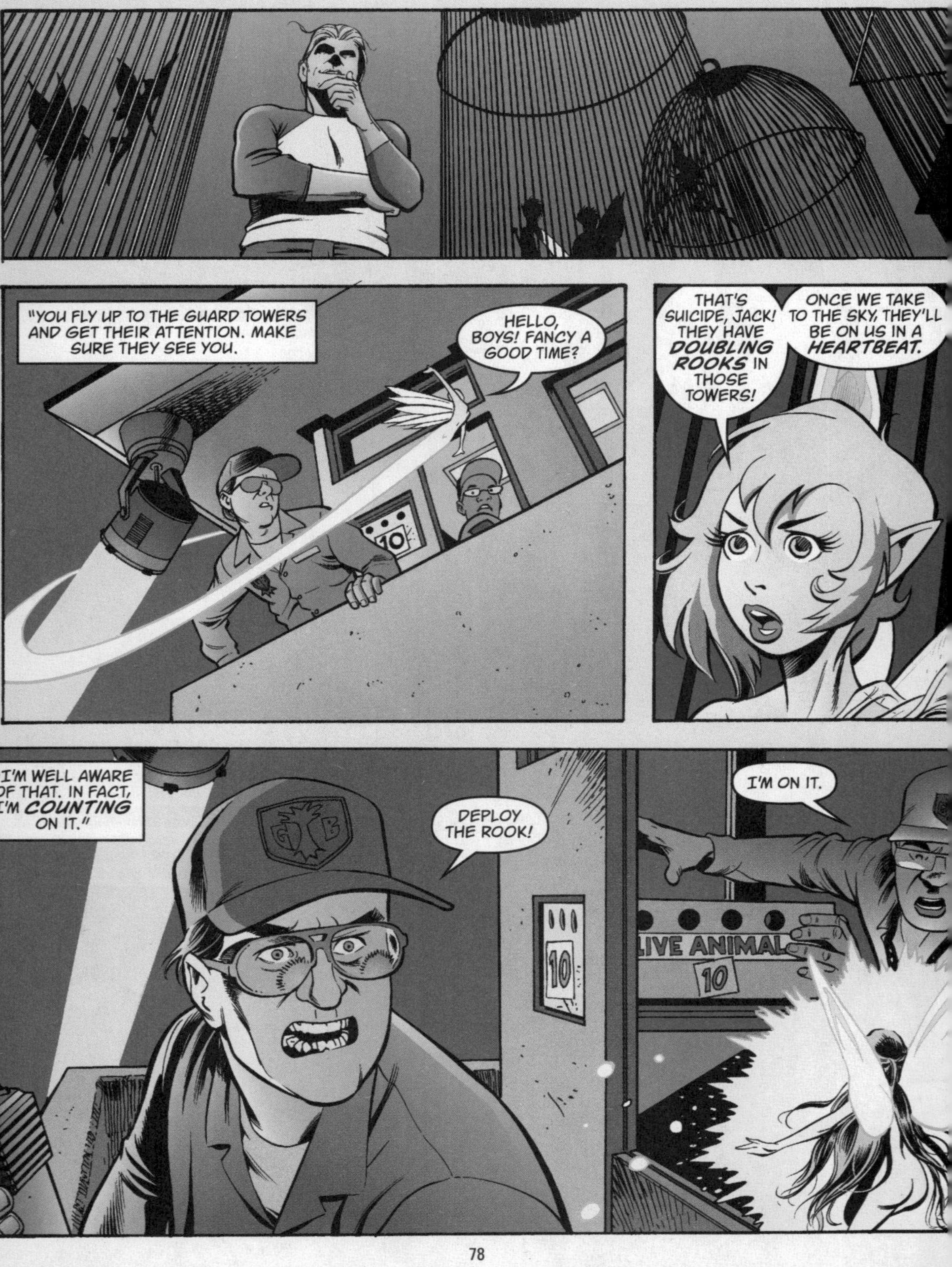
"YOU FLY UP TO THE GUARD TOWERS AND GET THEIR ATTENTION. MAKE SURE THEY SEE YOU.
HELLO, BOYS! FANCY A GOOD TIME?
10
THAT'S SUICIDE, JACK! THEY HAVE *DOUBLING ROOKS* IN THOSE TOWERS!
ONCE WE TAKE TO THE SKY, THEY'LL BE ON US IN A *HEARTBEAT.*
"I'M WELL AWARE OF THAT. IN FACT, I'M *COUNTING* ON IT."
DEPLOY THE ROOK!
10
I'M ON IT.
LIVE ANIMAL
10

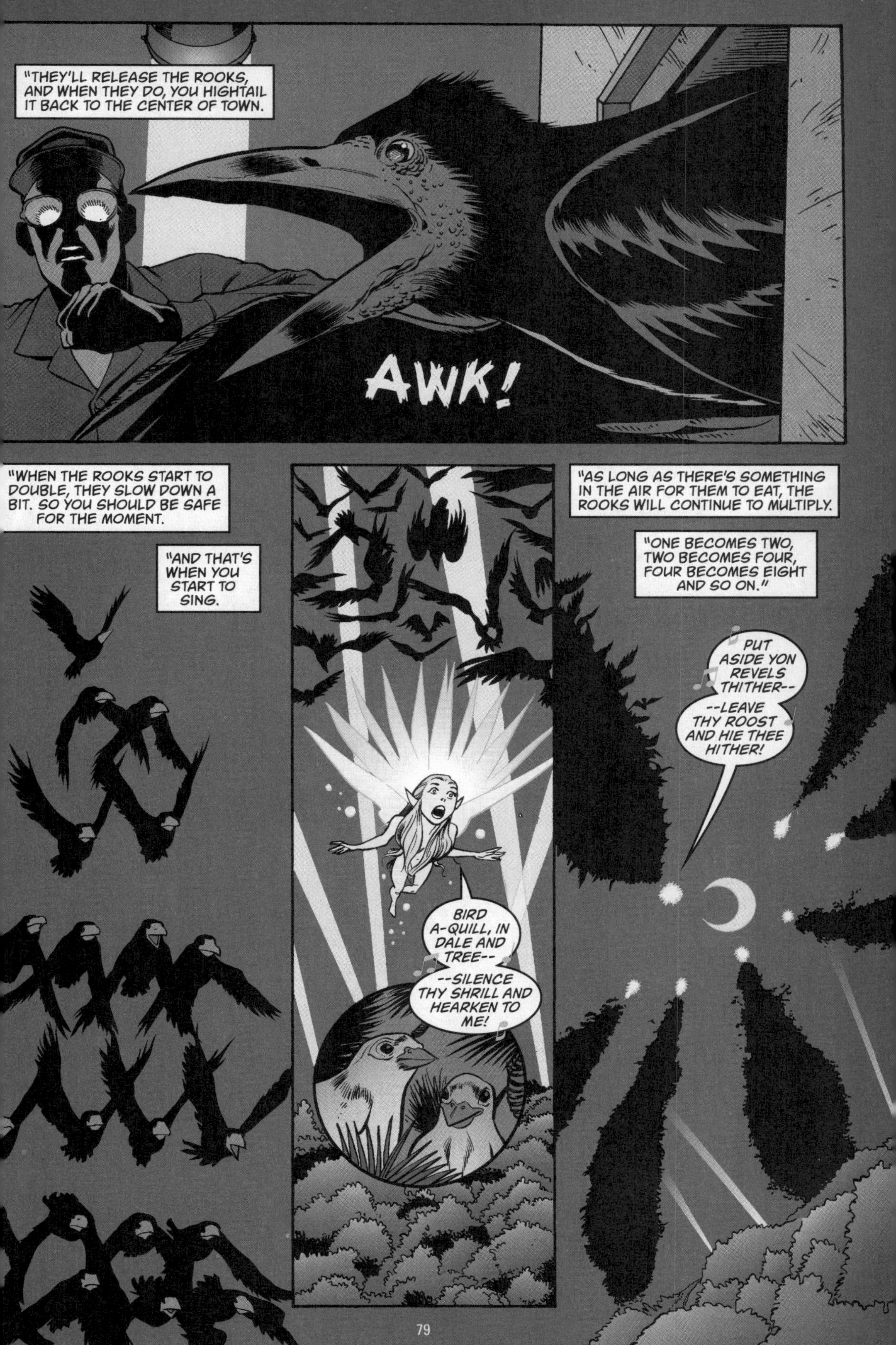
"THEY'LL RELEASE THE ROOKS, AND WHEN THEY DO, YOU HIGHTAIL IT BACK TO THE CENTER OF TOWN.
AWK!
"WHEN THE ROOKS START TO DOUBLE, THEY SLOW DOWN A BIT. SO YOU SHOULD BE SAFE FOR THE MOMENT.
"AND THAT'S WHEN YOU START TO SING.
BIRD A-QUILL, IN DALE AND TREE--
--SILENCE THY SHRILL AND HEARKEN TO ME!
"AS LONG AS THERE'S SOMETHING IN THE AIR FOR THEM TO EAT, THE ROOKS WILL CONTINUE TO MULTIPLY.
"ONE BECOMES TWO, TWO BECOMES FOUR, FOUR BECOMES EIGHT AND SO ON."
PUT ASIDE YON REVELS THITHER--
--LEAVE THY ROOST AND HIE THEE HITHER!

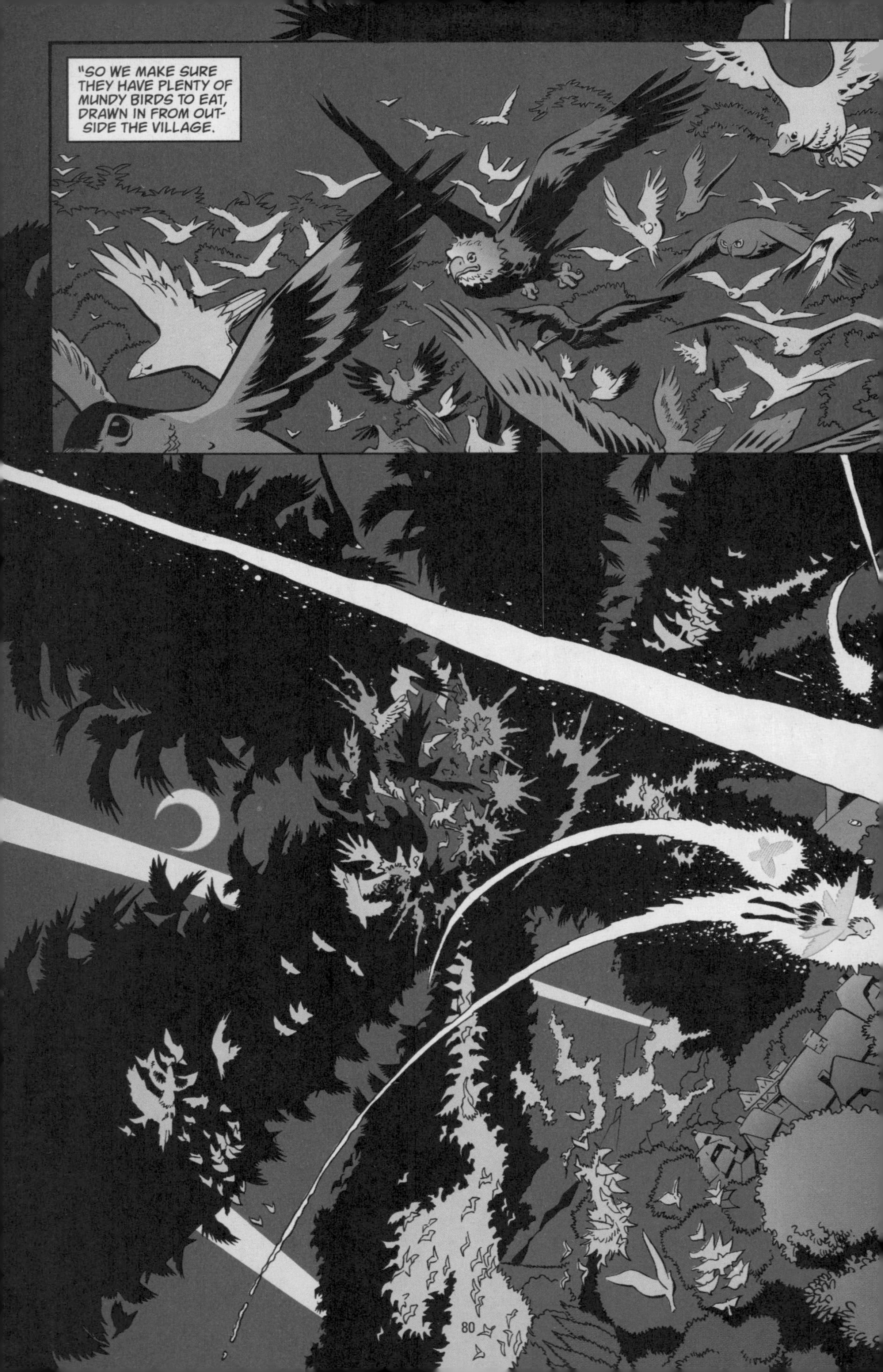
"SO WE MAKE SURE THEY HAVE PLENTY OF MUNDY BIRDS TO EAT, DRAWN IN FROM OUT-SIDE THE VILLAGE.

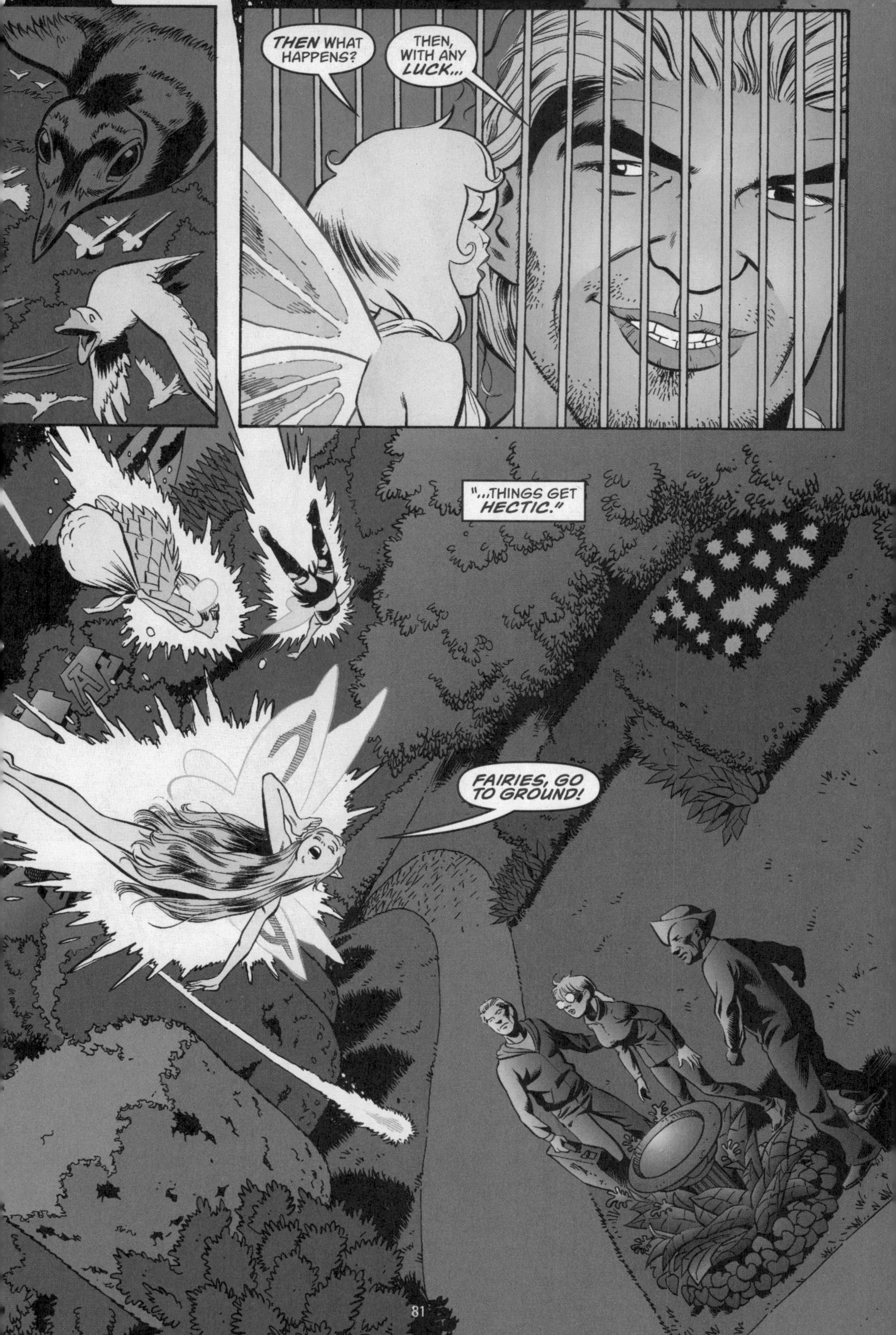
THEN WHAT HAPPENS?
THEN, WITH ANY LUCK...
"...THINGS GET HECTIC."
FAIRIES, GO TO GROUND!

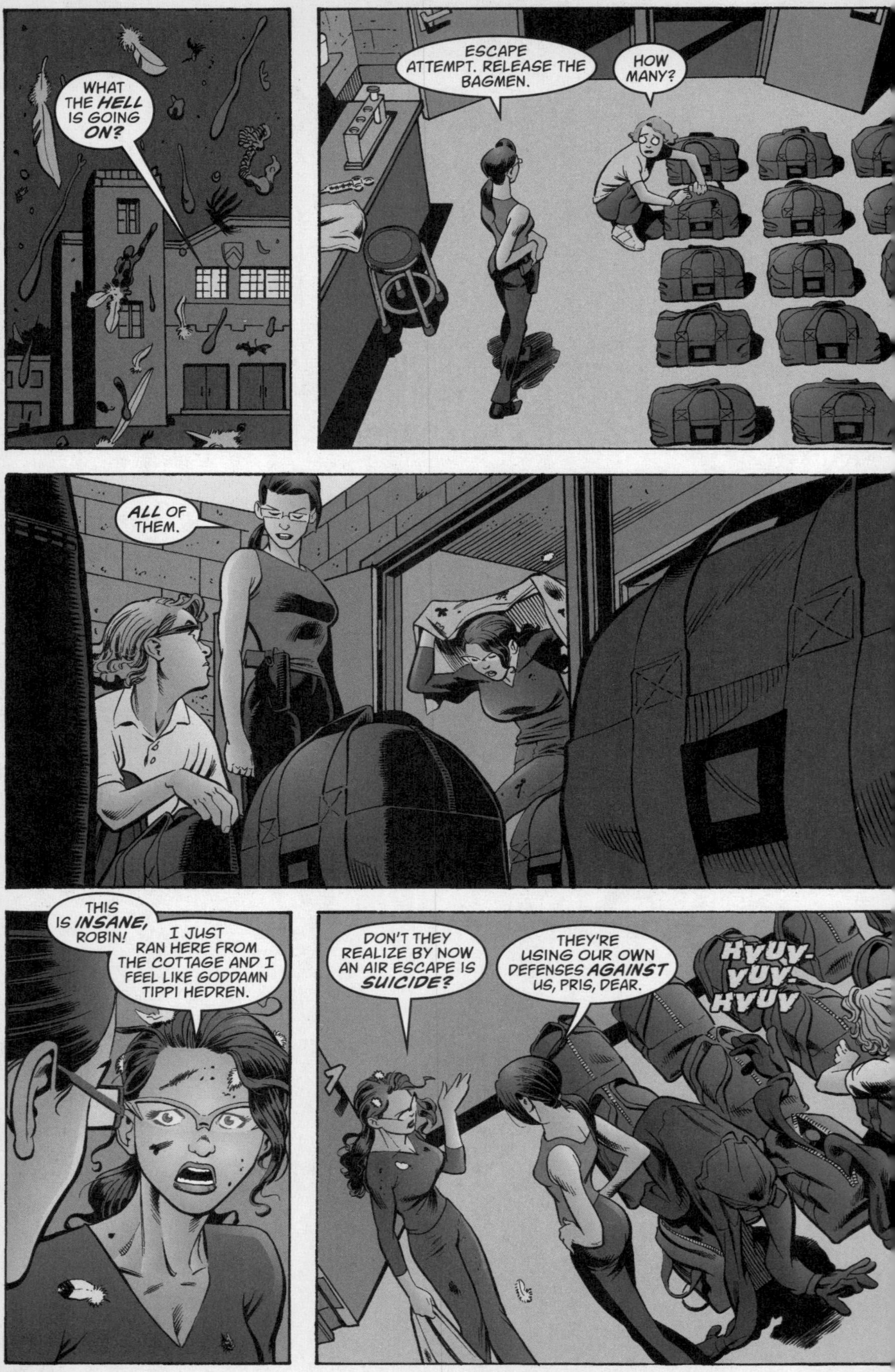
WHAT THE HELL IS GOING ON?
ESCAPE ATTEMPT. RELEASE THE BAGMEN.
HOW MANY?
ALL OF THEM.
THIS IS INSANE, ROBIN!
I JUST RAN HERE FROM THE COTTAGE AND I FEEL LIKE GODDAMN TIPPI HEDREN.
DON'T THEY REALIZE BY NOW AN AIR ESCAPE IS SUICIDE?
THEY'RE USING OUR OWN DEFENSES AGAINST US, PRIS, DEAR.
HVUV-VUV-HVUV

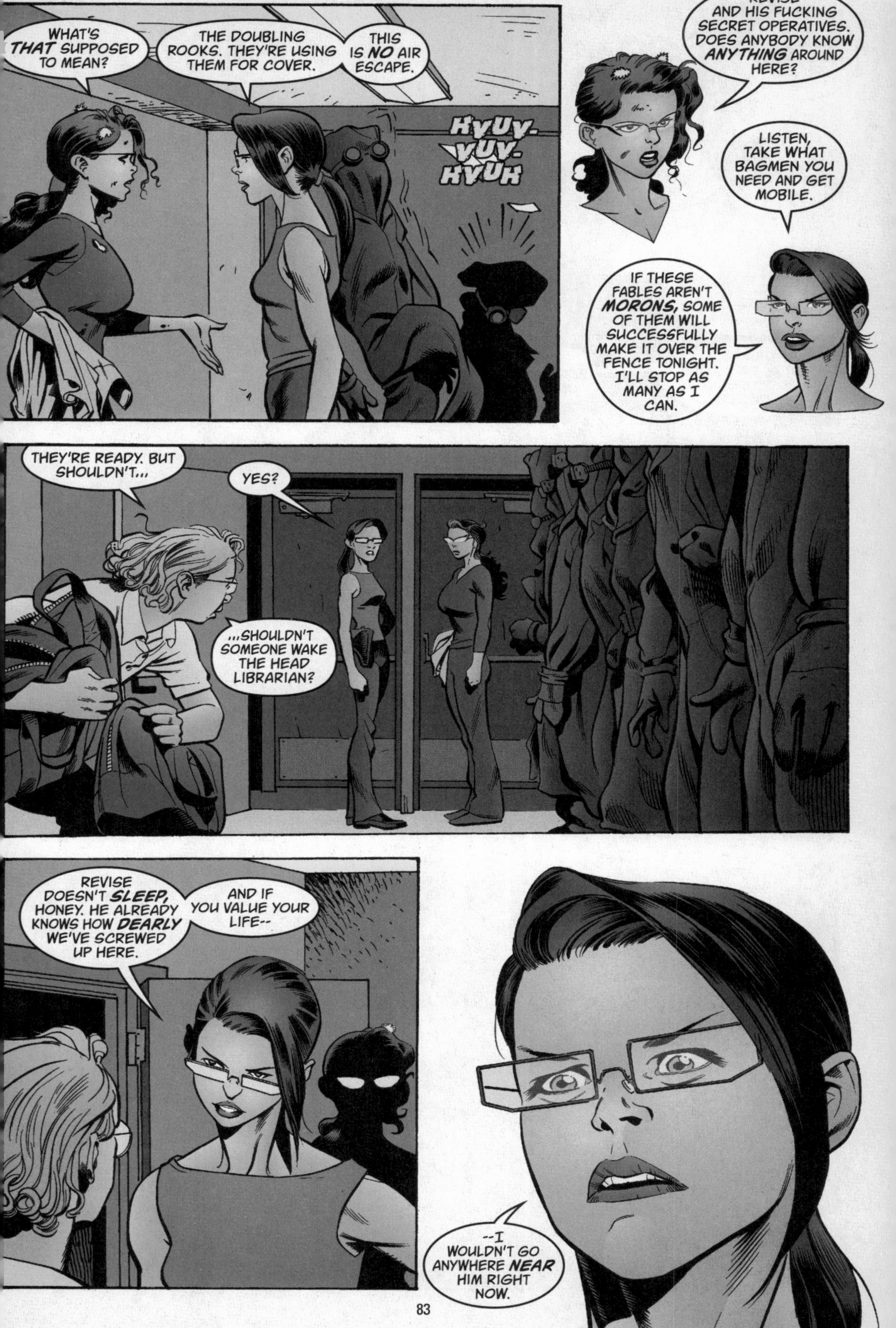
WHAT'S THAT SUPPOSED TO MEAN?
THE DOUBLING ROOKS. THEY'RE USING THEM FOR COVER.
THIS IS NO AIR ESCAPE.
HVUV-VUV-HVUK
REVISE AND HIS FUCKING SECRET OPERATIVES. DOES ANYBODY KNOW ANYTHING AROUND HERE?
LISTEN, TAKE WHAT BAGMEN YOU NEED AND GET MOBILE.
IF THESE FABLES AREN'T MORONS, SOME OF THEM WILL SUCCESSFULLY MAKE IT OVER THE FENCE TONIGHT. I'LL STOP AS MANY AS I CAN.
THEY'RE READY. BUT SHOULDN'T...
YES?
...SHOULDN'T SOMEONE WAKE THE HEAD LIBRARIAN?
REVISE DOESN'T SLEEP, HONEY. HE ALREADY KNOWS HOW DEARLY WE'VE SCREWED UP HERE.
AND IF YOU VALUE YOUR LIFE--
--I WOULDN'T GO ANYWHERE NEAR HIM RIGHT NOW.

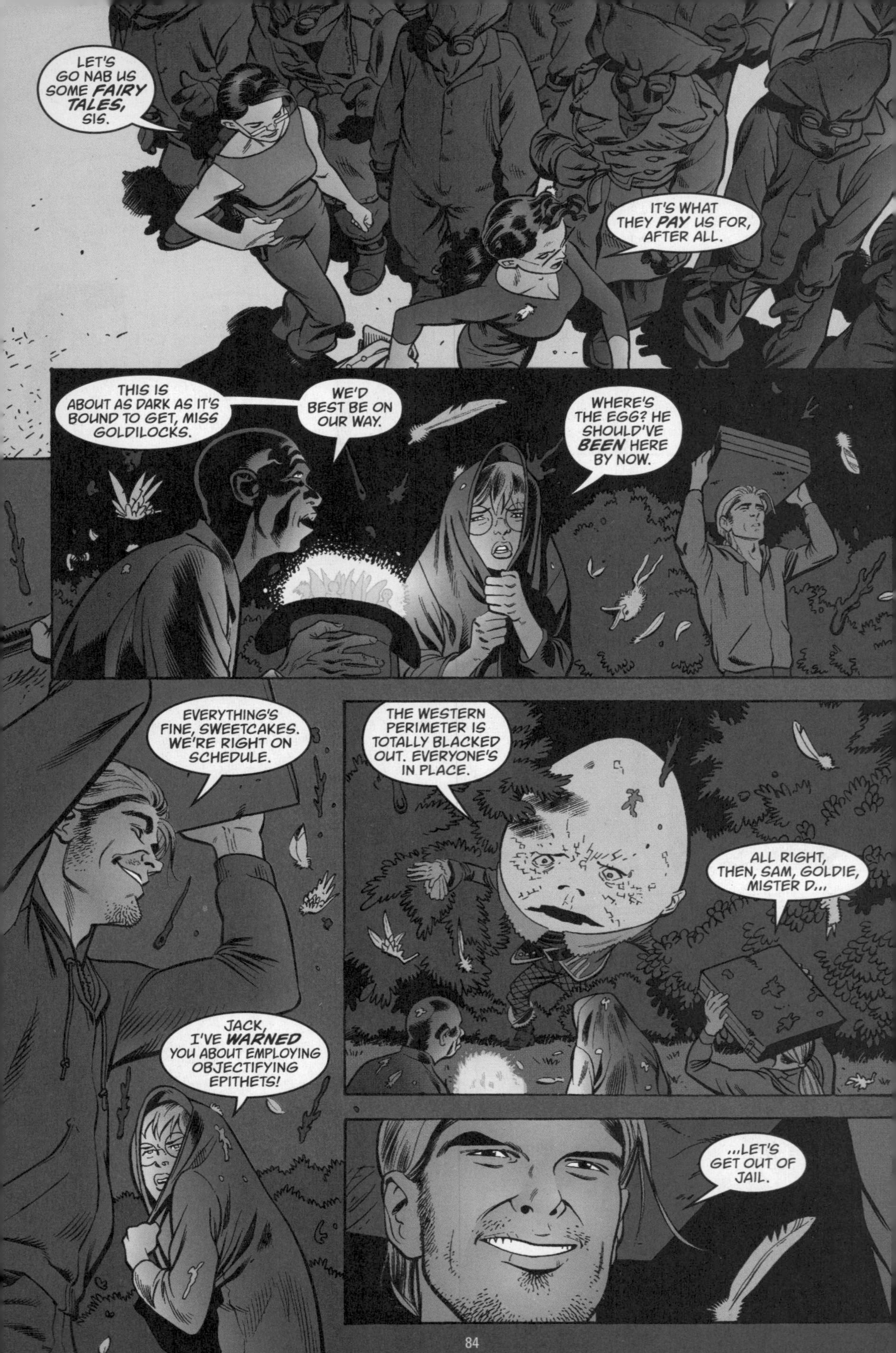
LET'S GO NAB US SOME FAIRY TALES, SIS.
IT'S WHAT THEY PAY US FOR, AFTER ALL.
THIS IS ABOUT AS DARK AS IT'S BOUND TO GET, MISS GOLDILOCKS.
WE'D BEST BE ON OUR WAY.
WHERE'S THE EGG? HE SHOULD'VE BEEN HERE BY NOW.
EVERYTHING'S FINE, SWEETCAKES. WE'RE RIGHT ON SCHEDULE.
JACK, I'VE WARNED YOU ABOUT EMPLOYING OBJECTIFYING EPITHETS!
THE WESTERN PERIMETER IS TOTALLY BLACKED OUT. EVERYONE'S IN PLACE.
ALL RIGHT, THEN, SAM, GOLDIE, MISTER D...
...LET'S GET OUT OF JAIL.

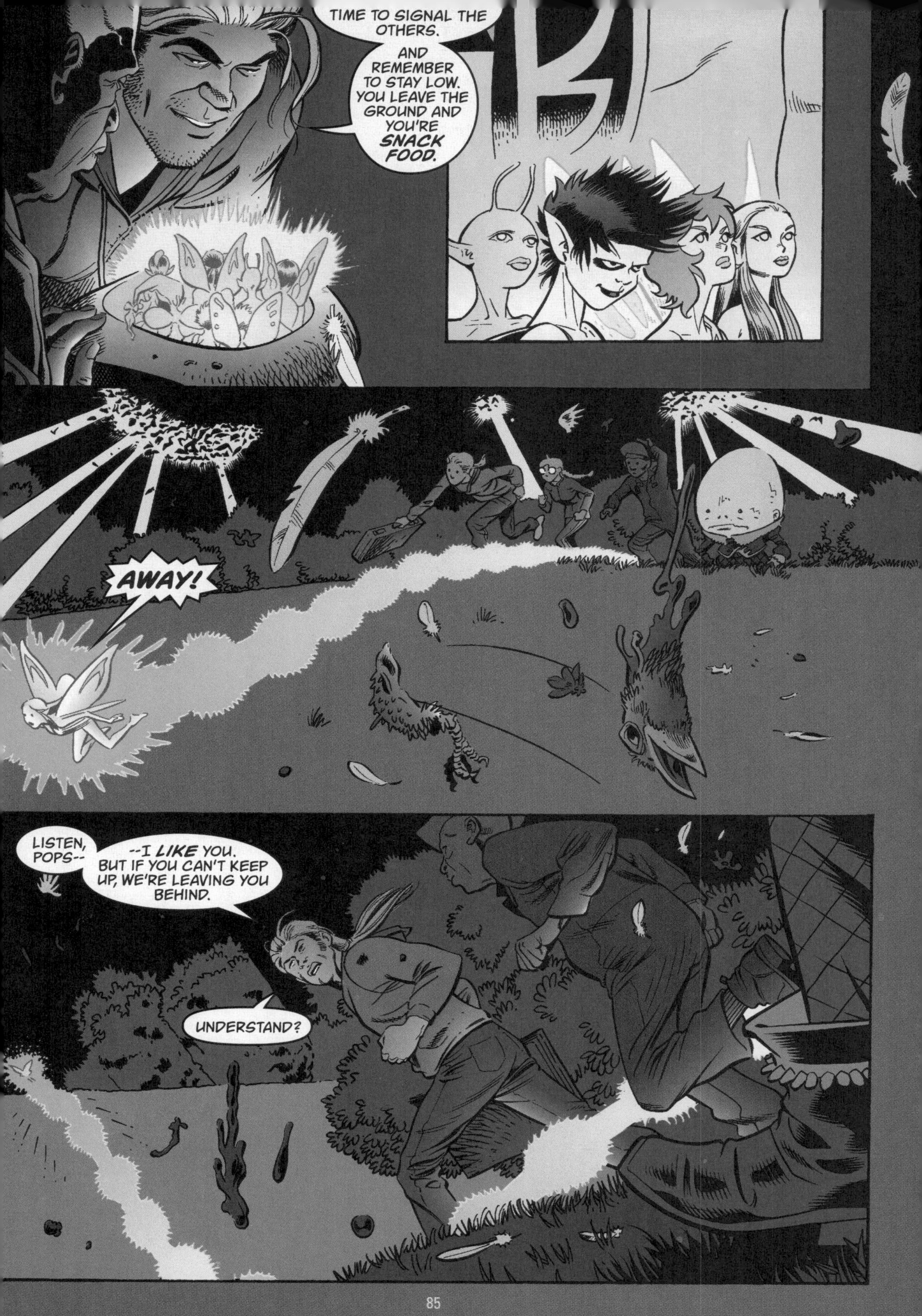
TIME TO SIGNAL THE OTHERS.
AND REMEMBER TO STAY LOW. YOU LEAVE THE GROUND AND YOU'RE *SNACK FOOD.*
AWAY!
LISTEN, POPS--
--I *LIKE* YOU. BUT IF YOU CAN'T KEEP UP, WE'RE LEAVING YOU BEHIND.
UNDERSTAND?

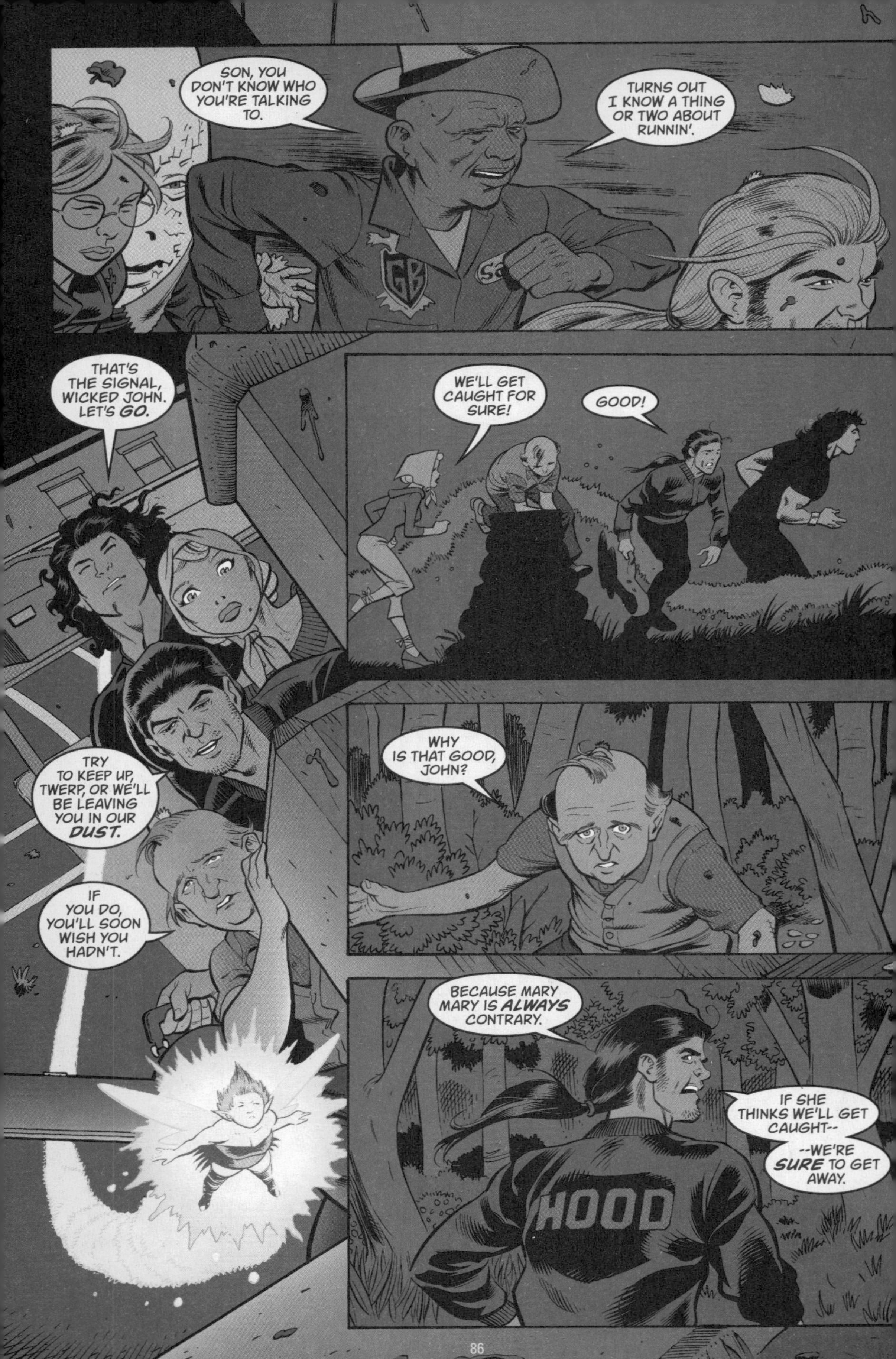
SON, YOU DON'T KNOW WHO YOU'RE TALKING TO.
TURNS OUT I KNOW A THING OR TWO ABOUT RUNNIN'.
THAT'S THE SIGNAL, WICKED JOHN. LET'S GO.
TRY TO KEEP UP, TWERP, OR WE'LL BE LEAVING YOU IN OUR DUST.
IF YOU DO, YOU'LL SOON WISH YOU HADN'T.
WE'LL GET CAUGHT FOR SURE!
GOOD!
WHY IS THAT GOOD, JOHN?
BECAUSE MARY MARY IS ALWAYS CONTRARY.
IF SHE THINKS WE'LL GET CAUGHT--
--WE'RE SURE TO GET AWAY.
HOOD

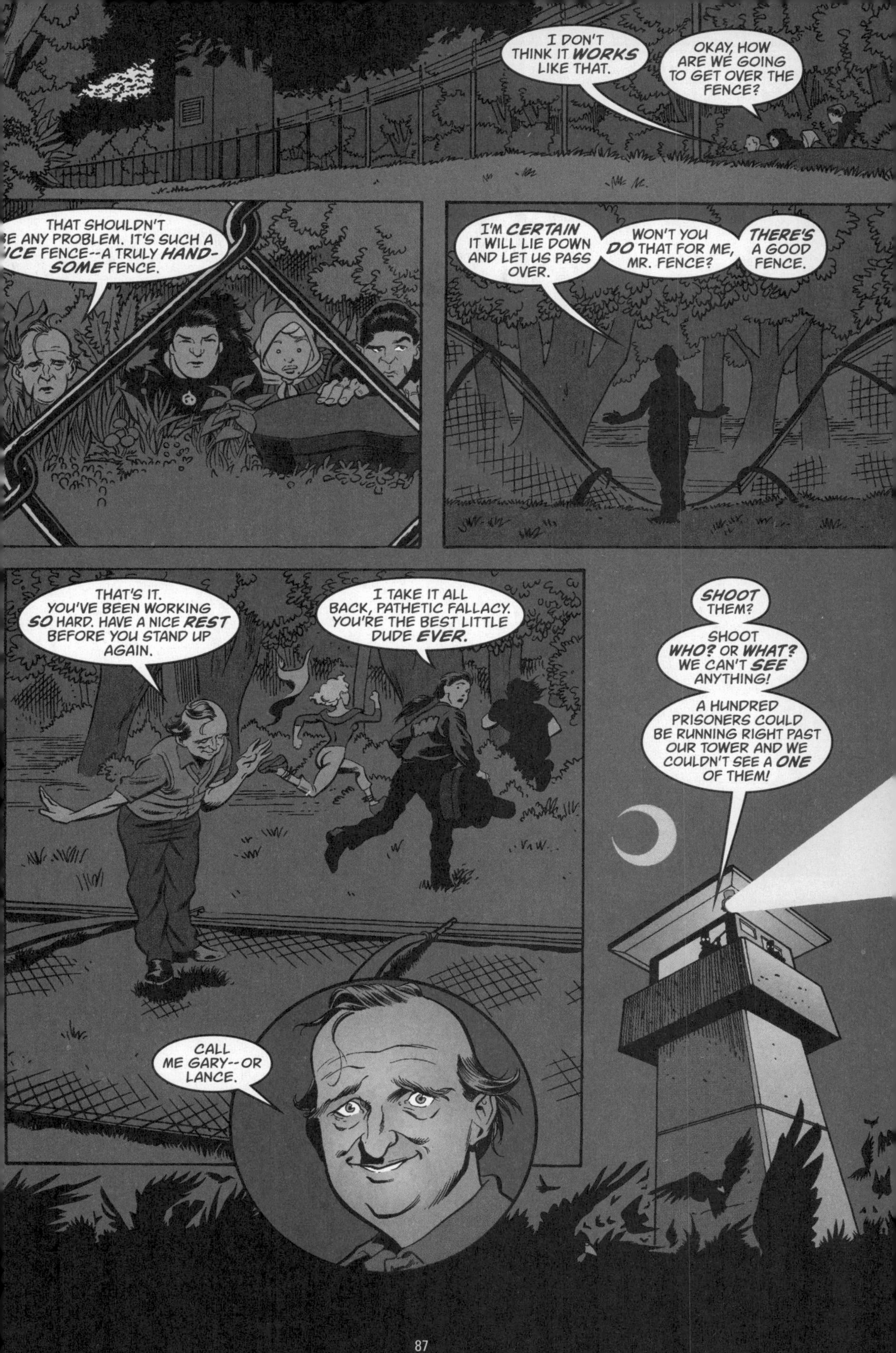

I DON'T THINK IT WORKS LIKE THAT.
OKAY, HOW ARE WE GOING TO GET OVER THE FENCE?
THAT SHOULDN'T BE ANY PROBLEM. IT'S SUCH A NICE FENCE--A TRULY HANDSOME FENCE.
I'M CERTAIN IT WILL LIE DOWN AND LET US PASS OVER.
WON'T YOU DO THAT FOR ME, MR. FENCE?
THERE'S A GOOD FENCE.
THAT'S IT. YOU'VE BEEN WORKING SO HARD. HAVE A NICE REST BEFORE YOU STAND UP AGAIN.
I TAKE IT ALL BACK, PATHETIC FALLACY. YOU'RE THE BEST LITTLE DUDE EVER.
CALL ME GARY--OR LANCE.
SHOOT THEM?
SHOOT WHO? OR WHAT? WE CAN'T SEE ANYTHING!
A HUNDRED PRISONERS COULD BE RUNNING RIGHT PAST OUR TOWER AND WE COULDN'T SEE A ONE OF THEM!

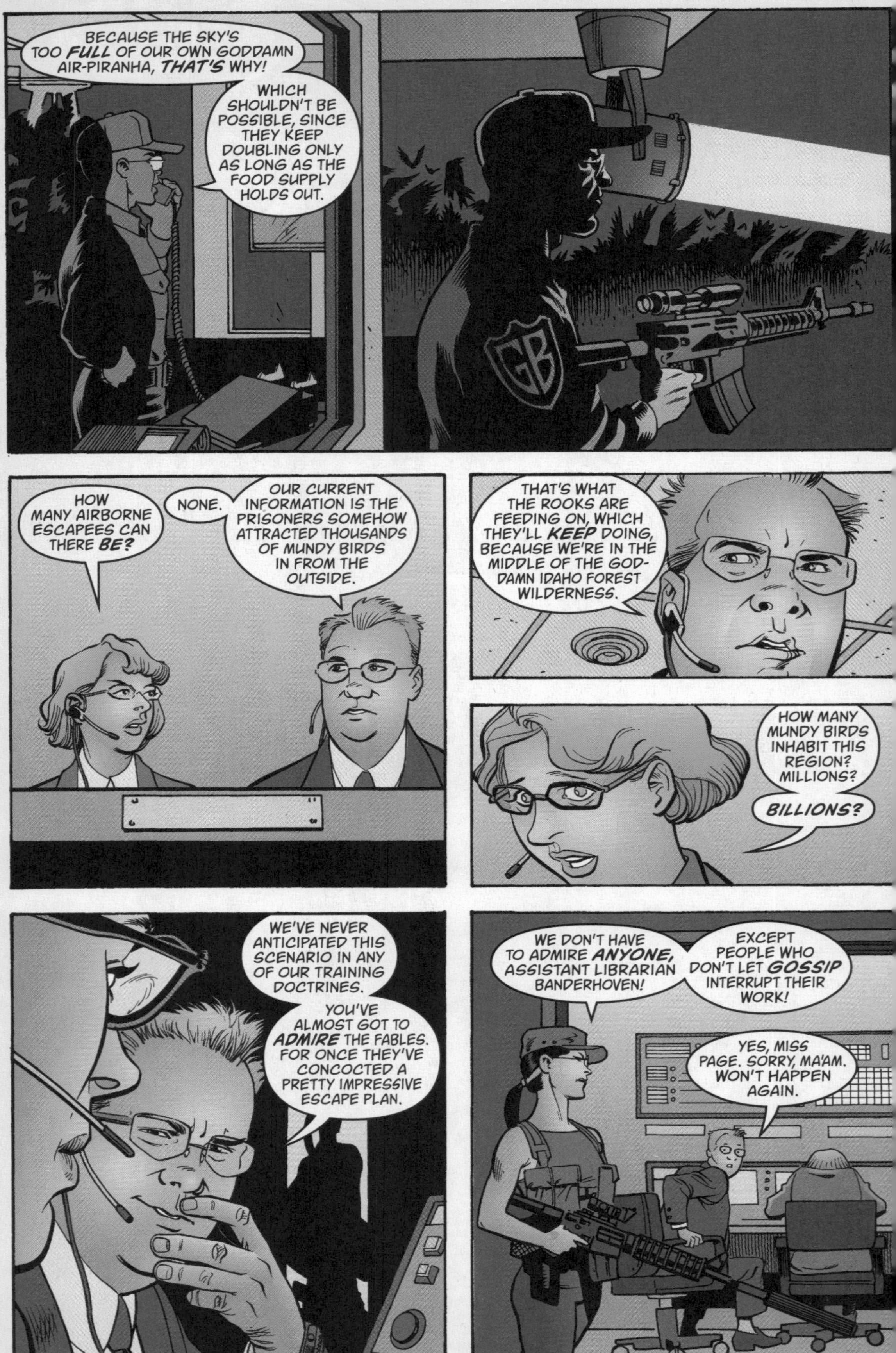
BECAUSE THE SKY'S TOO FULL OF OUR OWN GODDAMN AIR-PIRANHA, THAT'S WHY!
WHICH SHOULDN'T BE POSSIBLE, SINCE THEY KEEP DOUBLING ONLY AS LONG AS THE FOOD SUPPLY HOLDS OUT.
HOW MANY AIRBORNE ESCAPEES CAN THERE BE?
NONE.
OUR CURRENT INFORMATION IS THE PRISONERS SOMEHOW ATTRACTED THOUSANDS OF MUNDY BIRDS IN FROM THE OUTSIDE.
THAT'S WHAT THE ROOKS ARE FEEDING ON, WHICH THEY'LL KEEP DOING, BECAUSE WE'RE IN THE MIDDLE OF THE GOD-DAMN IDAHO FOREST WILDERNESS.
HOW MANY MUNDY BIRDS INHABIT THIS REGION? MILLIONS?
BILLIONS?
WE'VE NEVER ANTICIPATED THIS SCENARIO IN ANY OF OUR TRAINING DOCTRINES.
YOU'VE ALMOST GOT TO ADMIRE THE FABLES. FOR ONCE THEY'VE CONCOCTED A PRETTY IMPRESSIVE ESCAPE PLAN.
WE DON'T HAVE TO ADMIRE ANYONE, ASSISTANT LIBRARIAN BANDERHOVEN!
EXCEPT PEOPLE WHO DON'T LET GOSSIP INTERRUPT THEIR WORK!
YES, MISS PAGE. SORRY, MA'AM. WON'T HAPPEN AGAIN.

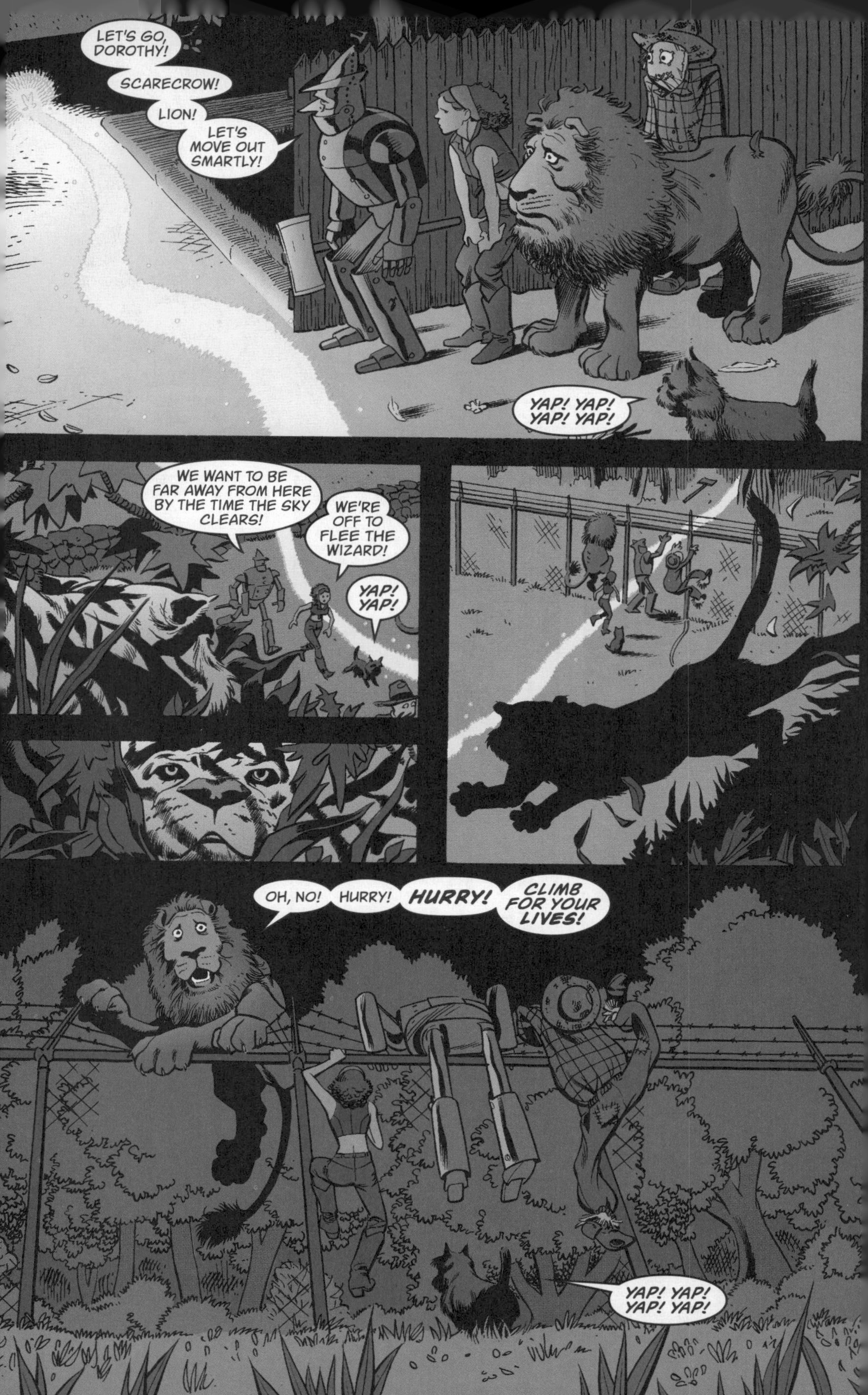
LET'S GO, DOROTHY!
SCARECROW!
LION!
LET'S MOVE OUT SMARTLY!
YAP! YAP! YAP! YAP!
WE WANT TO BE FAR AWAY FROM HERE BY THE TIME THE SKY CLEARS!
WE'RE OFF TO FLEE THE WIZARD!
YAP! YAP!
OH, NO!
HURRY!
HURRY!
CLIMB FOR YOUR LIVES!
YAP! YAP! YAP! YAP!

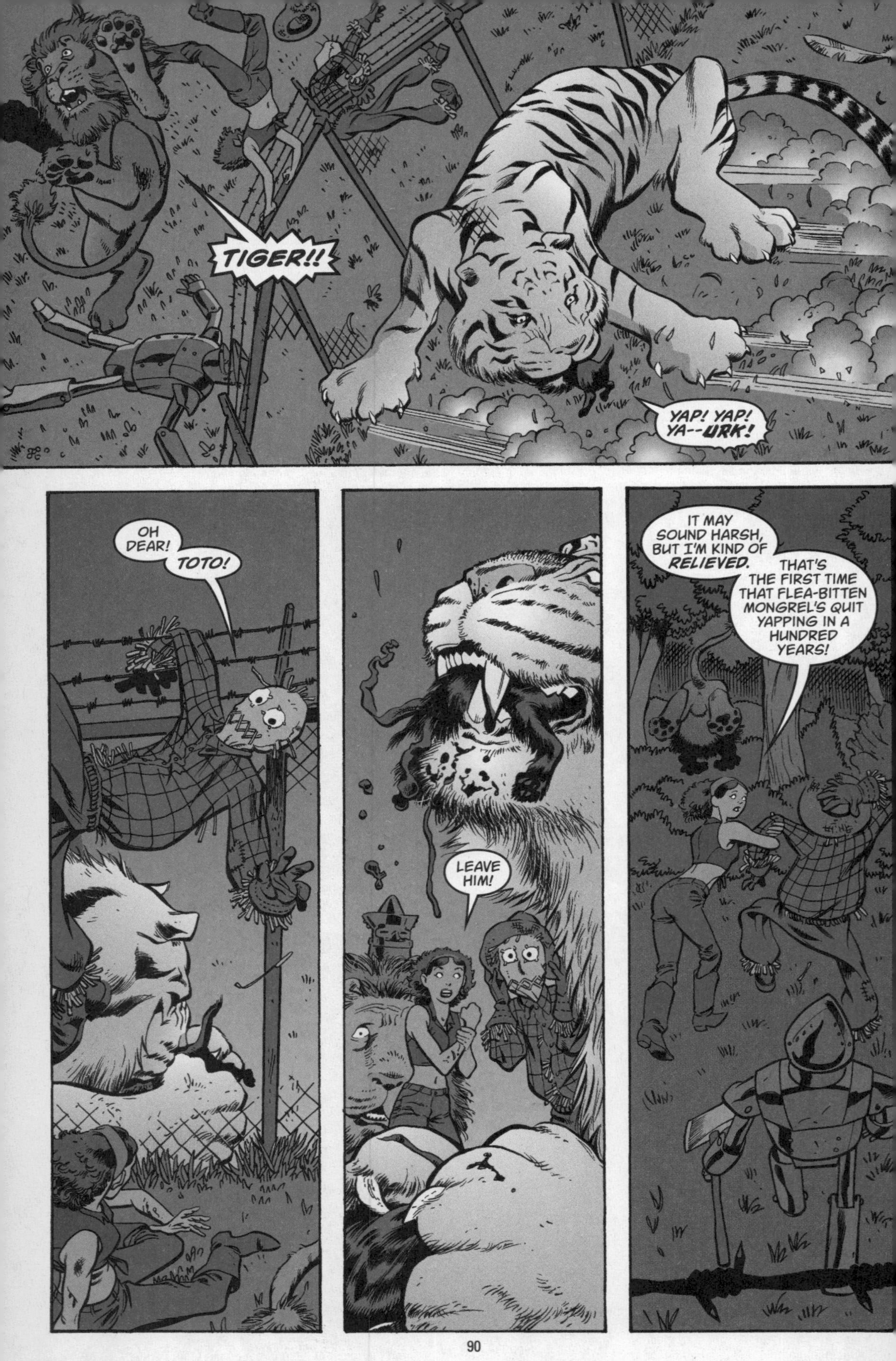
TIGER!!
YAP! YAP! YA--URK!
OH DEAR!
TOTO!
LEAVE HIM!
IT MAY SOUND HARSH, BUT I'M KIND OF RELIEVED.
THAT'S THE FIRST TIME THAT FLEA-BITTEN MONGREL'S QUIT YAPPING IN A HUNDRED YEARS!

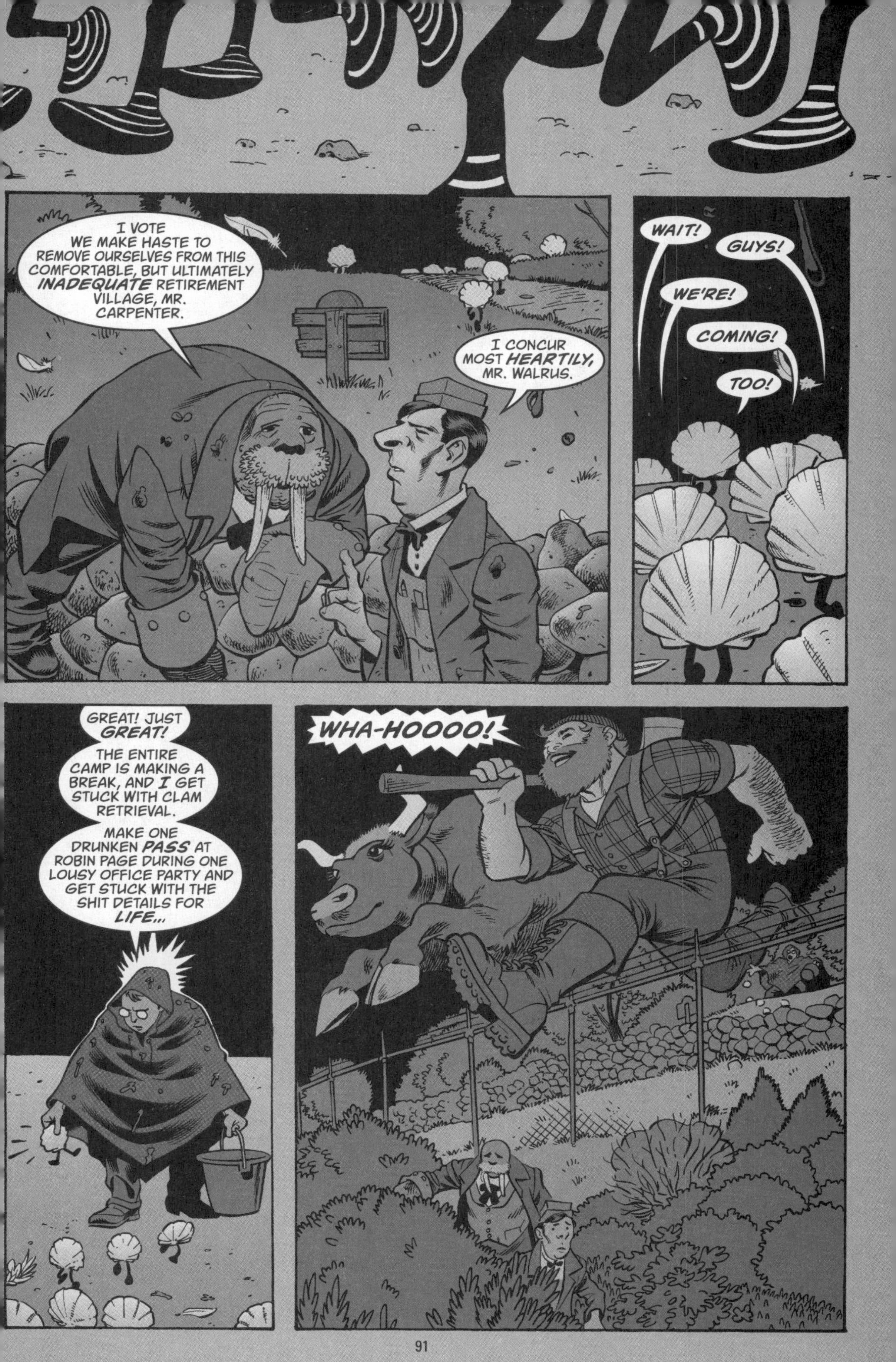
I VOTE WE MAKE HASTE TO REMOVE OURSELVES FROM THIS COMFORTABLE, BUT ULTIMATELY INADEQUATE RETIREMENT VILLAGE, MR. CARPENTER.
I CONCUR MOST HEARTILY, MR. WALRUS.
WAIT!
GUYS!
WE'RE!
COMING!
TOO!
GREAT! JUST GREAT!
THE ENTIRE CAMP IS MAKING A BREAK, AND I GET STUCK WITH CLAM RETRIEVAL.
MAKE ONE DRUNKEN PASS AT ROBIN PAGE DURING ONE LOUSY OFFICE PARTY AND GET STUCK WITH THE SHIT DETAILS FOR LIFE...
WHA-HOOOO!

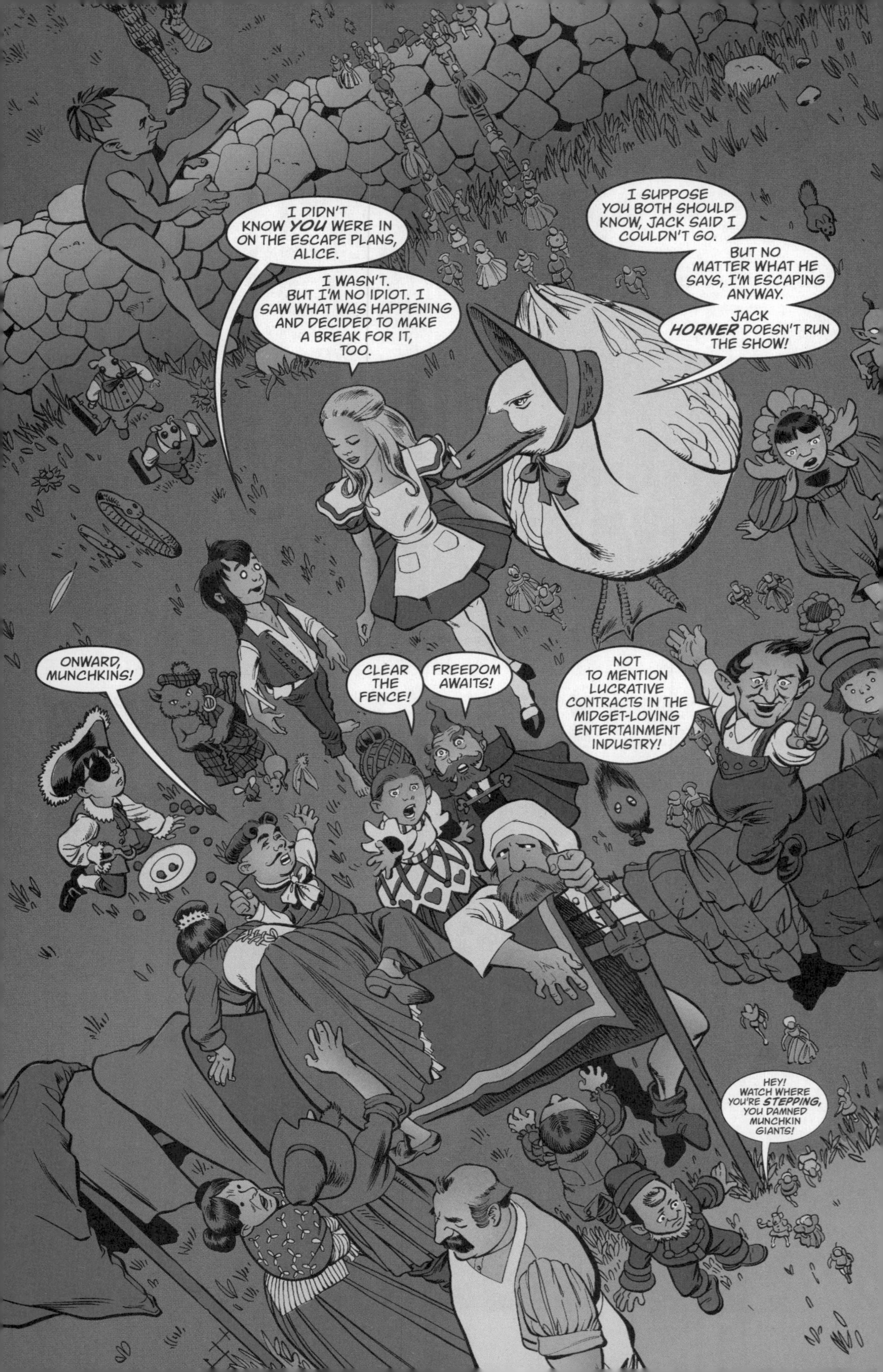
I DIDN'T KNOW YOU WERE IN ON THE ESCAPE PLANS, ALICE.
I WASN'T. BUT I'M NO IDIOT. I SAW WHAT WAS HAPPENING AND DECIDED TO MAKE A BREAK FOR IT, TOO.
I SUPPOSE YOU BOTH SHOULD KNOW, JACK SAID I COULDN'T GO.
BUT NO MATTER WHAT HE SAYS, I'M ESCAPING ANYWAY.
JACK HORNER DOESN'T RUN THE SHOW!
ONWARD, MUNCHKINS!
CLEAR THE FENCE!
FREEDOM AWAITS!
NOT TO MENTION LUCRATIVE CONTRACTS IN THE MIDGET-LOVING ENTERTAINMENT INDUSTRY!
HEY! WATCH WHERE YOU'RE STEPPING, YOU DAMNED MUNCHKIN GIANTS!

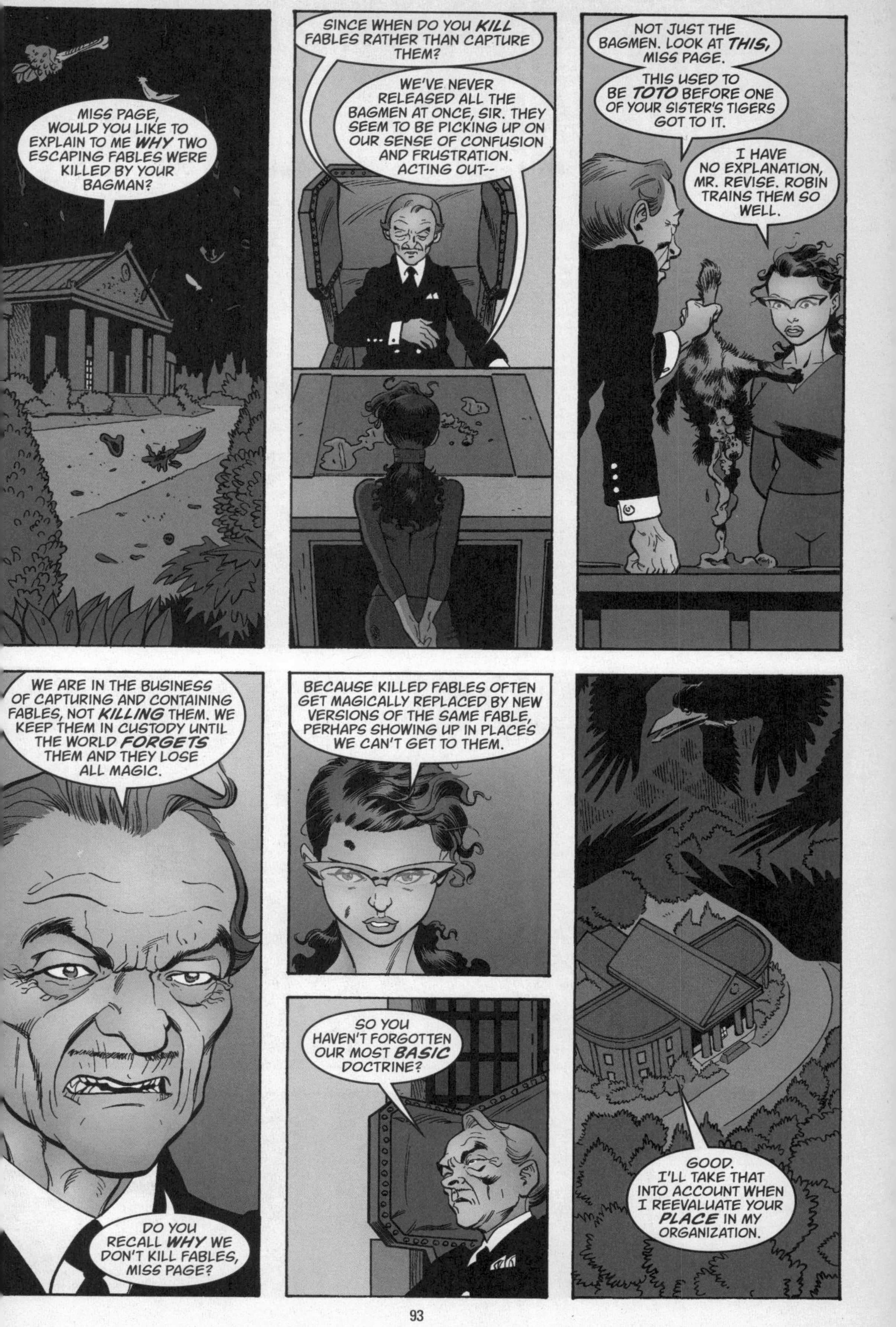
MISS PAGE, WOULD YOU LIKE TO EXPLAIN TO ME WHY TWO ESCAPING FABLES WERE KILLED BY YOUR BAGMAN?
SINCE WHEN DO YOU KILL FABLES RATHER THAN CAPTURE THEM?
WE'VE NEVER RELEASED ALL THE BAGMEN AT ONCE, SIR. THEY SEEM TO BE PICKING UP ON OUR SENSE OF CONFUSION AND FRUSTRATION. ACTING OUT--
NOT JUST THE BAGMEN. LOOK AT THIS, MISS PAGE.
THIS USED TO BE TOTO BEFORE ONE OF YOUR SISTER'S TIGERS GOT TO IT.
I HAVE NO EXPLANATION, MR. REVISE. ROBIN TRAINS THEM SO WELL.
WE ARE IN THE BUSINESS OF CAPTURING AND CONTAINING FABLES, NOT KILLING THEM. WE KEEP THEM IN CUSTODY UNTIL THE WORLD FORGETS THEM AND THEY LOSE ALL MAGIC.
DO YOU RECALL WHY WE DON'T KILL FABLES, MISS PAGE?
BECAUSE KILLED FABLES OFTEN GET MAGICALLY REPLACED BY NEW VERSIONS OF THE SAME FABLE, PERHAPS SHOWING UP IN PLACES WE CAN'T GET TO THEM.
SO YOU HAVEN'T FORGOTTEN OUR MOST BASIC DOCTRINE?
GOOD. I'LL TAKE THAT INTO ACCOUNT WHEN I REEVALUATE YOUR PLACE IN MY ORGANIZATION.

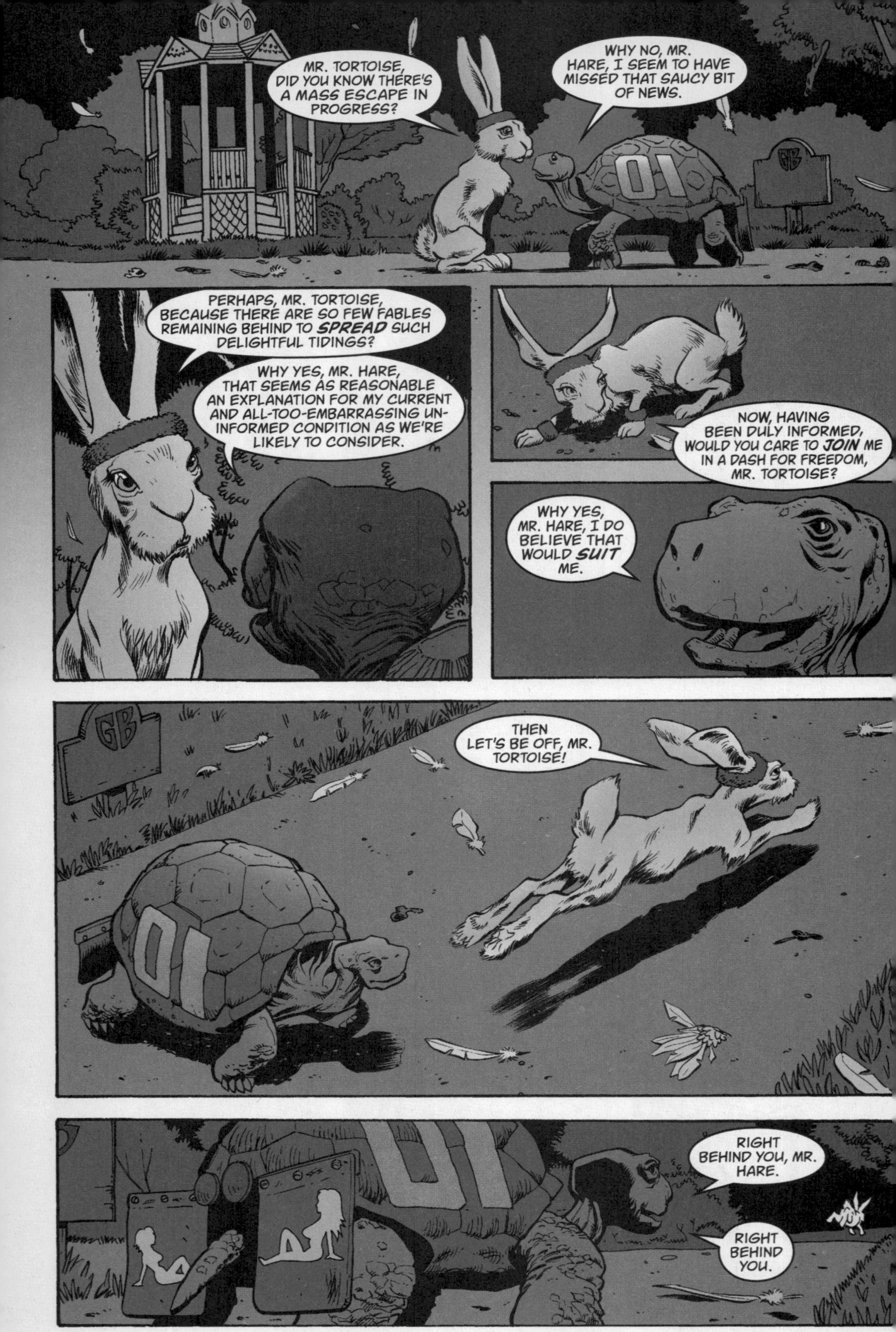
MR. TORTOISE, DID YOU KNOW THERE'S A MASS ESCAPE IN PROGRESS?
WHY NO, MR. HARE, I SEEM TO HAVE MISSED THAT SAUCY BIT OF NEWS.
PERHAPS, MR. TORTOISE, BECAUSE THERE ARE SO FEW FABLES REMAINING BEHIND TO SPREAD SUCH DELIGHTFUL TIDINGS?
WHY YES, MR. HARE, THAT SEEMS AS REASONABLE AN EXPLANATION FOR MY CURRENT AND ALL-TOO-EMBARRASSING UN-INFORMED CONDITION AS WE'RE LIKELY TO CONSIDER.
NOW, HAVING BEEN DULY INFORMED, WOULD YOU CARE TO JOIN ME IN A DASH FOR FREEDOM, MR. TORTOISE?
WHY YES, MR. HARE, I DO BELIEVE THAT WOULD SUIT ME.
THEN LET'S BE OFF, MR. TORTOISE!
RIGHT BEHIND YOU, MR. HARE.
RIGHT BEHIND YOU.

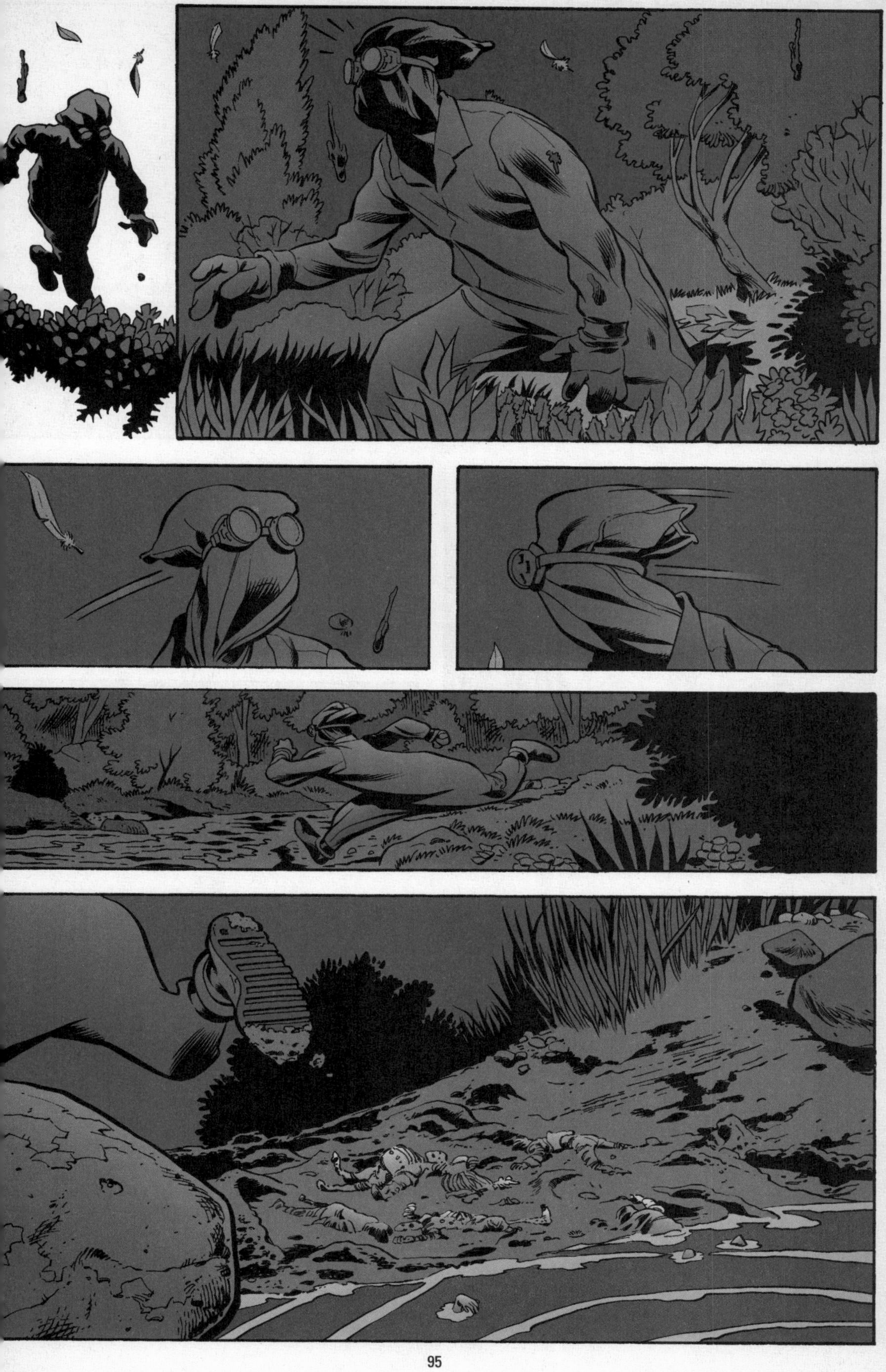

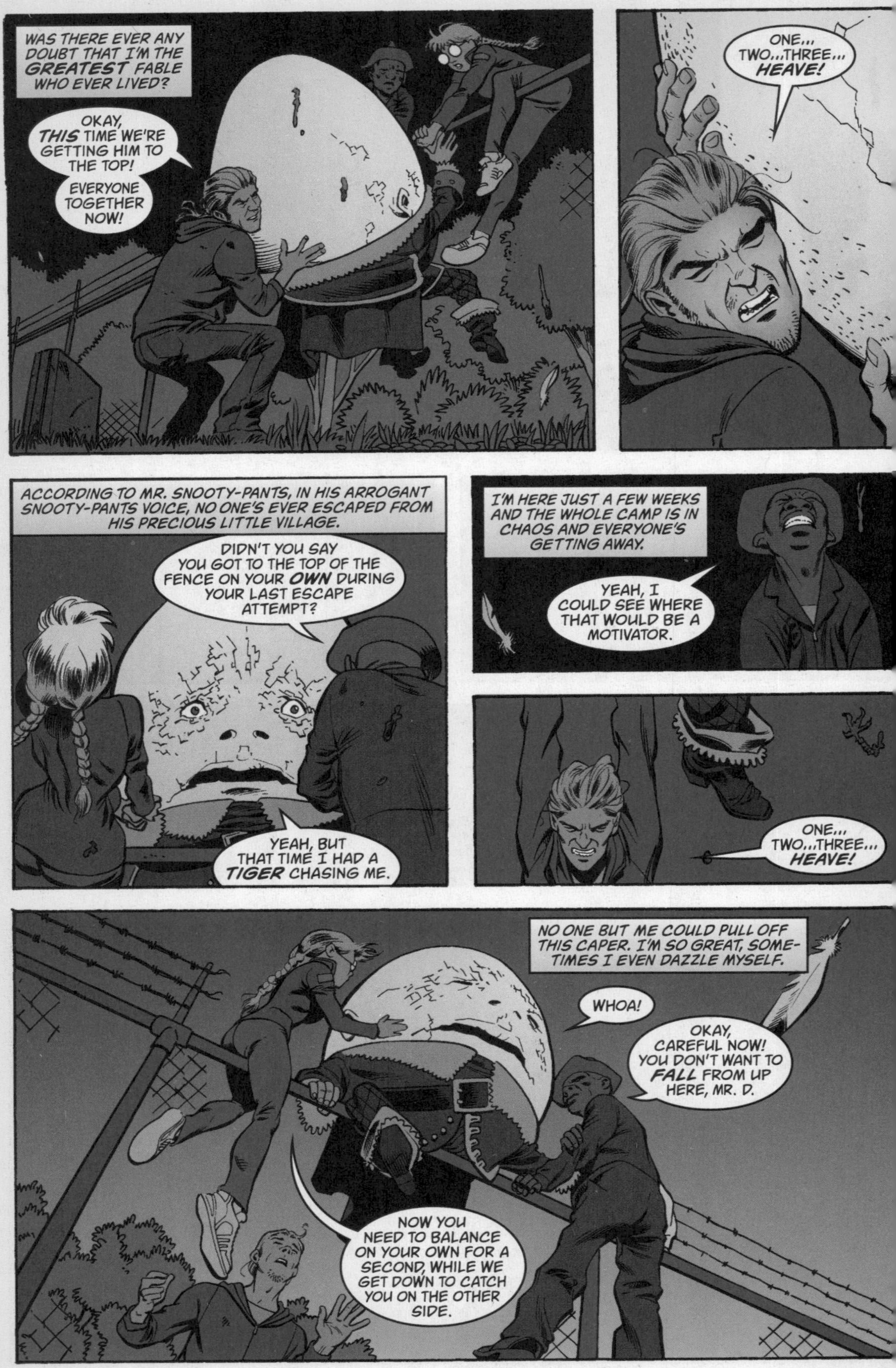
WAS THERE EVER ANY DOUBT THAT I'M THE GREATEST FABLE WHO EVER LIVED?
OKAY, THIS TIME WE'RE GETTING HIM TO THE TOP!
EVERYONE TOGETHER NOW!
ONE... TWO...THREE... HEAVE!
ACCORDING TO MR. SNOOTY-PANTS, IN HIS ARROGANT SNOOTY-PANTS VOICE, NO ONE'S EVER ESCAPED FROM HIS PRECIOUS LITTLE VILLAGE.
DIDN'T YOU SAY YOU GOT TO THE TOP OF THE FENCE ON YOUR OWN DURING YOUR LAST ESCAPE ATTEMPT?
YEAH, BUT THAT TIME I HAD A TIGER CHASING ME.
I'M HERE JUST A FEW WEEKS AND THE WHOLE CAMP IS IN CHAOS AND EVERYONE'S GETTING AWAY.
YEAH, I COULD SEE WHERE THAT WOULD BE A MOTIVATOR.
ONE... TWO...THREE... HEAVE!
NO ONE BUT ME COULD PULL OFF THIS CAPER. I'M SO GREAT, SOMETIMES I EVEN DAZZLE MYSELF.
WHOA!
OKAY, CAREFUL NOW! YOU DON'T WANT TO FALL FROM UP HERE, MR. D.
NOW YOU NEED TO BALANCE ON YOUR OWN FOR A SECOND, WHILE WE GET DOWN TO CATCH YOU ON THE OTHER SIDE.

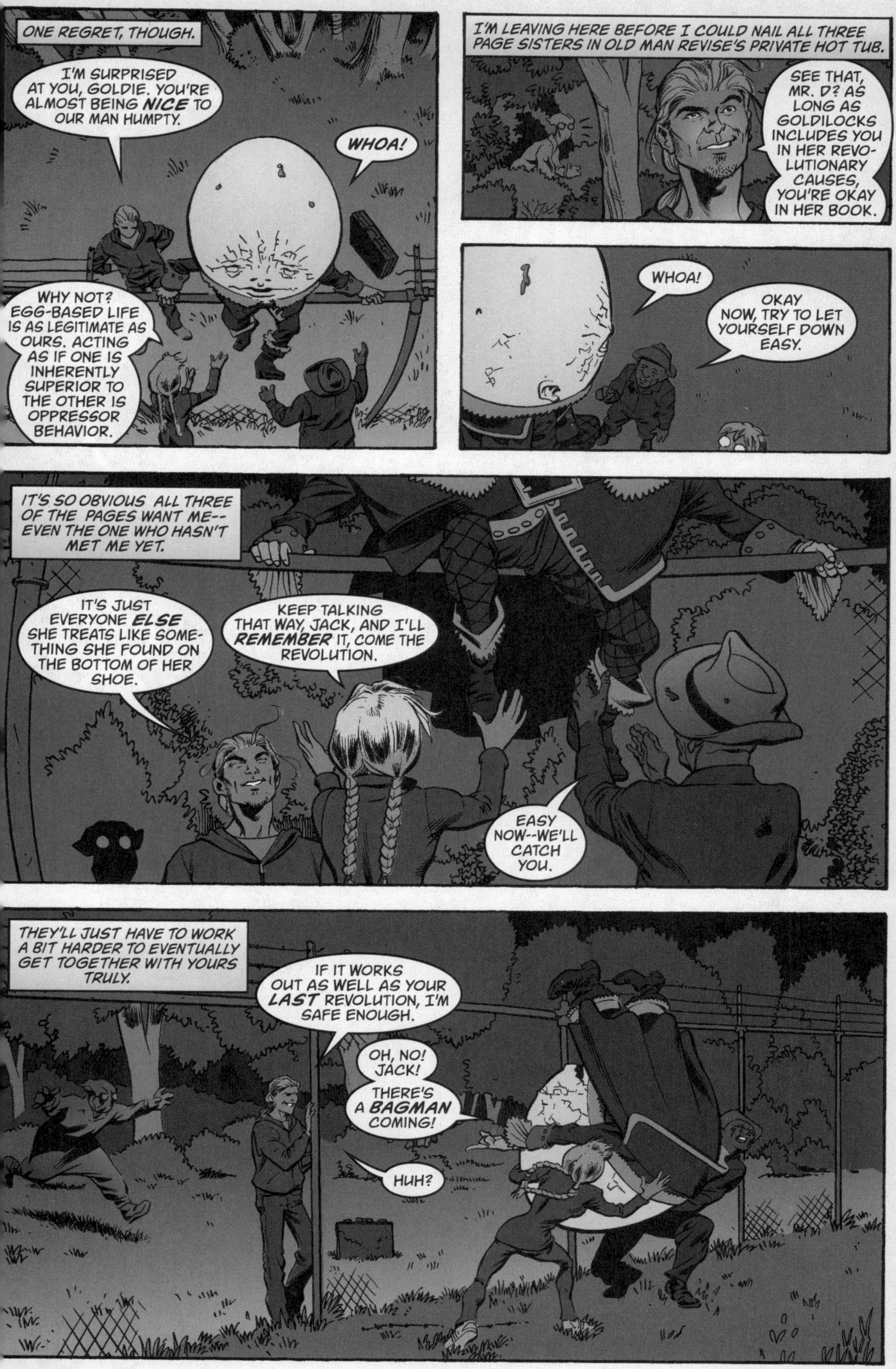
ONE REGRET, THOUGH.
I'M SURPRISED AT YOU, GOLDIE. YOU'RE ALMOST BEING NICE TO OUR MAN HUMPTY.
WHOA!
WHY NOT? EGG-BASED LIFE IS AS LEGITIMATE AS OURS. ACTING AS IF ONE IS INHERENTLY SUPERIOR TO THE OTHER IS OPPRESSOR BEHAVIOR.
I'M LEAVING HERE BEFORE I COULD NAIL ALL THREE PAGE SISTERS IN OLD MAN REVISE'S PRIVATE HOT TUB.
SEE THAT, MR. D? AS LONG AS GOLDILOCKS INCLUDES YOU IN HER REVOLUTIONARY CAUSES, YOU'RE OKAY IN HER BOOK.
WHOA!
OKAY NOW, TRY TO LET YOURSELF DOWN EASY.
IT'S SO OBVIOUS ALL THREE OF THE PAGES WANT ME-- EVEN THE ONE WHO HASN'T MET ME YET.
IT'S JUST EVERYONE ELSE SHE TREATS LIKE SOMETHING SHE FOUND ON THE BOTTOM OF HER SHOE.
KEEP TALKING THAT WAY, JACK, AND I'LL REMEMBER IT, COME THE REVOLUTION.
EASY NOW--WE'LL CATCH YOU.
THEY'LL JUST HAVE TO WORK A BIT HARDER TO EVENTUALLY GET TOGETHER WITH YOURS TRULY.
IF IT WORKS OUT AS WELL AS YOUR LAST REVOLUTION, I'M SAFE ENOUGH.
OH, NO! JACK!
THERE'S A BAGMAN COMING!
HUH?

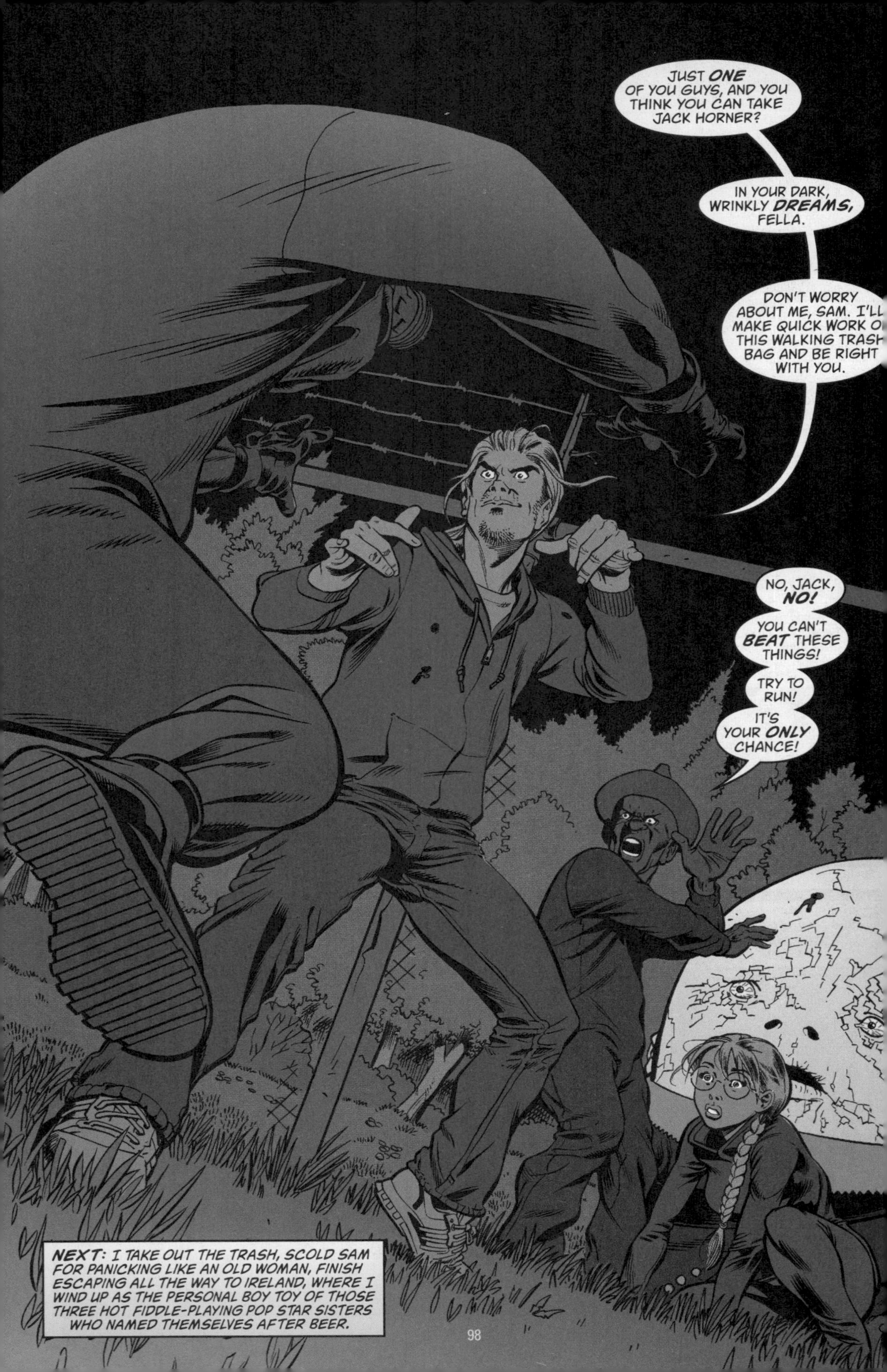
JUST ONE OF YOU GUYS, AND YOU THINK YOU CAN TAKE JACK HORNER?
IN YOUR DARK, WRINKLY DREAMS, FELLA.
DON'T WORRY ABOUT ME, SAM. I'LL MAKE QUICK WORK O THIS WALKING TRASH BAG AND BE RIGHT WITH YOU.
NO, JACK, NO!
YOU CAN'T BEAT THESE THINGS!
TRY TO RUN!
IT'S YOUR ONLY CHANCE!
NEXT: I TAKE OUT THE TRASH, SCOLD SAM FOR PANICKING LIKE AN OLD WOMAN, FINISH ESCAPING ALL THE WAY TO IRELAND, WHERE I WIND UP AS THE PERSONAL BOY TOY OF THOSE THREE HOT FIDDLE-PLAYING POP STAR SISTERS WHO NAMED THEMSELVES AFTER BEER.

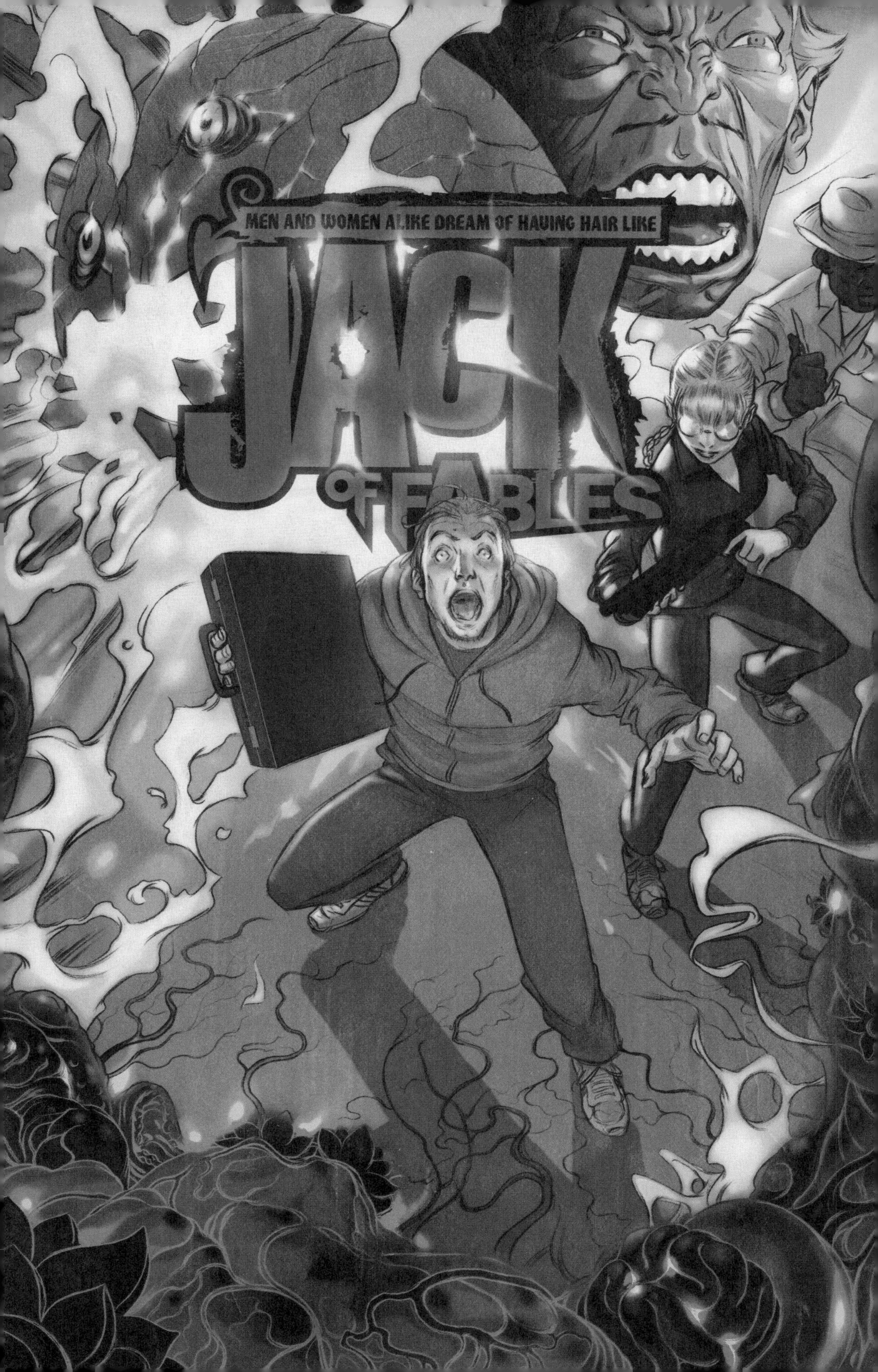
MEN AND WOMEN ALIKE DREAM OF HAVING HAIR LIKE
JACK OF FABLES

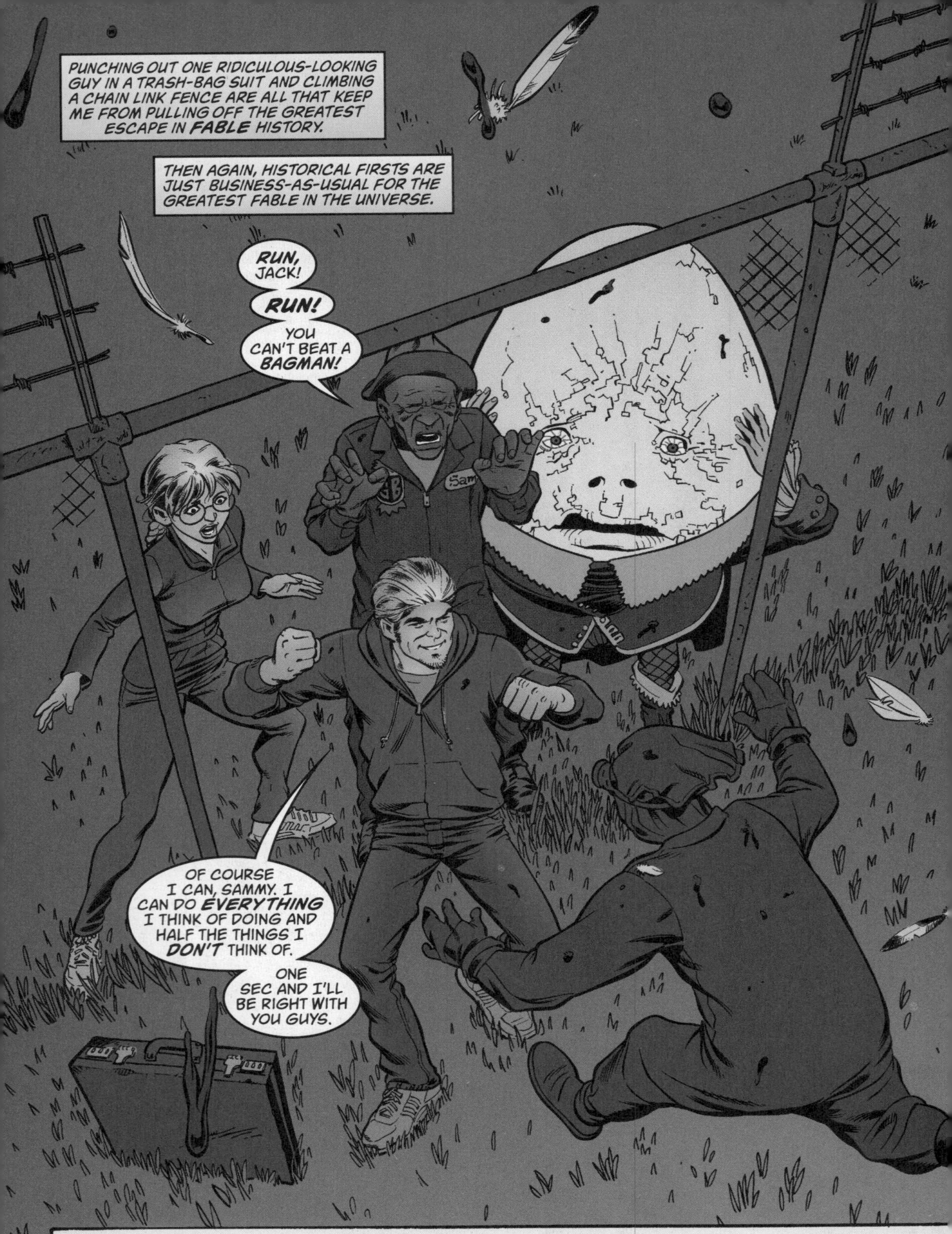
PUNCHING OUT ONE RIDICULOUS-LOOKING GUY IN A TRASH-BAG SUIT AND CLIMBING A CHAIN LINK FENCE ARE ALL THAT KEEP ME FROM PULLING OFF THE GREATEST ESCAPE IN FABLE HISTORY.
THEN AGAIN, HISTORICAL FIRSTS ARE JUST BUSINESS-AS-USUAL FOR THE GREATEST FABLE IN THE UNIVERSE.
RUN, JACK!
RUN!
YOU CAN'T BEAT A BAGMAN!
OF COURSE I CAN, SAMMY. I CAN DO EVERYTHING I THINK OF DOING AND HALF THE THINGS I DON'T THINK OF.
ONE SEC AND I'LL BE RIGHT WITH YOU GUYS.

JACK, OFF

In which both readers and main characters get all choked up, eggs crack, tigers turn, and Dodge is gotten the hell out of.

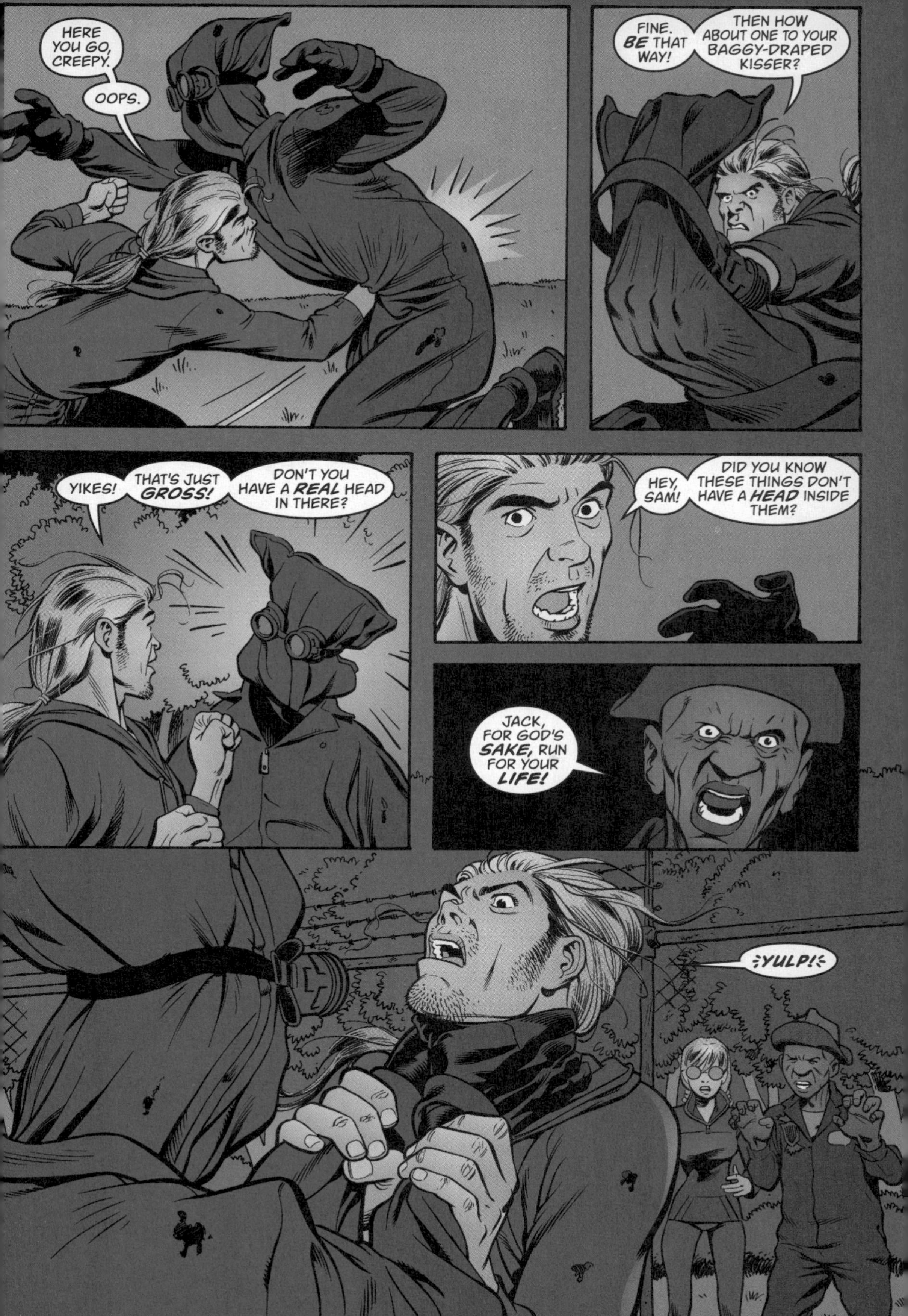
HERE YOU GO, CREEPY.
OOPS.
FINE. BE THAT WAY!
THEN HOW ABOUT ONE TO YOUR BAGGY-DRAPED KISSER?
YIKES!
THAT'S JUST GROSS!
DON'T YOU HAVE A REAL HEAD IN THERE?
HEY, SAM!
DID YOU KNOW THESE THINGS DON'T HAVE A HEAD INSIDE THEM?
JACK, FOR GOD'S SAKE, RUN FOR YOUR LIFE!
YULP!

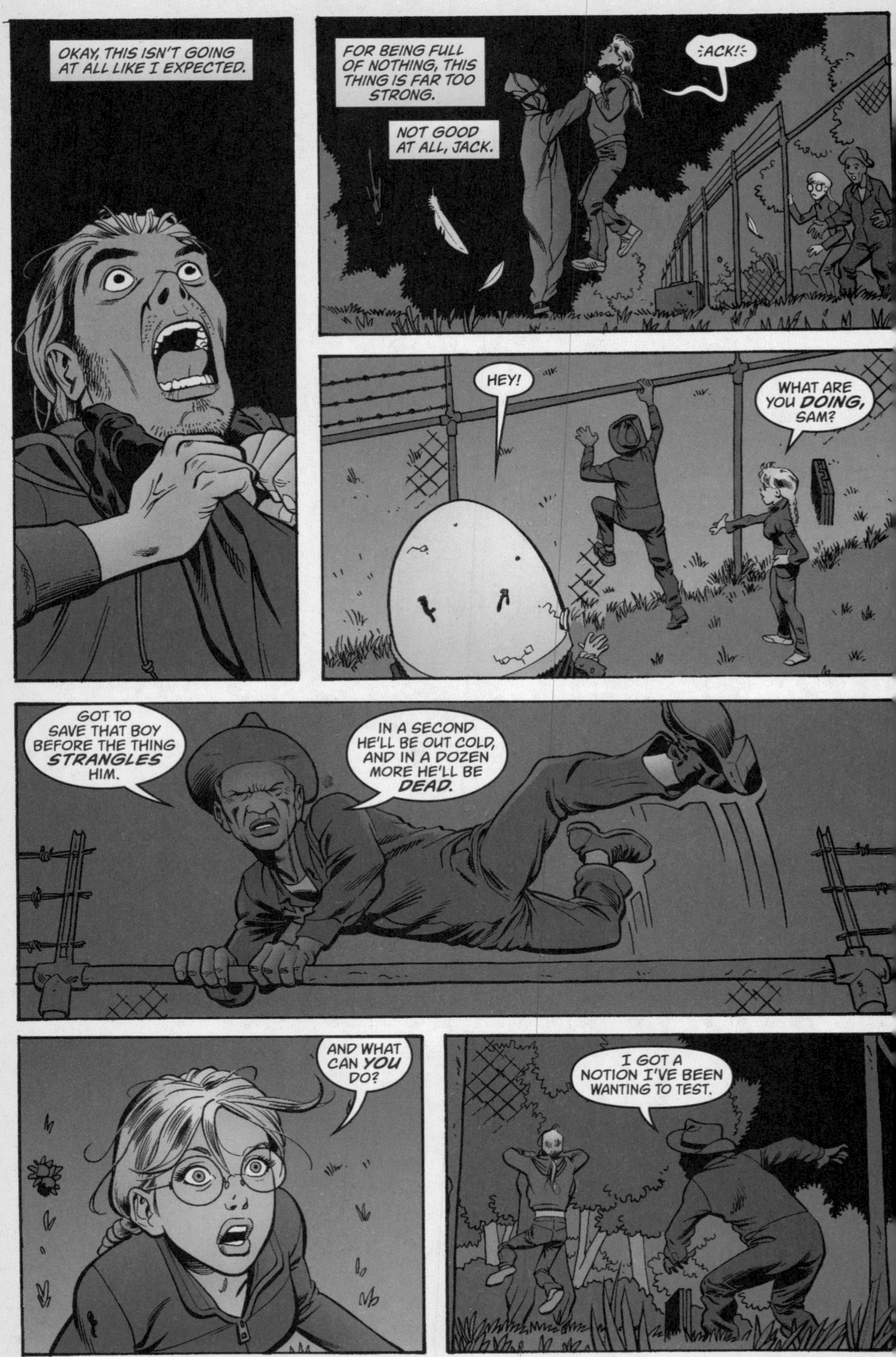
OKAY, THIS ISN'T GOING AT ALL LIKE I EXPECTED.
FOR BEING FULL OF NOTHING, THIS THING IS FAR TOO STRONG.
NOT GOOD AT ALL, JACK.
ACK!
HEY!
WHAT ARE YOU DOING, SAM?
GOT TO SAVE THAT BOY BEFORE THE THING STRANGLES HIM.
IN A SECOND HE'LL BE OUT COLD, AND IN A DOZEN MORE HE'LL BE DEAD.
AND WHAT CAN YOU DO?
I GOT A NOTION I'VE BEEN WANTING TO TEST.

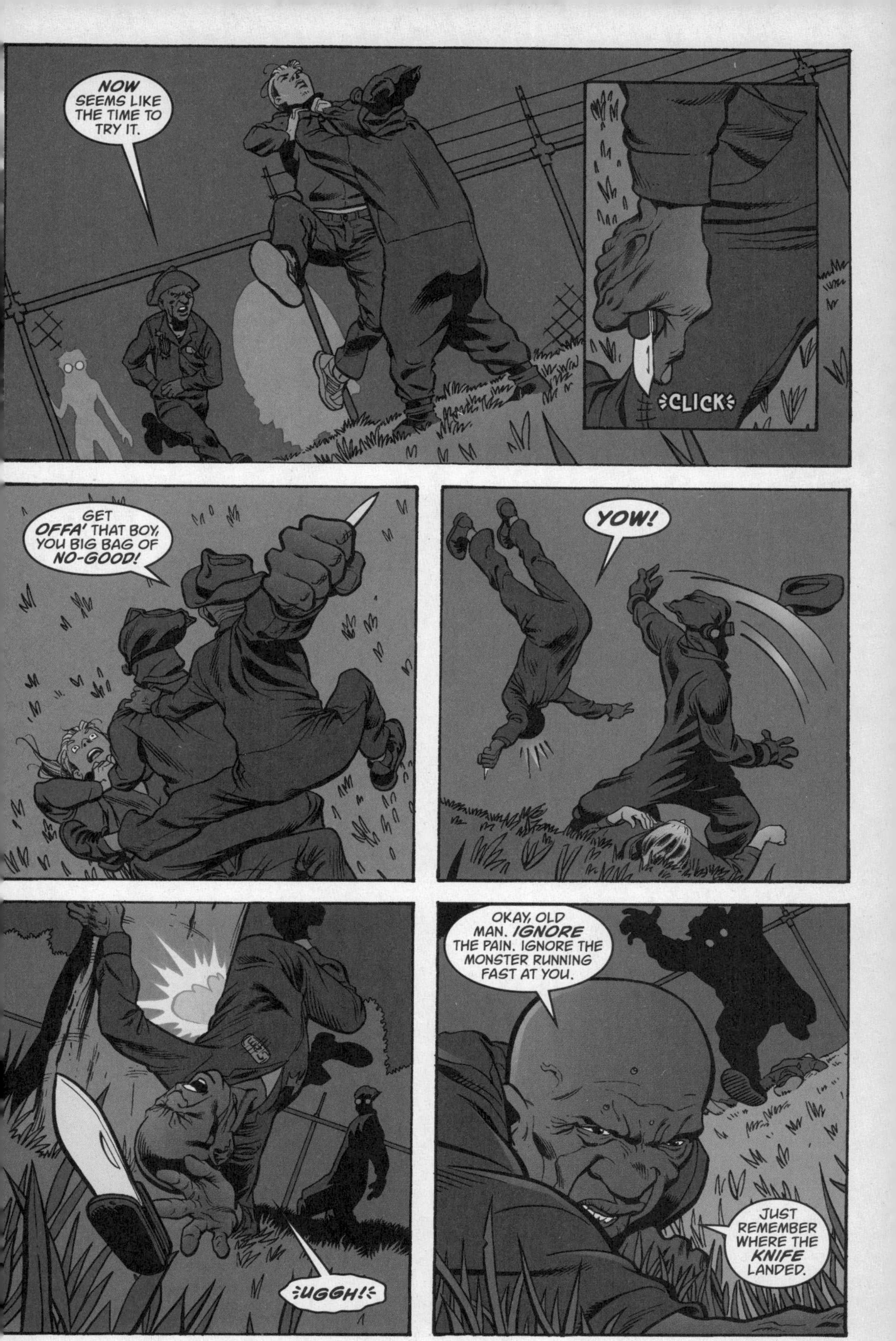
NOW SEEMS LIKE THE TIME TO TRY IT.
CLICK
GET OFFA' THAT BOY, YOU BIG BAG OF NO-GOOD!
YOW!
UGGH!
OKAY, OLD MAN. IGNORE THE PAIN. IGNORE THE MONSTER RUNNING FAST AT YOU.
JUST REMEMBER WHERE THE KNIFE LANDED.

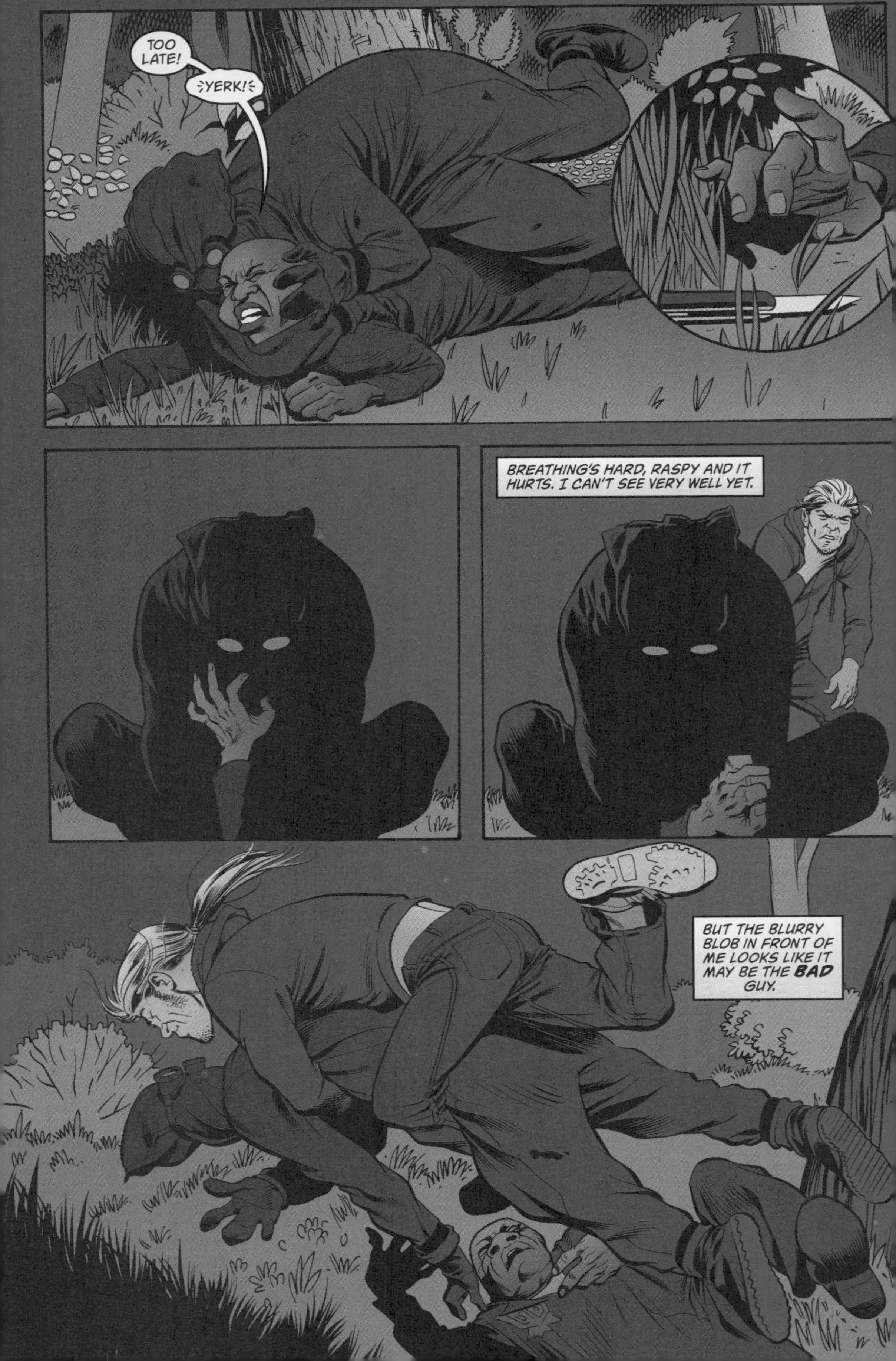
TOO LATE!
YERK!
BREATHING'S HARD, RASPY AND IT HURTS. I CAN'T SEE VERY WELL YET.
BUT THE BLURRY BLOB IN FRONT OF ME LOOKS LIKE IT MAY BE THE **BAD** GUY.

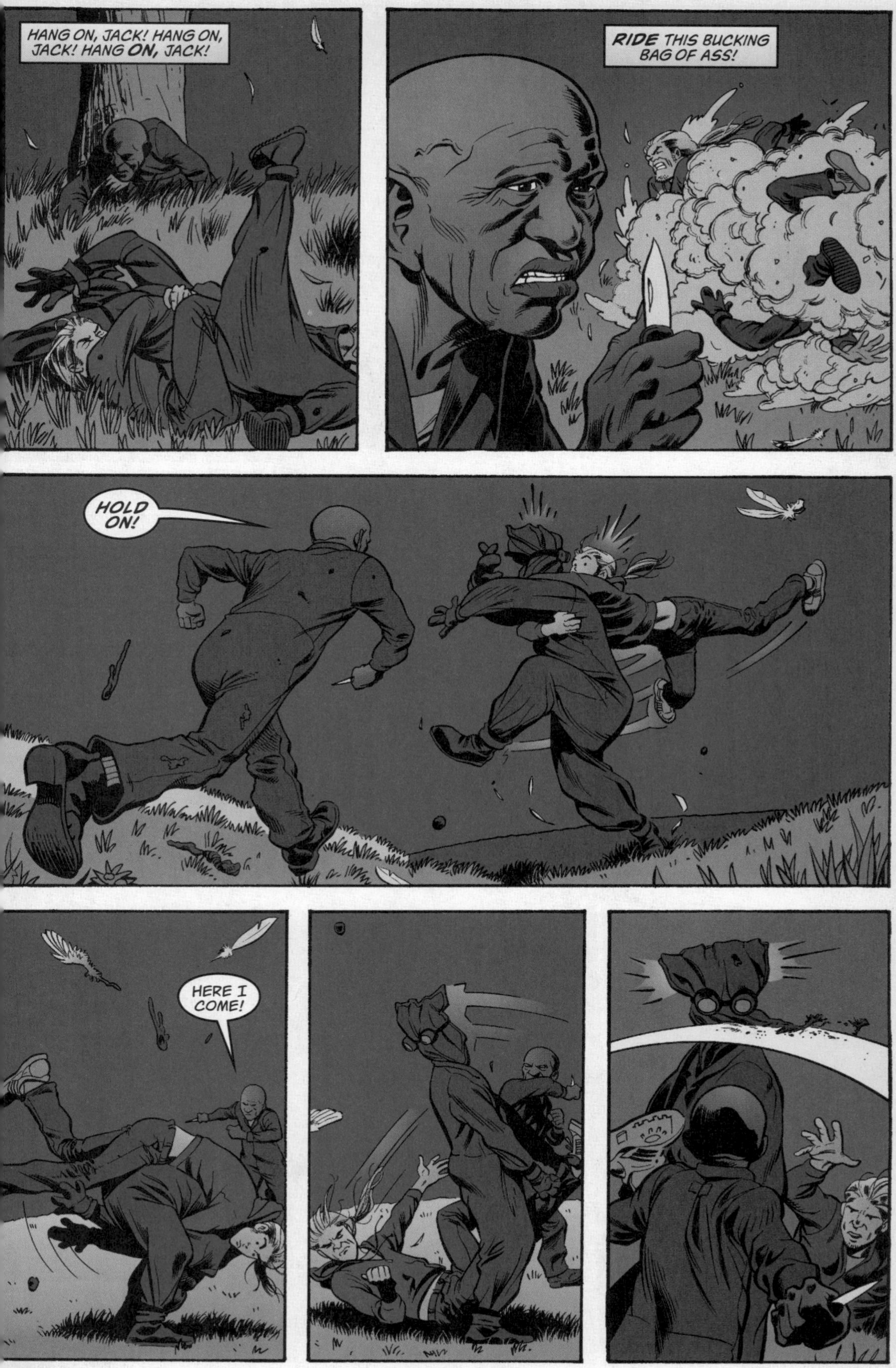
HANG ON, JACK! HANG ON, JACK! HANG ON, JACK!
RIDE THIS BUCKING BAG OF ASS!
HOLD ON!
HERE I COME!

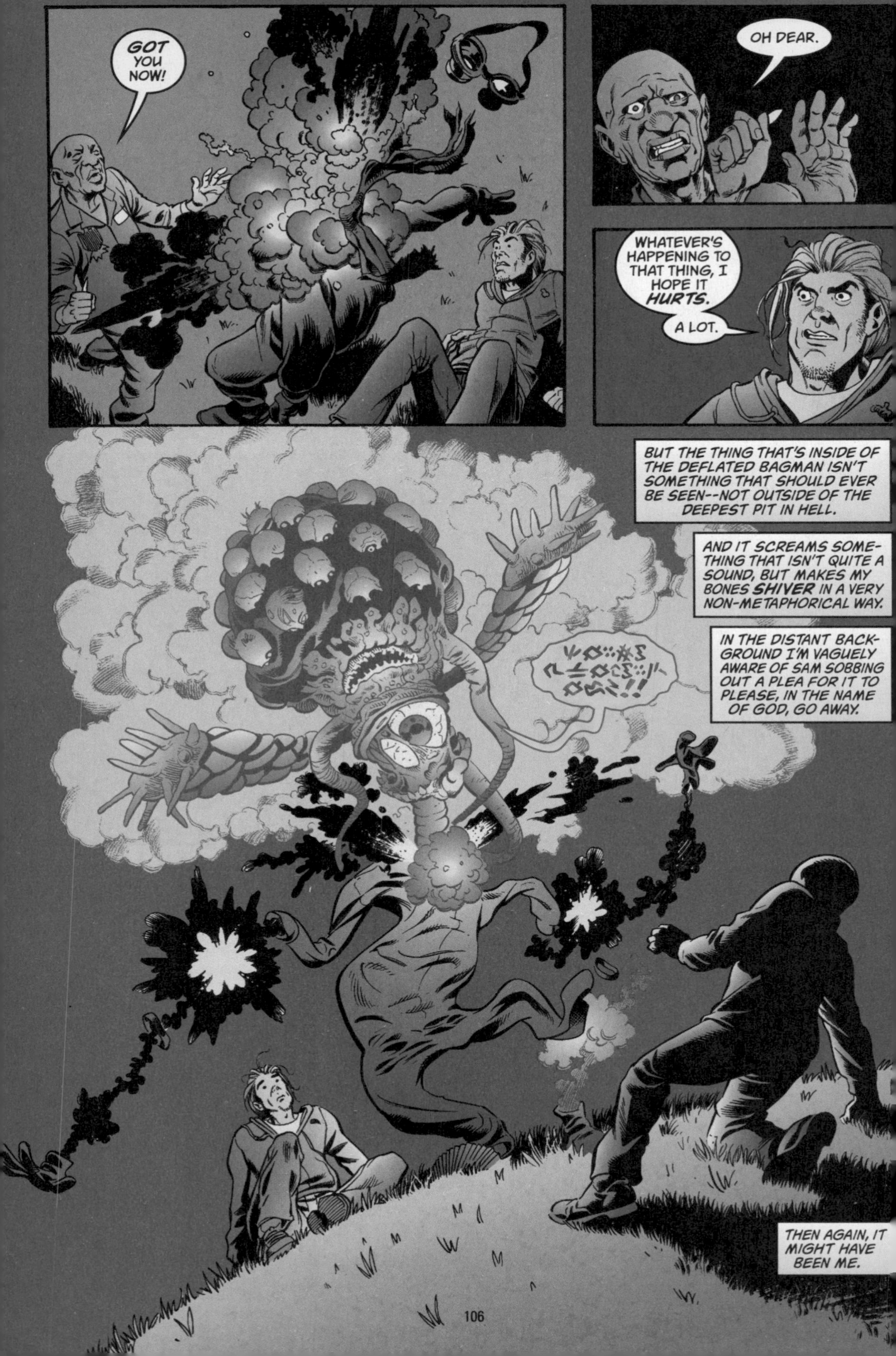
GOT YOU NOW!
OH DEAR.
WHATEVER'S HAPPENING TO THAT THING, I HOPE IT HURTS.
A LOT.
BUT THE THING THAT'S INSIDE OF THE DEFLATED BAGMAN ISN'T SOMETHING THAT SHOULD EVER BE SEEN--NOT OUTSIDE OF THE DEEPEST PIT IN HELL.
AND IT SCREAMS SOMETHING THAT ISN'T QUITE A SOUND, BUT MAKES MY BONES SHIVER IN A VERY NON-METAPHORICAL WAY.
IN THE DISTANT BACKGROUND I'M VAGUELY AWARE OF SAM SOBBING OUT A PLEA FOR IT TO PLEASE, IN THE NAME OF GOD, GO AWAY.
THEN AGAIN, IT MIGHT HAVE BEEN ME.

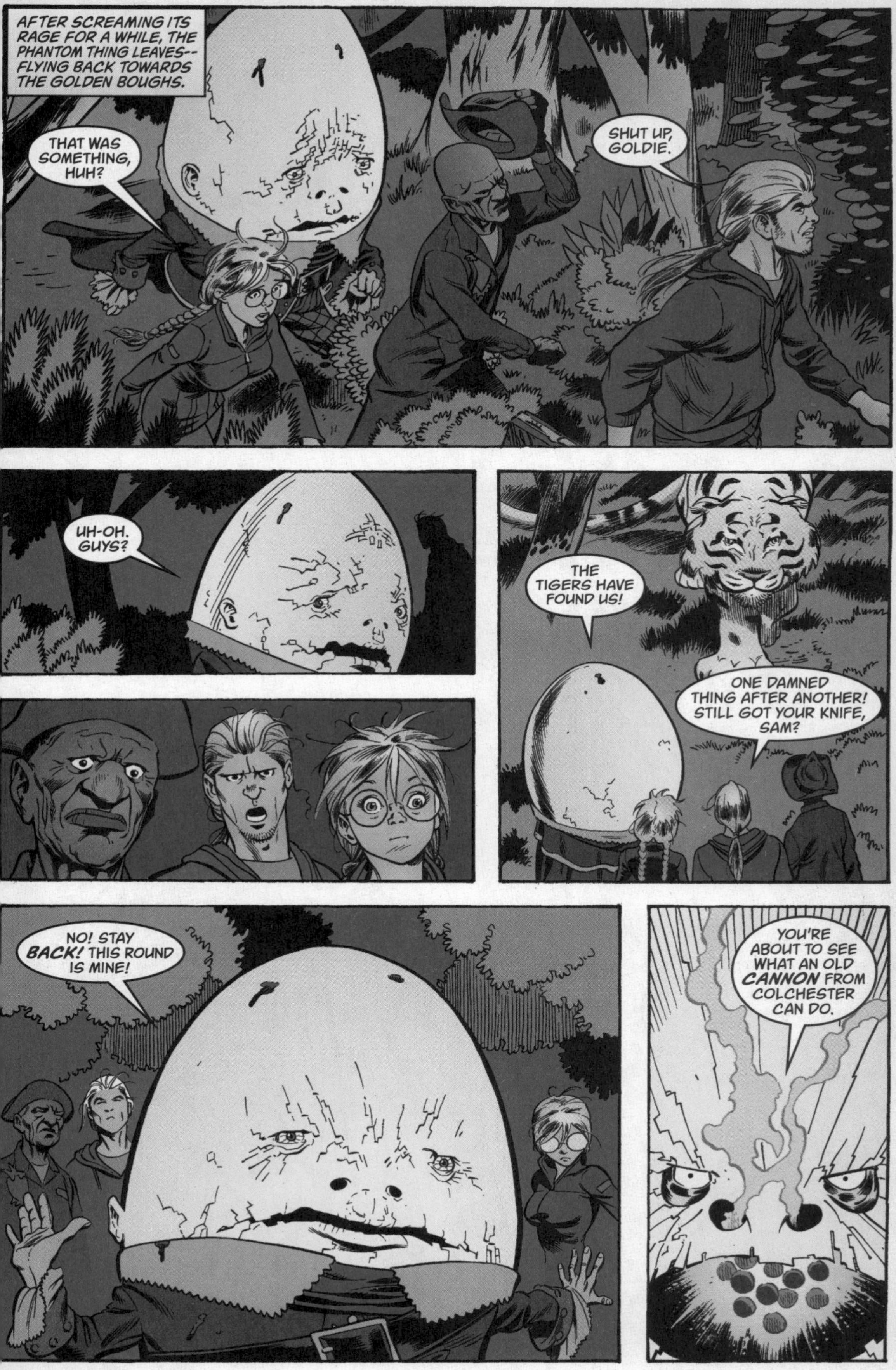
AFTER SCREAMING ITS RAGE FOR A WHILE, THE PHANTOM THING LEAVES-- FLYING BACK TOWARDS THE GOLDEN BOUGHS.
THAT WAS SOMETHING, HUH?
SHUT UP, GOLDIE.
UH-OH. GUYS?
THE TIGERS HAVE FOUND US!
ONE DAMNED THING AFTER ANOTHER! STILL GOT YOUR KNIFE, SAM?
NO! STAY BACK! THIS ROUND IS MINE!
YOU'RE ABOUT TO SEE WHAT AN OLD CANNON FROM COLCHESTER CAN DO.

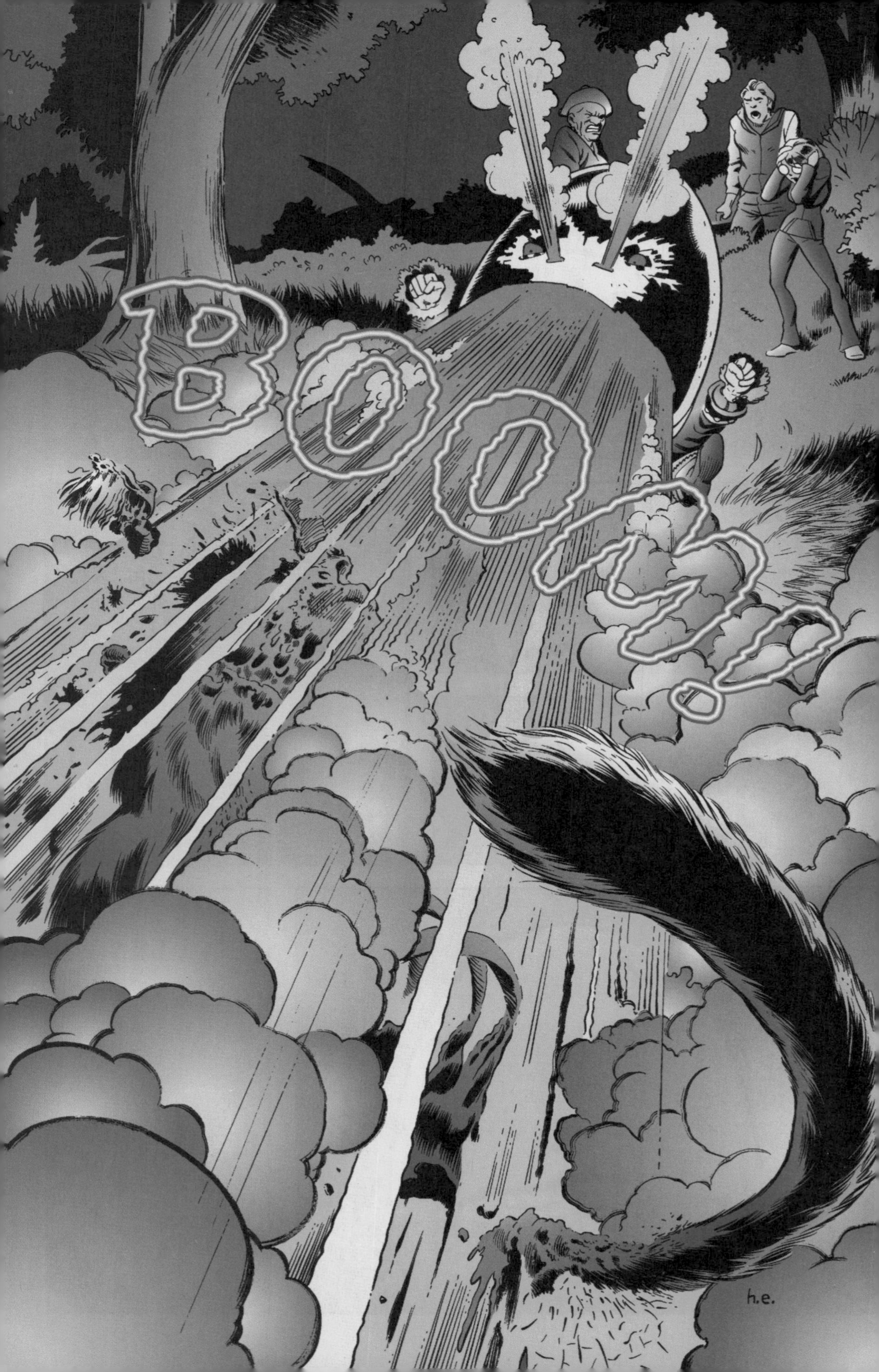
BOOM!!
h.e.

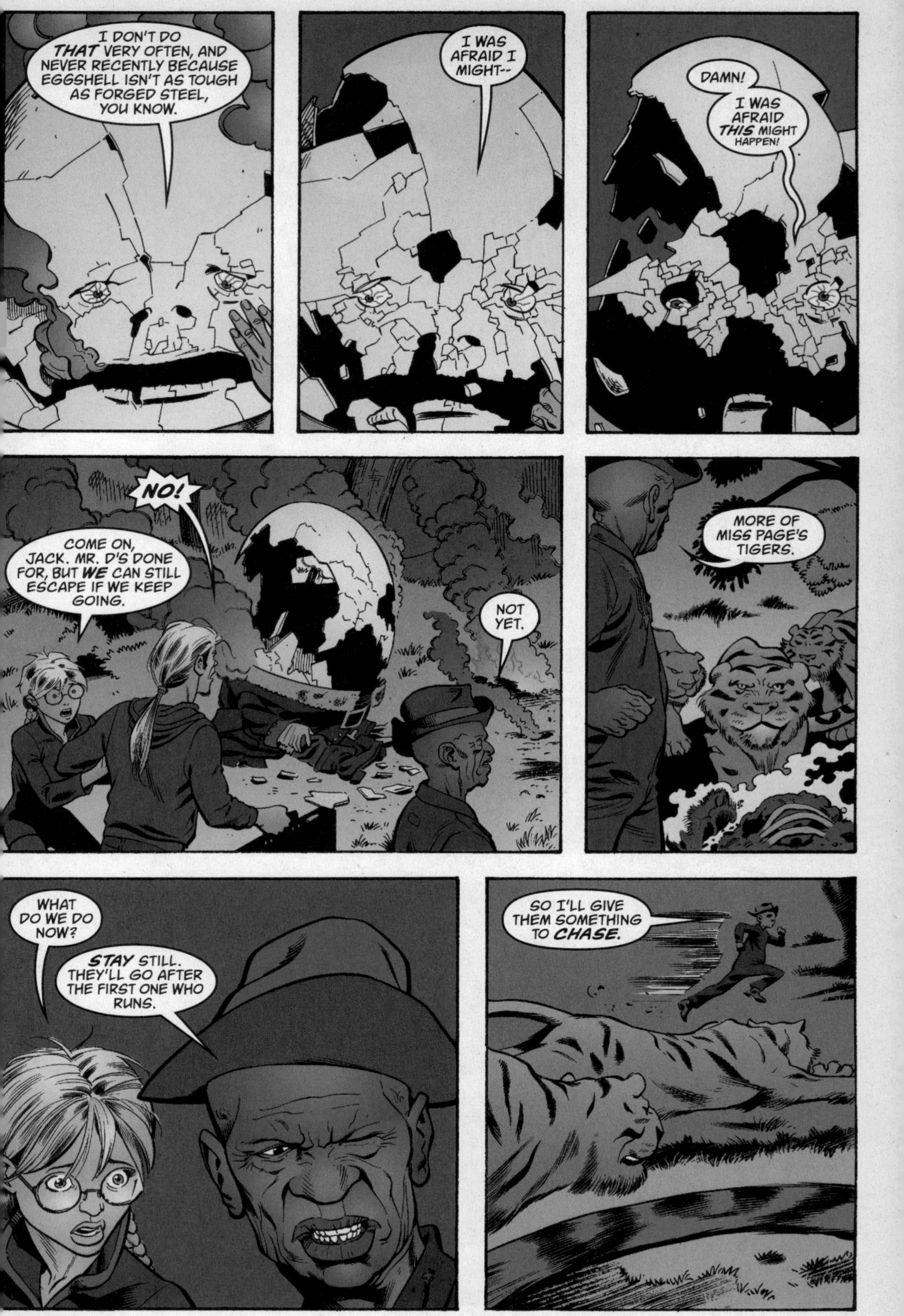
I DON'T DO THAT VERY OFTEN, AND NEVER RECENTLY BECAUSE EGGSHELL ISN'T AS TOUGH AS FORGED STEEL, YOU KNOW.
I WAS AFRAID I MIGHT--
DAMN!
I WAS AFRAID THIS MIGHT HAPPEN!
NO!
COME ON, JACK. MR. D'S DONE FOR, BUT WE CAN STILL ESCAPE IF WE KEEP GOING.
NOT YET.
MORE OF MISS PAGE'S TIGERS.
WHAT DO WE DO NOW?
STAY STILL. THEY'LL GO AFTER THE FIRST ONE WHO RUNS.
SO I'LL GIVE THEM SOMETHING TO CHASE.

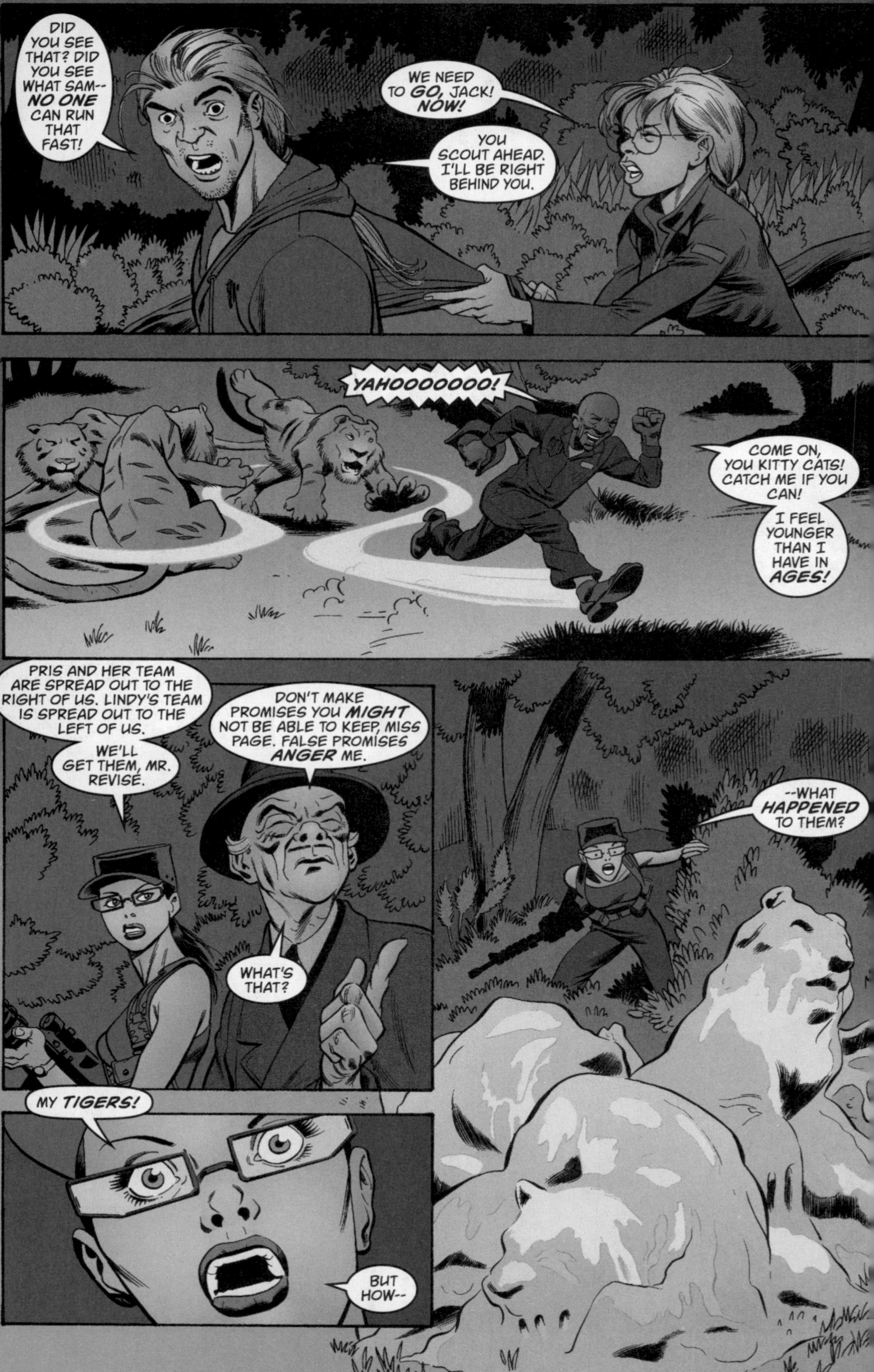
DID YOU SEE THAT? DID YOU SEE WHAT SAM-- NO ONE CAN RUN THAT FAST!
WE NEED TO GO, JACK! NOW!
YOU SCOUT AHEAD. I'LL BE RIGHT BEHIND YOU.
YAHOOOOOOOO!
COME ON, YOU KITTY CATS! CATCH ME IF YOU CAN!
I FEEL YOUNGER THAN I HAVE IN AGES!
PRIS AND HER TEAM ARE SPREAD OUT TO THE RIGHT OF US. LINDY'S TEAM IS SPREAD OUT TO THE LEFT OF US.
WE'LL GET THEM, MR. REVISE.
DON'T MAKE PROMISES YOU MIGHT NOT BE ABLE TO KEEP, MISS PAGE. FALSE PROMISES ANGER ME.
WHAT'S THAT?
--WHAT HAPPENED TO THEM?
MY TIGERS!
BUT HOW--

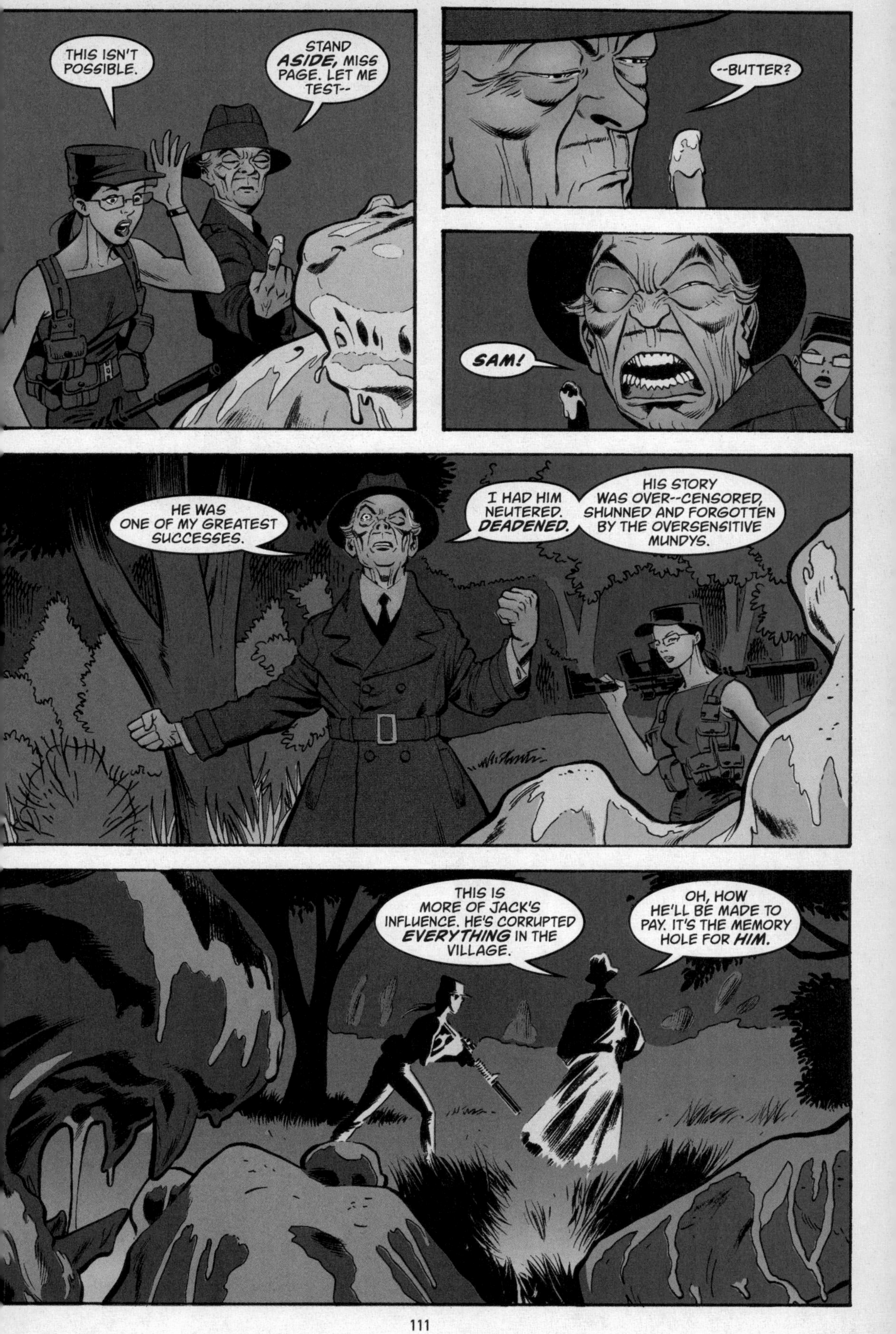
THIS ISN'T POSSIBLE.
STAND ASIDE, MISS PAGE. LET ME TEST--
--BUTTER?
SAM!
HE WAS ONE OF MY GREATEST SUCCESSES.
I HAD HIM NEUTERED. DEADENED.
HIS STORY WAS OVER--CENSORED, SHUNNED AND FORGOTTEN BY THE OVERSENSITIVE MUNDYS.
THIS IS MORE OF JACK'S INFLUENCE. HE'S CORRUPTED EVERYTHING IN THE VILLAGE.
OH, HOW HE'LL BE MADE TO PAY. IT'S THE MEMORY HOLE FOR HIM.

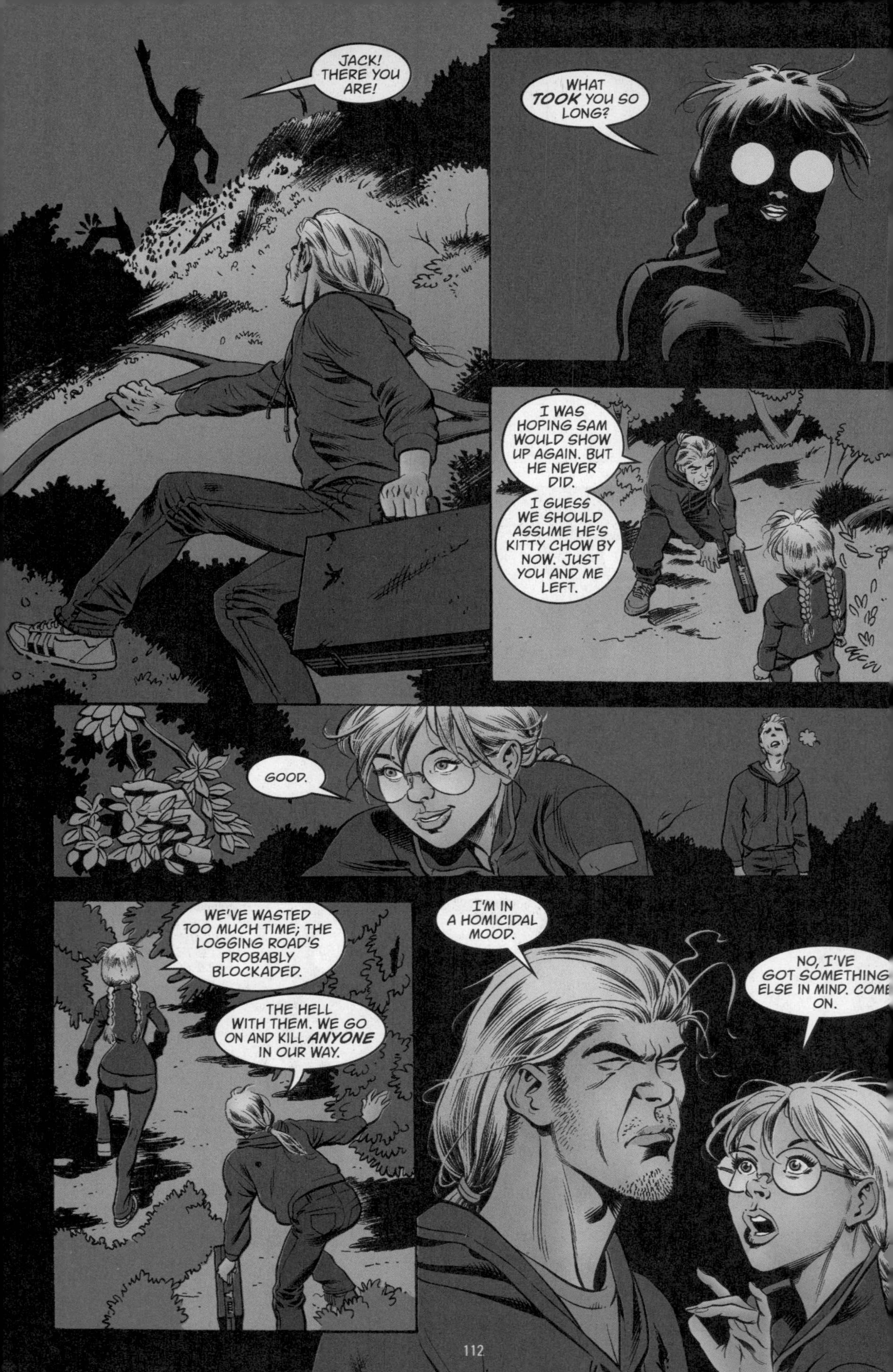
JACK! THERE YOU ARE!
WHAT TOOK YOU SO LONG?
I WAS HOPING SAM WOULD SHOW UP AGAIN. BUT HE NEVER DID.
I GUESS WE SHOULD ASSUME HE'S KITTY CHOW BY NOW. JUST YOU AND ME LEFT.
GOOD.
WE'VE WASTED TOO MUCH TIME; THE LOGGING ROAD'S PROBABLY BLOCKADED.
THE HELL WITH THEM. WE GO ON AND KILL ANYONE IN OUR WAY.
I'M IN A HOMICIDAL MOOD.
NO, I'VE GOT SOMETHING ELSE IN MIND. COME ON.

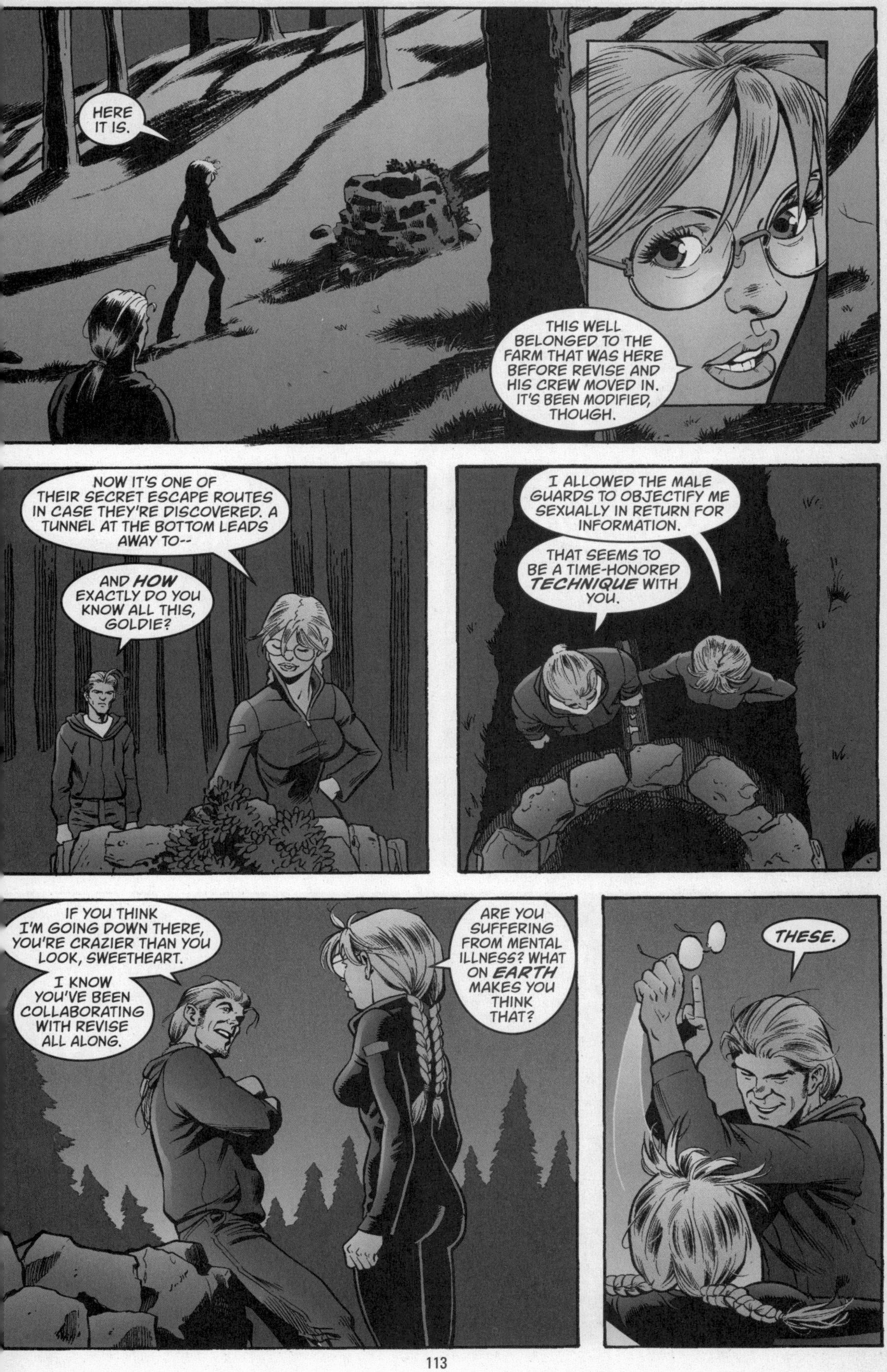
HERE IT IS.
THIS WELL BELONGED TO THE FARM THAT WAS HERE BEFORE REVISE AND HIS CREW MOVED IN. IT'S BEEN MODIFIED, THOUGH.
NOW IT'S ONE OF THEIR SECRET ESCAPE ROUTES IN CASE THEY'RE DISCOVERED. A TUNNEL AT THE BOTTOM LEADS AWAY TO--
AND HOW EXACTLY DO YOU KNOW ALL THIS, GOLDIE?
I ALLOWED THE MALE GUARDS TO OBJECTIFY ME SEXUALLY IN RETURN FOR INFORMATION.
THAT SEEMS TO BE A TIME-HONORED TECHNIQUE WITH YOU.
IF YOU THINK I'M GOING DOWN THERE, YOU'RE CRAZIER THAN YOU LOOK, SWEETHEART.
I KNOW YOU'VE BEEN COLLABORATING WITH REVISE ALL ALONG.
ARE YOU SUFFERING FROM MENTAL ILLNESS? WHAT ON EARTH MAKES YOU THINK THAT?
THESE.

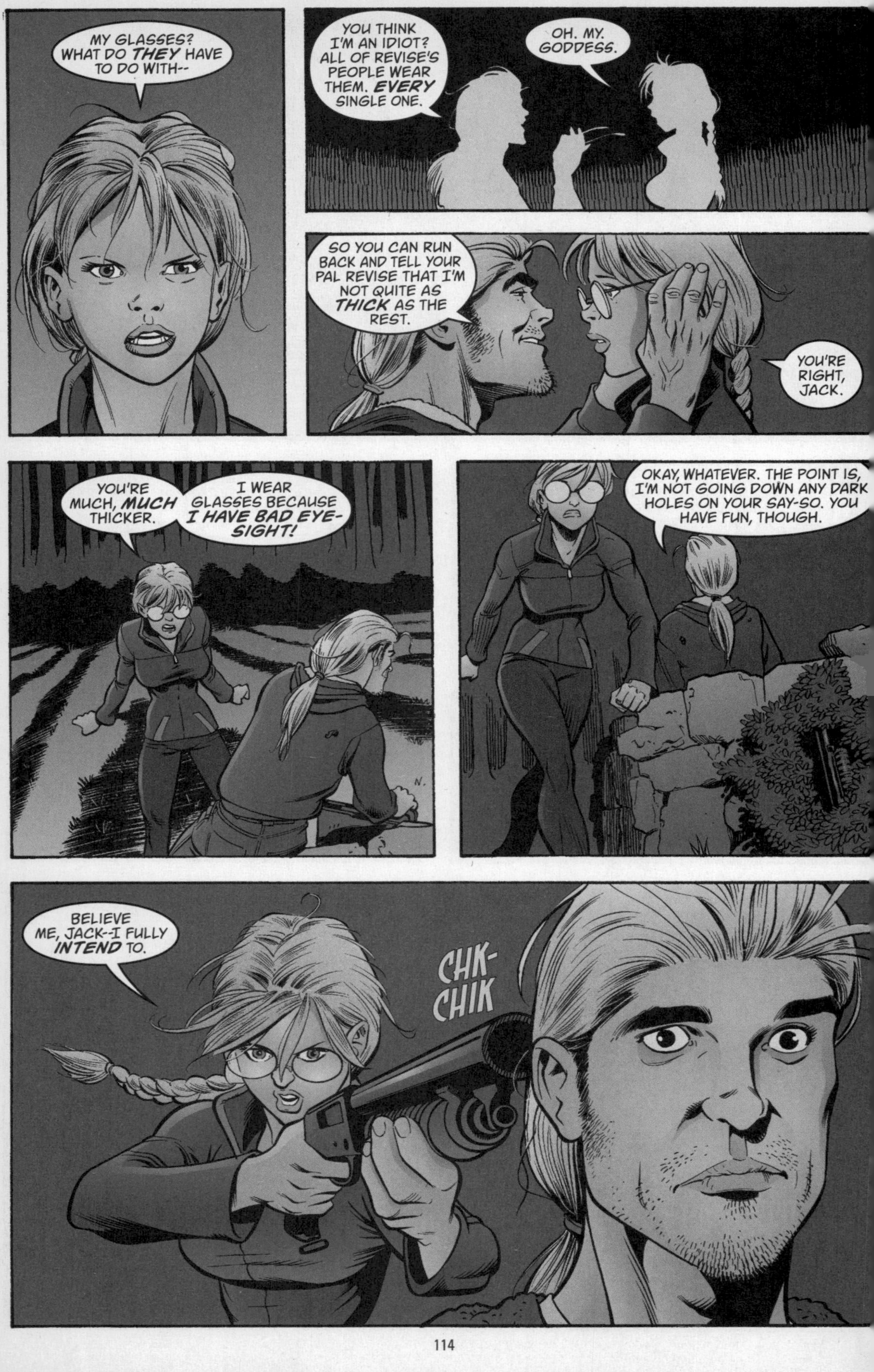
MY GLASSES? WHAT DO THEY HAVE TO DO WITH--
YOU THINK I'M AN IDIOT? ALL OF REVISE'S PEOPLE WEAR THEM. EVERY SINGLE ONE.
OH. MY. GODDESS.
SO YOU CAN RUN BACK AND TELL YOUR PAL REVISE THAT I'M NOT QUITE AS THICK AS THE REST.
YOU'RE RIGHT, JACK.
YOU'RE MUCH, MUCH THICKER.
I WEAR GLASSES BECAUSE I HAVE BAD EYE-SIGHT!
OKAY, WHATEVER. THE POINT IS, I'M NOT GOING DOWN ANY DARK HOLES ON YOUR SAY-SO. YOU HAVE FUN, THOUGH.
BELIEVE ME, JACK--I FULLY INTEND TO.
CHK-CHIK

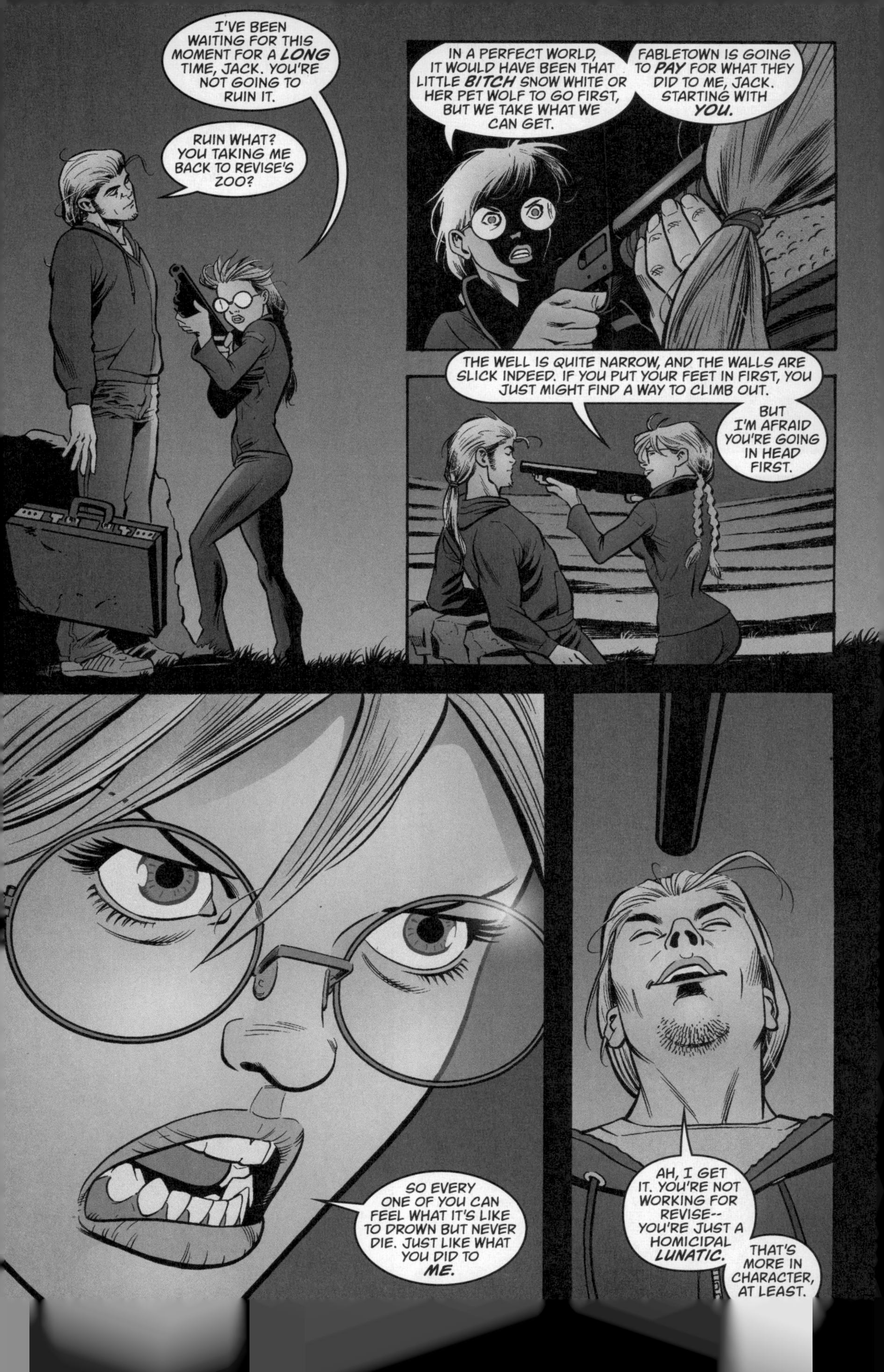
I'VE BEEN WAITING FOR THIS MOMENT FOR A LONG TIME, JACK. YOU'RE NOT GOING TO RUIN IT.
RUIN WHAT? YOU TAKING ME BACK TO REVISE'S ZOO?
IN A PERFECT WORLD, IT WOULD HAVE BEEN THAT LITTLE BITCH SNOW WHITE OR HER PET WOLF TO GO FIRST, BUT WE TAKE WHAT WE CAN GET.
FABLETOWN IS GOING TO PAY FOR WHAT THEY DID TO ME, JACK. STARTING WITH YOU.
THE WELL IS QUITE NARROW, AND THE WALLS ARE SLICK INDEED. IF YOU PUT YOUR FEET IN FIRST, YOU JUST MIGHT FIND A WAY TO CLIMB OUT.
BUT I'M AFRAID YOU'RE GOING IN HEAD FIRST.
SO EVERY ONE OF YOU CAN FEEL WHAT IT'S LIKE TO DROWN BUT NEVER DIE. JUST LIKE WHAT YOU DID TO ME.
AH, I GET IT. YOU'RE NOT WORKING FOR REVISE-- YOU'RE JUST A HOMICIDAL LUNATIC.
THAT'S MORE IN CHARACTER, AT LEAST.

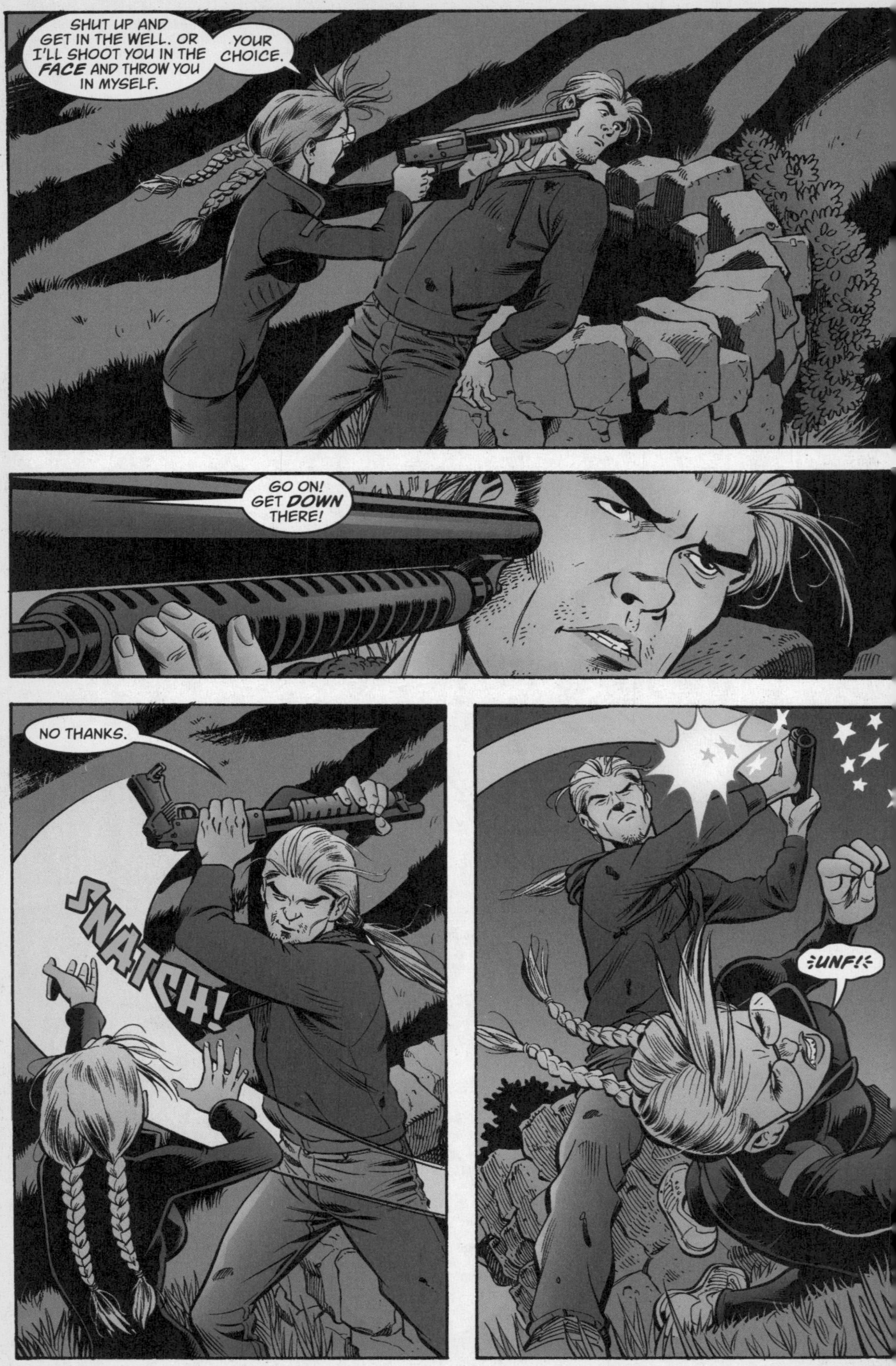
SHUT UP AND GET IN THE WELL. OR I'LL SHOOT YOU IN THE FACE AND THROW YOU IN MYSELF.
YOUR CHOICE.
GO ON! GET DOWN THERE!
NO THANKS.
SNATCH!
UNF!

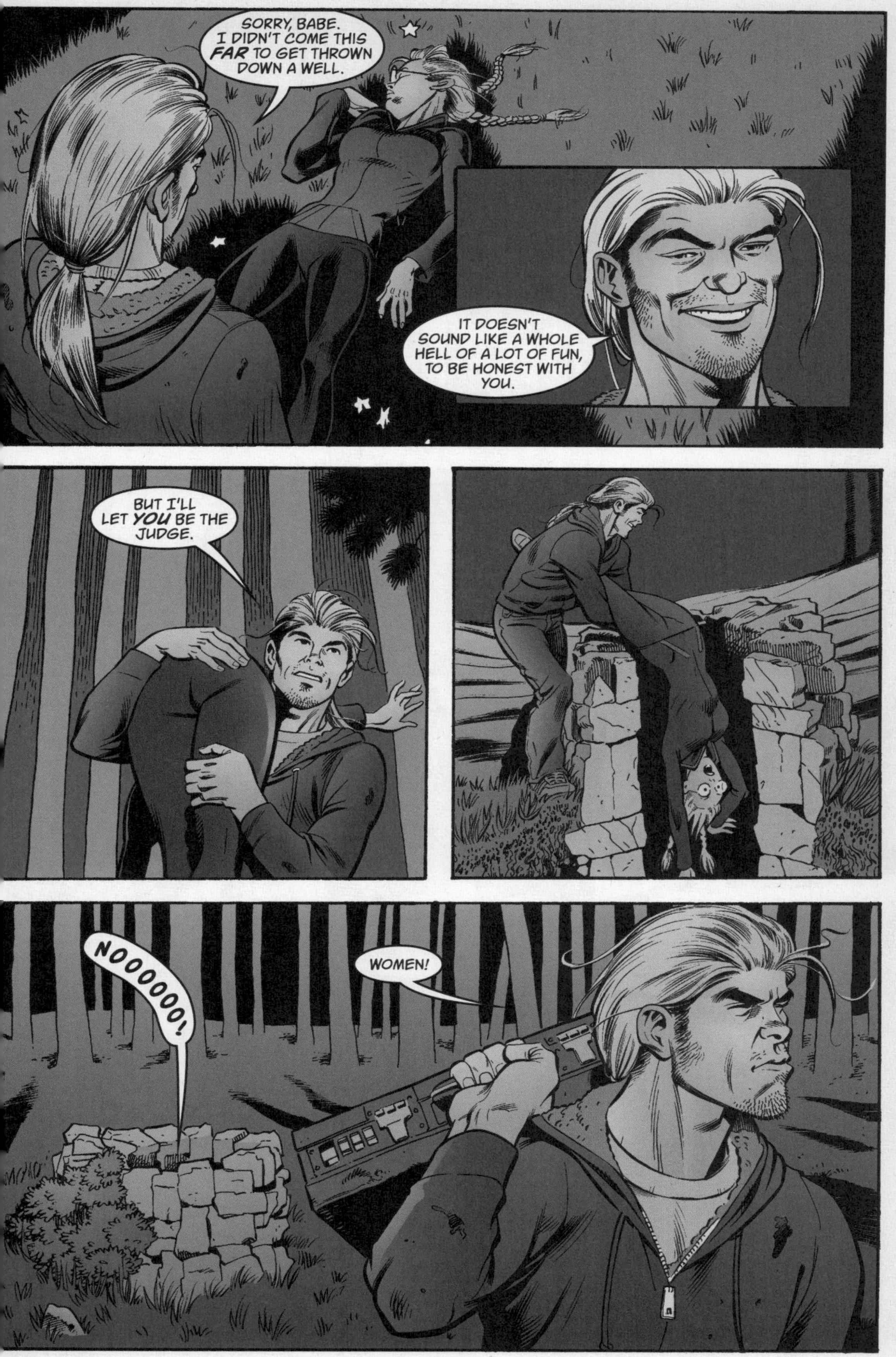
SORRY, BABE. I DIDN'T COME THIS FAR TO GET THROWN DOWN A WELL.
IT DOESN'T SOUND LIKE A WHOLE HELL OF A LOT OF FUN, TO BE HONEST WITH YOU.
BUT I'LL LET YOU BE THE JUDGE.
NOOOOOO!
WOMEN!

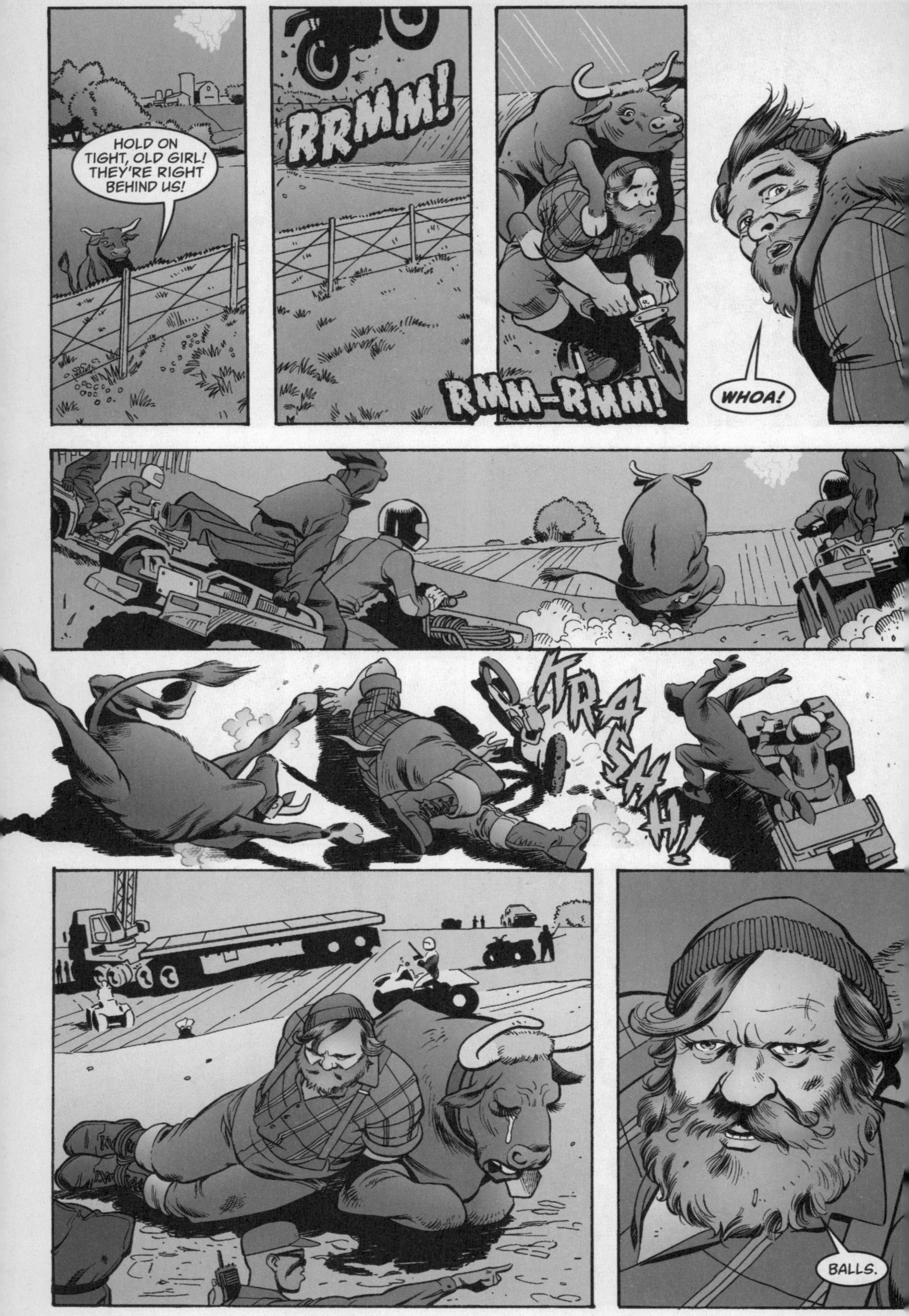
HOLD ON TIGHT, OLD GIRL! THEY'RE RIGHT BEHIND US!
RRMM!
RMM-RMM!
WHOA!
KRASHH!
BALLS.

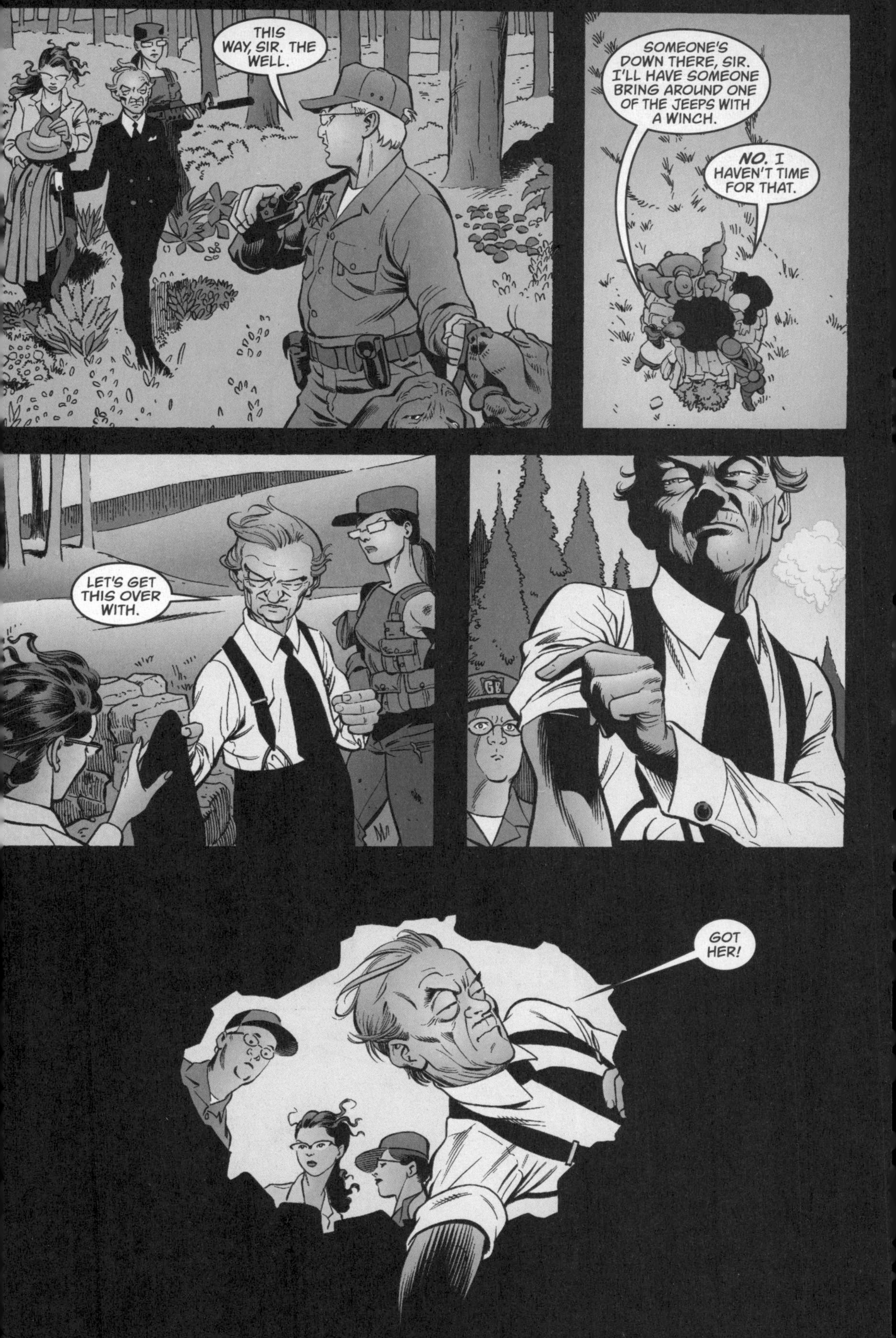
THIS WAY, SIR. THE WELL.
SOMEONE'S DOWN THERE, SIR. I'LL HAVE SOMEONE BRING AROUND ONE OF THE JEEPS WITH A WINCH.
NO. I HAVEN'T TIME FOR THAT.
LET'S GET THIS OVER WITH.
GOT HER!

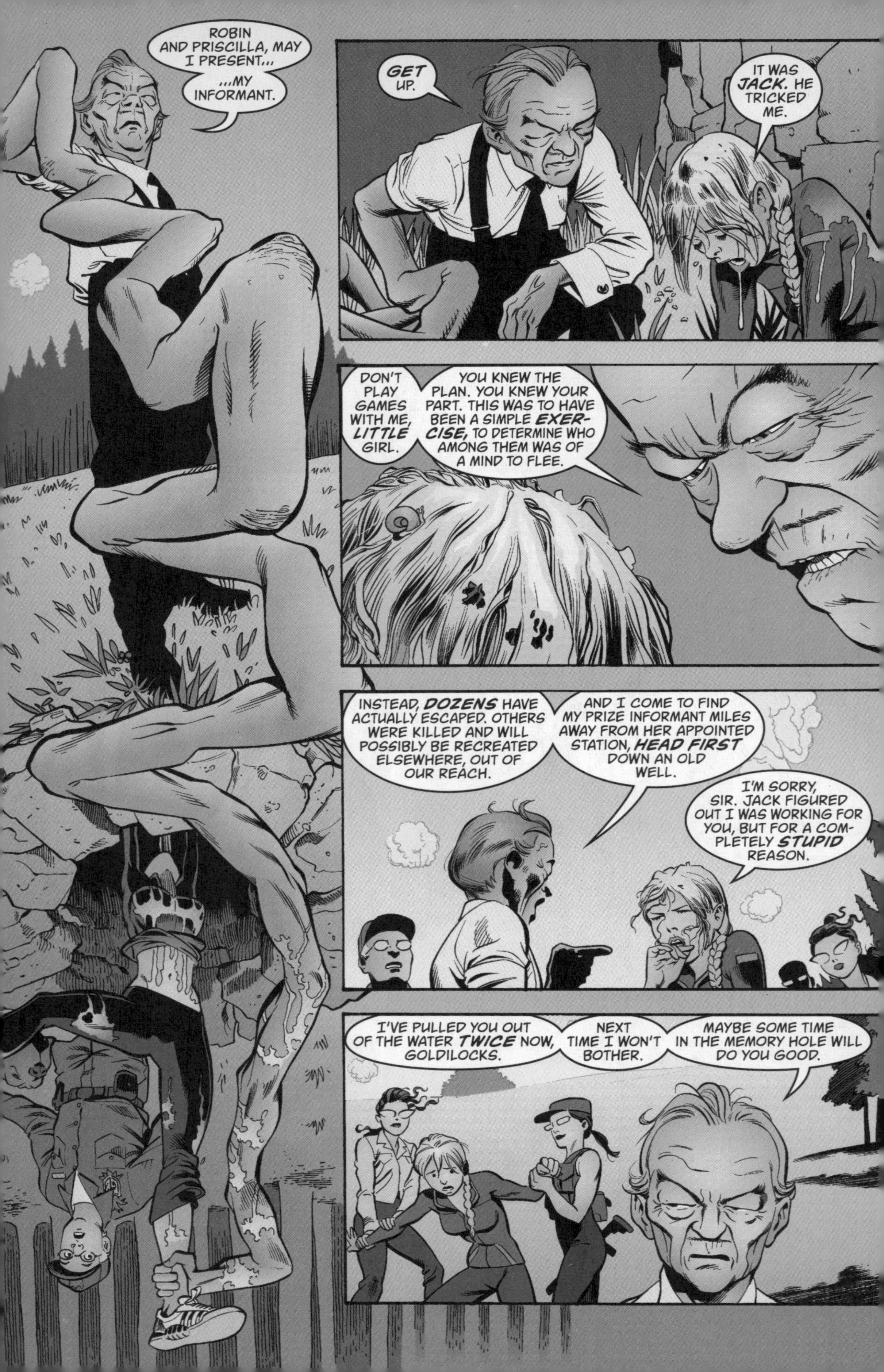
ROBIN AND PRISCILLA, MAY I PRESENT...
...MY INFORMANT.
GET UP.
IT WAS JACK. HE TRICKED ME.
DON'T PLAY GAMES WITH ME, LITTLE GIRL.
YOU KNEW THE PLAN. YOU KNEW YOUR PART. THIS WAS TO HAVE BEEN A SIMPLE EXERCISE, TO DETERMINE WHO AMONG THEM WAS OF A MIND TO FLEE.
INSTEAD, DOZENS HAVE ACTUALLY ESCAPED. OTHERS WERE KILLED AND WILL POSSIBLY BE RECREATED ELSEWHERE, OUT OF OUR REACH.
AND I COME TO FIND MY PRIZE INFORMANT MILES AWAY FROM HER APPOINTED STATION, HEAD FIRST DOWN AN OLD WELL.
I'M SORRY, SIR. JACK FIGURED OUT I WAS WORKING FOR YOU, BUT FOR A COMPLETELY STUPID REASON.
I'VE PULLED YOU OUT OF THE WATER TWICE NOW, GOLDILOCKS.
NEXT TIME I WON'T BOTHER.
MAYBE SOME TIME IN THE MEMORY HOLE WILL DO YOU GOOD.

YOU ARE NOW LEAVING
IDAHO
COME BACK SOON!
OKAY, ONE OF YOU MUNDY ASSHOLES PULL OVER AND GIVE ME A RIDE.
PEPOY 2006
SEE? I PROMISED YOU I'D GET AWAY, AND I DID. SO, NYAH, NYAH TO ALL OF YOU WHO THOUGHT THIS SERIES WOULD JUST BE A RIPOFF OF THAT SILLY BRIT SHOW WITH THE VILLAGE AND THE GIANT GUARDIAN BUBBLE. THIS TALE'S OVER, KIDS. A NEW STORY WILL START SOON ENOUGH. SO COOL YOUR JETS ALREADY.

PICTURE THIS
CHARACTER DESIGNS

by **Tony Akins**

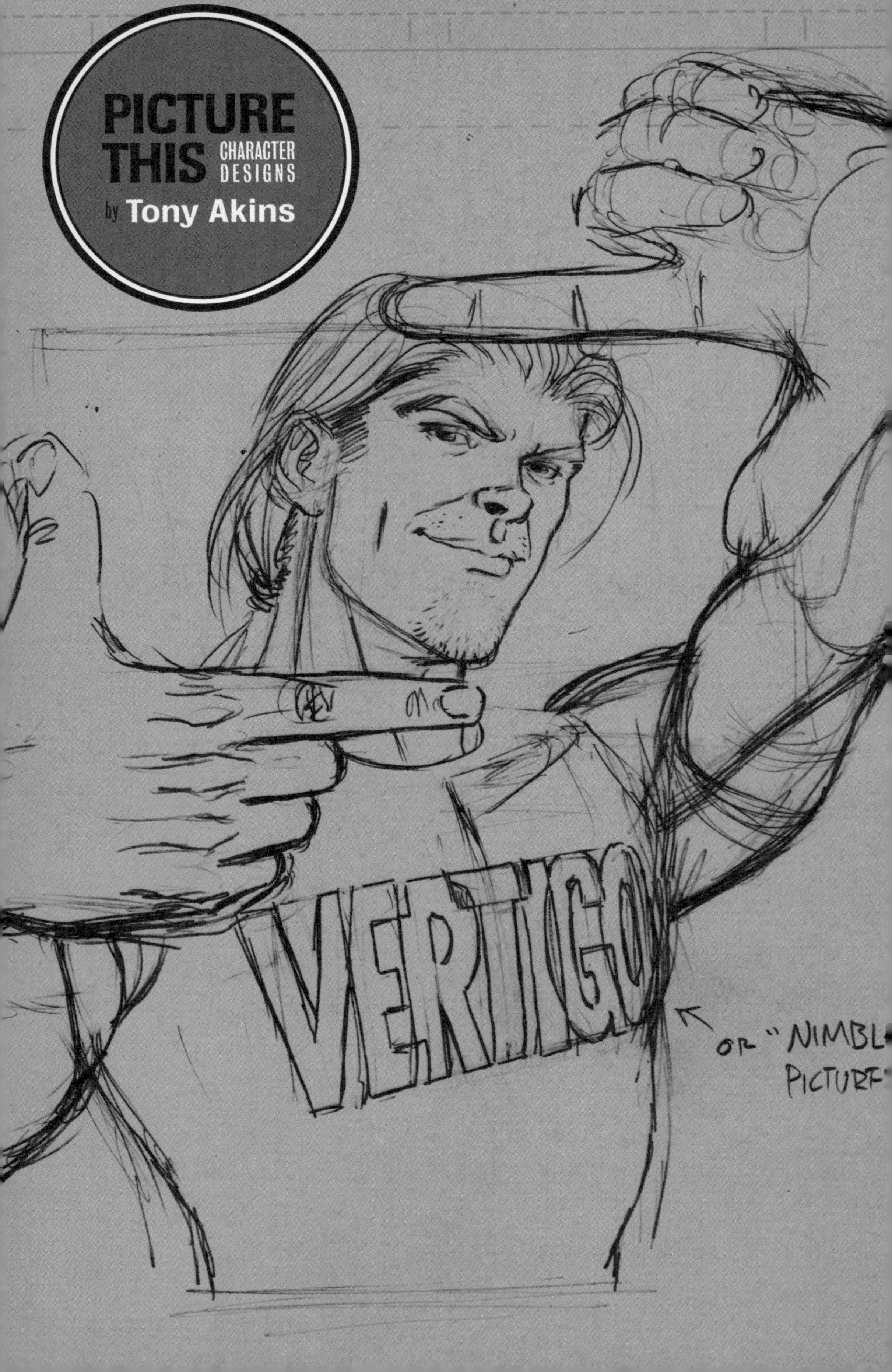
VERTIGO
OR "NIMBL
PICTUR

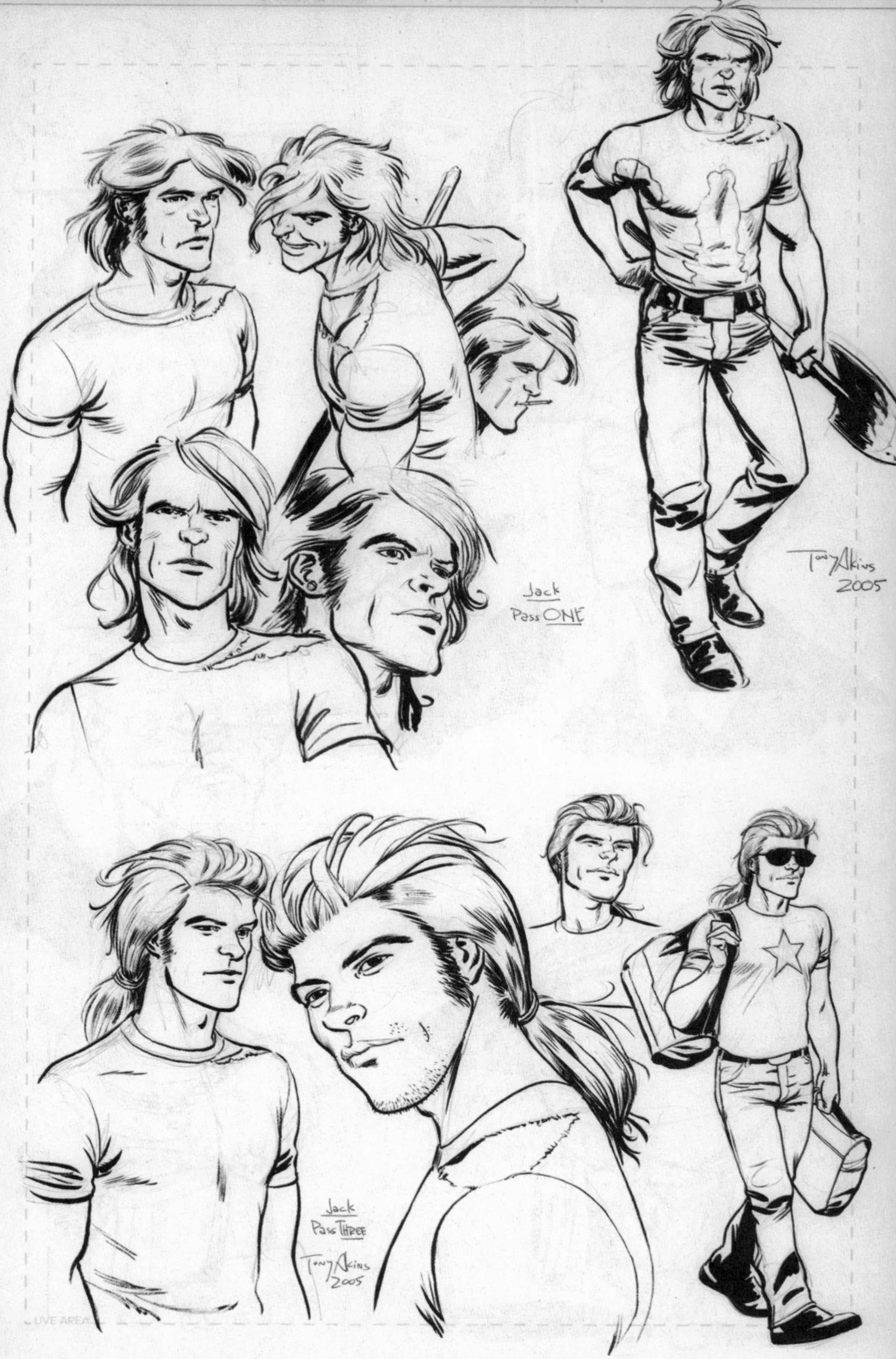
Jack
Pass ONE
Tony Akins
2005
Jack
Pass THREE
Tony Akins
2005
LIVE AREA
CROP
BLEED

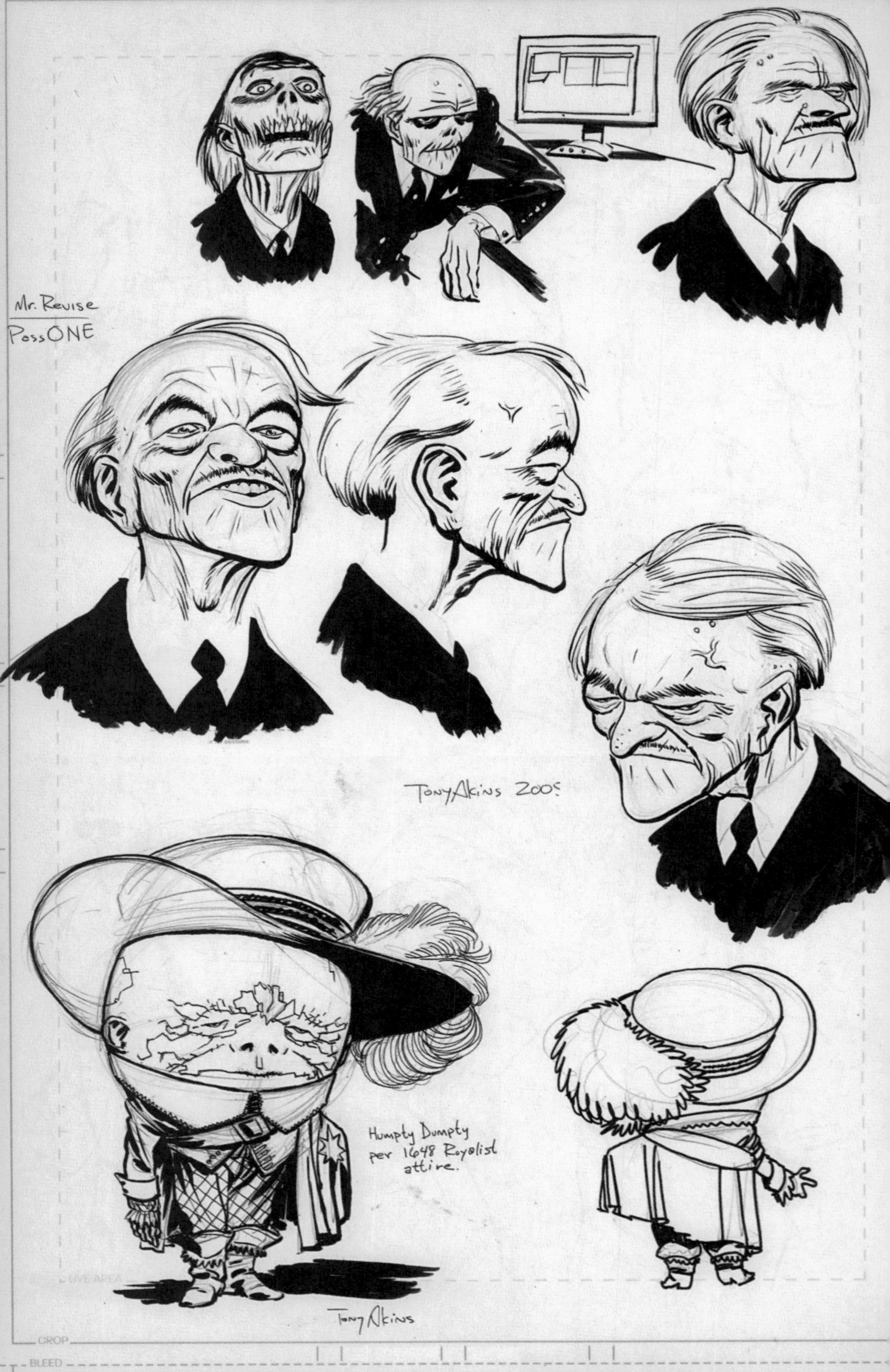
Mr. Revise
Poss ONE
Tony Akins 2009
Humpty Dumpty
per 1648 Royalist
attire.
LIVE AREA
Tony Akins
CROP
BLEED

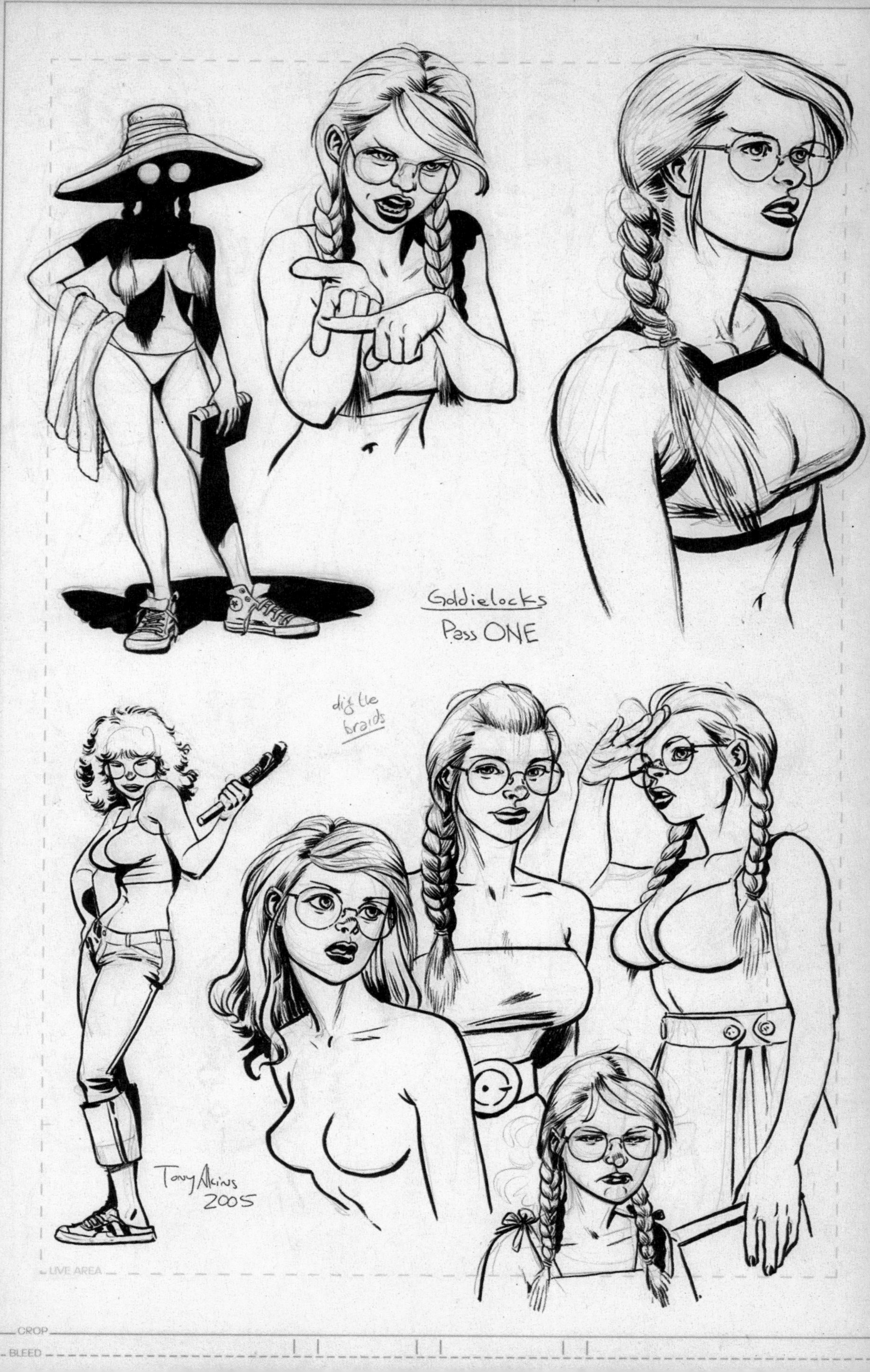

Goldielocks
Pass ONE
dig the braids
Tony Akins
2005
LIVE AREA
CROP
BLEED

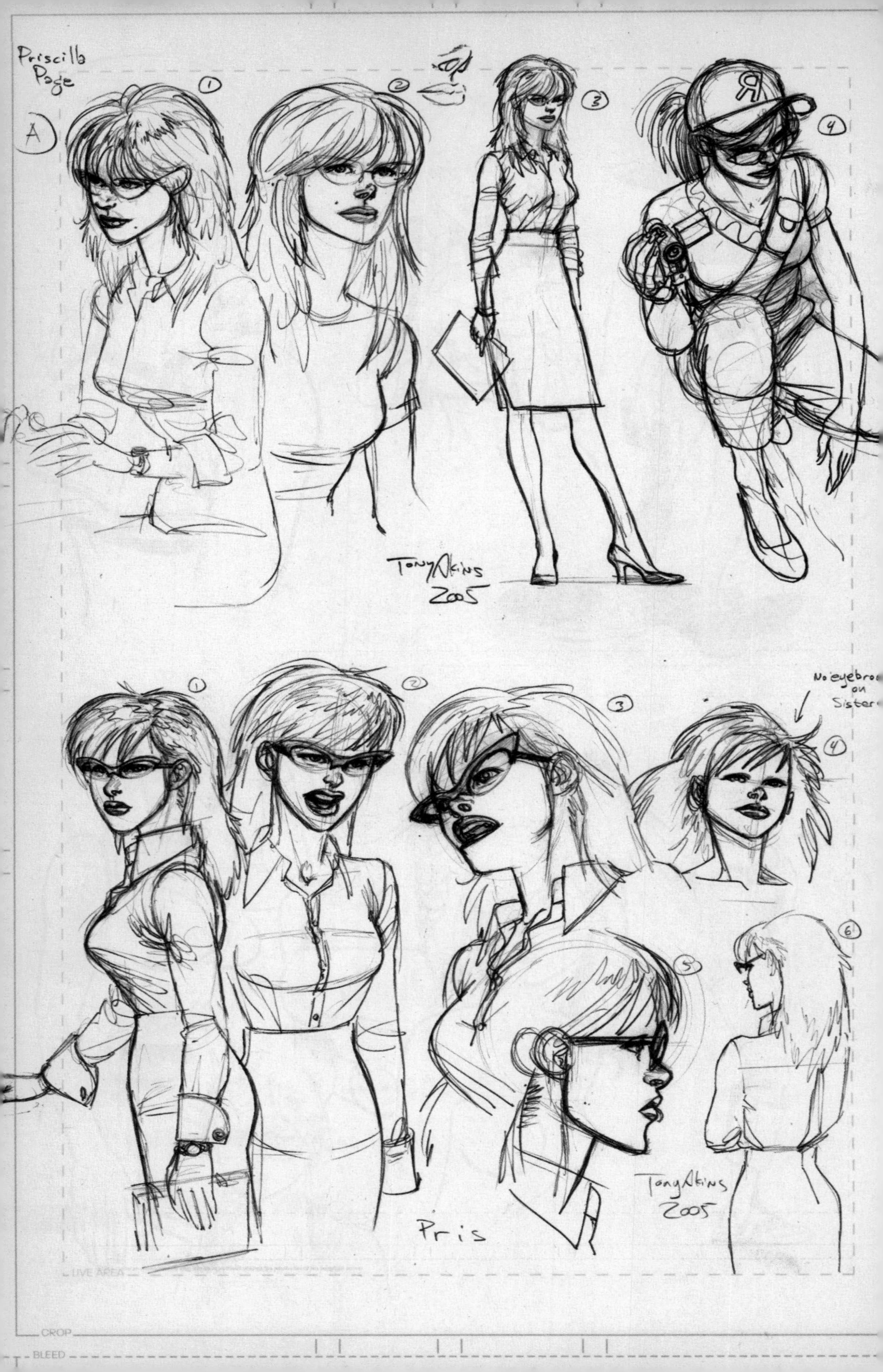
Priscilla Page
A
1
2
3
4
Tony Akins 2005
1
2
3
No eyebrows on Sister
4
5
6
Tony Akins 2005
Pris
LIVE AREA
CROP
BLEED

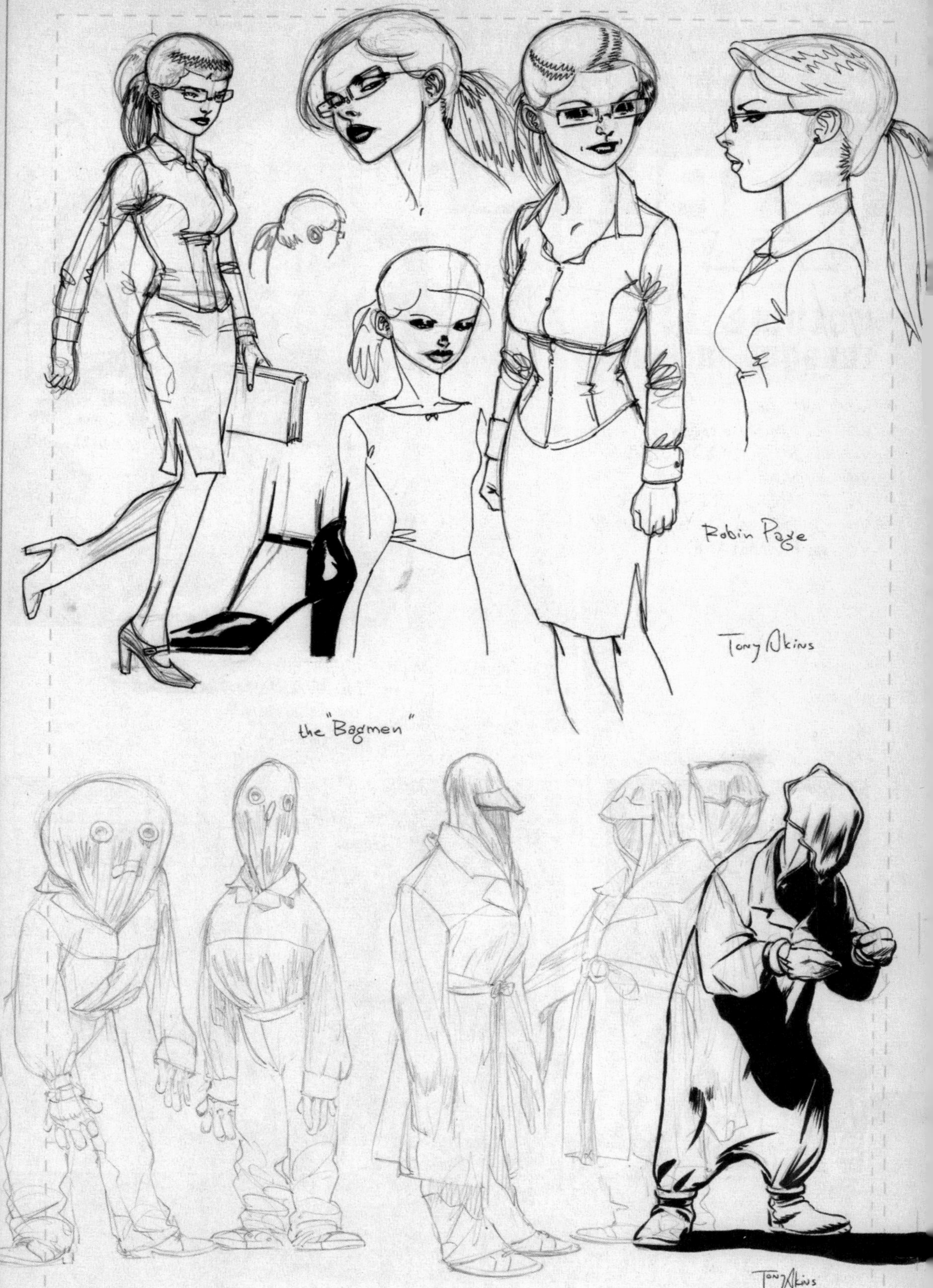
Robin Page
Tony Akins
the "Bagmen"
Tony Akins
2005

LIVE AREA
CROP
BLEED